Singing to the Dead

Singing to the Dead

A MISSIONER'S LIFE AMONG

REFUGEES FROM

BURMA

Victoria Armour-Hileman

THE UNIVERSITY OF GEORGIA PRESS

ATHENS AND LONDON

Published by the University of Georgia Press

Athens, Georgia 30602

© 2002 by Victoria Armour-Hileman

Designed by Betty Palmer McDaniel

Set in 10/14 Minion by Bookcomp, Inc.

Printed and bound by Maple-Vail Book Group

The paper in this book meets the guidelines for
permanence and durability of the Committee on
Production Guidelines for Book Longevity of the
Council on Library Resources.

Printed in the United States of America

06 05 04 03 02 C 5 4 3 2 1

Library of Congress Cataloging-in-Publication Data

Armour-Hileman, Victoria, 1958–
Singing to the dead : a missioner's life among refugees from Burma / Victoria Armour-Hileman.
p. cm.
ISBN 0-8203-2358-6 (hardcover : alk. paper)
1. Armour-Hileman, Victoria, 1958–.   2. Mon (Southeast Asian
people)—Thailand—Bangkok.   3. Church work with refugees—Thailand—Bangkok.
4. Refugees—Burma.   5. Catholic Church—Missions—Thailand—Bangkok.
6. Missionaries—Thailand—Bangkok—Biography.   I. Title.
BV3317.A76 A3 2003
261.8'328—dc21   2001008022

British Library Cataloging-in-Publication Data available

The golden sheldrake, or Bob Htaw, used as an ornament in this book is the
national symbol of the Mon people. Appearing on their flag and referred to in songs
and stories throughout Mon history, the Bob Htaw represents the Mon pride
in their cultural identity as well as their struggle for freedom from oppression.

Contents

Preface

On August 8, 1988, Burma came to the attention of the world when soldiers opened fire on unarmed demonstrators who were calling for democracy and an end to twenty-six years of military dictatorship. The massacre drew international condemnation and within the country spurred widespread protests. In response to the growing unrest, on September 18, 1988, the Burmese government staged a mock coup and declared power to be in the hands of the newly formed State Law and Order Restoration Council (SLORC). The SLORC changed the country's official English name to Myanmar, a change rejected by most opposition groups and democracy-movement leaders who do not recognize the legitimacy of the government or its authority to make such a change, especially without consultation of the populace. Throughout the book, I refer to the country as Burma, rather than as Myanmar.

The first act of the SLORC was to quell the nationwide demonstrations through a crackdown on protestors. Tactics included firing machine guns at unarmed crowds, as well as arrest, torture, and imprisonment of known dissidents. Although objective numbers of casualties are impossible to verify, some sources estimate that as many as ten thousand people may have been killed in the massacres of August and September 1988.

Despite the change in the name and some shuffling of individuals at the highest levels of power, the SLORC was still a military-led regime whose agenda was essentially the same as the Burma Socialist Programme Party (BSPP), which had ruled since 1962, stifling freedom of expression, committing gross human rights violations, and bringing the once strong economy to the brink of disaster. The only note of hope was that the SLORC promised to hold free elections once "peace and tranquility" had been restored.

The next snapshots of Burma that the Western media gave the world came two years later, when national elections resulted in a decisive victory for a popular opposition party, the National League for Democracy (NLD), which won more than 80 percent of the contested parliamentary seats.

The landslide victory of the NLD no doubt came as a surprise to the SLORC, which had placed the NLD's most prominent leader, Daw Aung San Suu Kyi, under house arrest in July 1989 and had harassed or arrested other opposition leaders and dissidents. Despite the election results, the SLORC refused to hand over power to a civilian government, and Daw Aung San Suu Kyi remained under house arrest until 1995.

Famous daughter of an equally famous father, and Nobel Peace Prize winner of 1991, Daw Aung San Suu Kyi is arguably Burma's best-known citizen. To the world, she became the central symbol of the struggle in Burma, and "democracy" became its battle cry.

ETHNIC CONFLICT

The above history summarizes the highlights of the conflict in Burma as represented in the Western media. The real story is more complicated. Much of the struggle has taken place out of sight of the Western media and far from the capital city. Further, the leaders of the democracy movement were not only students, as is the common perception, but also workers, monks, and most of all members of Burma's ethnic groups, who bore the worst of the oppression of its military socialist dictatorship before 1988 and continue to bear the worst of the oppression today.

According to official Burmese statistics, approximately 60 percent of Burma's population of forty-seven million people are Burmans. The other 40 percent belong to one of the more than twenty ethnic minorities who live in rural areas and along the border between Burma and Thailand.

The ethnic dimension of the struggle in Burma is often difficult for Americans to grasp fully. Although the ethnic groups are concerned with familiar issues—the struggle for democracy, human rights, return to civilian rule, and a halt of Burma's disastrous economic policies—they are also involved in a struggle to preserve their own cultures, and to maintain some degree of autonomy. These struggles go back much further than 1988.

In 1947, during Burma's transition from British colony to independent nation, General Aung San negotiated with the ethnic minorities to form the Panlong Agreement, which granted the minority groups a certain degree of autonomy and power-sharing. Unfortunately, General Aung San was assassinated, and the agreement was never fully honored, leaving the ethnic peoples in a difficult situation—they were officially citizens of Burma but enjoyed few rights and privileges of that citizenship. Ethnic tensions intensified when the initial parliamentary government of Burma was overthrown by the BSPP in 1962. Since then, the government, which is military-led and predominantly ethnically Burman, has carried on severe cultural, political, and economic oppression of the ethnic minorities. Subsequent ethnic rebellions and brutal military retaliations plunged the country into what amounts to an ethnic civil war that has continued more or less unabated for the last forty years.

The international community has condemned the Burmese government for its treatment of its citizens, especially the ethnic minorities. The United States banned new investments in Burma in 1997, and more than twenty American states and municipalities have issued selective purchasing laws. Also in 1997, the European Commission, under the Generalized System of Preferences, suspended Burma's import quotas. However, the efforts of Western governments, especially that of the United States, have been undermined by the active military assistance provided to the Burmese regime by China, as well as by the decision of the Association of Southeast Asian Nations (ASEAN) to admit Burma as a member.

THE MON

Along with refugees belonging to the Karen, the Shan, the Karenni, the Kachin, the Wah, the Rohingyas, and other ethnic groups of Burma, Mon refugees are among the more than 300,000 people who have fled Burma since 1988, spilling over the borders into Thailand.

I had never heard of the Mon people before I lived among them. What's more, like many Americans, I would have had trouble pinpointing Burma on a blank map. The Mon (pronounced "mawn") are often confused with the Hmong, who are better known in the United States.

Once I began working with the Mon, they became my whole world. It therefore came as something of a surprise to realize that they are one of the smaller ethnic minorities, consisting of about 4 percent of the Burmese population, or a little under two million in number. Mon sources estimate there may be closer to four million, but without an accurate census in Burma, there's no way to know for certain.

Linguistically and culturally related to the Khmer, the Mon-Khmer were once one of the most powerful forces in Southeast Asia. The Mon have the oldest extant written language in the region, and other languages throughout Southeast Asia borrowed much of their alphabet and basic vocabulary. They are also credited with having helped spread Buddhism throughout the region, and much of Mon literature and legend is filled with stories about the Buddha.

The Mon ancestral homeland occupies the lower southeast section of Burma, and the Mon population straddles the two modern nations of Thailand and Burma. Like other ethnic minorities along the border, the Mon are vulnerable to political and military movements between the two countries.

The number of Mon in Thailand is no easier to determine than the number on the Burmese side. The number of people of Mon ancestry may be very large, but the number who speak the language or who live in largely self-contained Mon communities is dwindling. As refugees, the Mon from Burma have frequently turned to the Thai-Mon community for help, though like other refugees, they are largely dependent for financial assistance on the various international agencies situated both along the border and in Bangkok.

As with other ethnic groups, the tensions between the Mon and the Burmans have existed for centuries. The Mon people still speak of their greatest kingdom, Hongsawatoi, which ended in 1757 with what they refer to as a holocaust. They claim that more than three thousand monks and thousands of laypeople were killed by the invading Burmese army.

During the time I worked with them, the Mon, along with the other ethnic groups of Burma, were engaged in a conflict with the SLORC. The conflict continues to this day. Under the rule of the SLORC, the Mon were pushed to the brink of starvation. Many Mon villagers were literally placed in shackles and forced to build the Ye-to-Tavoy railroad. They were also captured and made to work as porters and sometimes even as human minesweepers for the army.

The hardest-hit among the Mon were those living in what were labeled "Black Areas" by the Burmese military. Identified as places likely to be harboring and supporting ethnic guerrilla forces, Black Areas were deprived of even the minimal rights that might be granted elsewhere. In Black Areas, the army claimed the right to confiscate property and to arrest, torture, imprison, or execute people suspected of helping ethnic armed forces. These tactics were part of the "Four Cuts campaign," which sought to undermine ethnic insurgence by removing the source of four essential supports for opposition groups: food, money, recruits, and information.

In addition to direct military conflict, the Mon have been affected by both Burmese and international economic interests. Though now listed as a Least Developed Country, Burma is rich in natural resources, most of which are located in what has traditionally been indigenous territory. Burma was once a leading exporter of rice, but by 1988 the BSPP's economic policies had led to severe rice shortages. The SLORC continued the trend of economic decline by selling off teak forests, fishing rights, and other nonrenewable resources to international companies. The exploitation of such natural resources on indigenous lands has had a negative impact on the environment and has deprived ethnic peoples of traditional livelihoods. Further, the areas surrounding these rich lands are often highly militarized, and forced labor and relocation of local inhabitants is common.

Perhaps the best example of how economic policies have affected the Mon is the billion-dollar natural gas pipeline that carries gas from Burma to Thailand. Stretching from the Gulf of Martaban across southeastern Burma and into Kanchanaburi, Thailand, the pipeline cuts straight through the heart of Mon State. The Mon claim that potential negative effects such a pipeline might have on the environment and on the local population were not given due consideration. They also claim that their villages were relocated or burned and that their forced labor was used to clear the land and build the roads and railway that would facilitate construction, maintenance, and defense of the pipeline.

THE SITUATION IN THAILAND

Most of the stories in this book occur not in Burma but in Thailand, where the majority of refugees from Burma have sought shelter. While the book may seem critical of Thai refugee policy, Thailand has been continually saddled with the burden of hosting refugees from its more volatile neighbors. Over the last few decades, Thailand has hosted Laotian, Cambodian, and, since 1988, Burmese refugees along its borders. Refugees and economic migrants often are little worse off financially than the poorest of Thailand's own people. But the local residents do not get the visible international attention or assistance granted refugees, and this creates resentment among Thai nationals.

In addition to being the major recipient of the natural gas being piped into Kanchanaburi province, Thailand has a long history of border disputes with Burma. Security concerns have been especially high over the past few decades as Burma has become increasingly militarized with weapons from China and an ever-growing army, which has more than doubled in size since 1988.

Like that of other nations in Asia, the Thai government has chosen to respond to this combination of issues through "constructive engagement" with Burma, a policy of open trade without sanctions. Most opposition groups within Burma question this tactic and see it as a means of giving the SLORC the foreign exchange it needs to maintain the army and infrastructure that oppresses the Burmese peoples.

Given the complicated political and economic interests of Thailand, life for refugees there is less secure than it might be in other host nations, though realistically, insecurity is a hallmark of refugee life everywhere. One tangible insecurity is the difficulty of applying for resettlement in a third country. Refugees must apply at embassies located in Bangkok, but refugees are illegal in the city and risk arrest if they are caught outside the confines of the camps along the border.

While the Mon and other refugees in Bangkok face arrest and detention, the situation for those in the border camps has been even more precarious. In January 1994, the Thai government forced more than six thousand Mon refugees from the Lohloe camp in Thailand to relocate on the Burmese side of the border. The new camp, called Halockhani, was situated less than an hour's march from a Burmese military outpost.

On July 21, 1994, the camp at Halockhani was attacked by one hundred Burmese soldiers from the 62nd Battalion. Sixteen Mon refugees were kidnapped, and a section of the camp was burned to the ground. This incident and others like it led many of the most politically active monks and other prominent Mon refugees to seek resettlement in Western countries, but the process is long and by no means assured—would-be emigrants far outnumber refugee quotas in Western nations.

MY INVOLVEMENT

I was introduced to the situation in Burma while working for six years in Asia as a Catholic missioner (the politically correct term among liberal Catholics for what is otherwise known as a "missionary"). Initially assigned in 1988 to work with Vietnamese boat people in Hong Kong, I transferred in 1992 to Thailand, where I spent two and a half years working at a Buddhist temple. I helped out at a small medical program that cared for tortured, sick, and wounded Mon refugees from Burma who were seeking asylum.

To correct a common misperception, my work had nothing to do with converting people to Catholicism. On a day-to-day basis our work has very little to do with institutional religion at all, but rather with our own obligation, as people of faith, to promote global peace and justice.

My experience of refugee work in Thailand was atypical in that I was placed not on the border but in a small Buddhist temple in Bangkok. My coworkers were indigenous Mon monks, themselves refugees, who invited our missionary community to work at their side. Each month, risking imprisonment and torture, the monks returned to Burma, frequently bringing back not only news to share with international human rights groups but also torture victims, war-wounded refugees, and war orphans, many of whom needed medical care.

The Mon monks had set up a medical project that would transport refugees to doctors around the city. Because the refugees were not allowed in the city unless they had papers authorizing them to be there (which very few had), the police often raided the temple and arrested the refugees sheltering there. Arrested refugees were then taken to an overcrowded detention center, where they stayed for periods ranging from a few weeks to several months, after which they were sent back to camps along the border.

Throughout the book, names and identifying details of both the refugees and my Catholic coworkers have been changed to protect their privacy and to ensure their safety.

UPDATE SINCE 1994

I left Thailand at the end of 1994, but surprisingly little has changed in Burma or along the border since then. Aung San Suu Kyi was officially released from house arrest in 1995; however, she was forcibly prevented from leaving the Burmese capital of Rangoon in September 2000, and she has since been granted so little freedom of movement that her situation is not much better than when she was officially under house arrest. She is currently in dialogue with the Burmese government, continuing to work toward civilian rule, democracy, and responsible economic development of the country.

In 1997 the name of the Burmese regime changed to the State Peace and Development Council (SPDC), certainly a more pleasant title, but with the same people in charge and an unchanged national agenda.

In recent years there has been some economic improvement in Rangoon, but outside the city, widespread poverty is still the norm. Many international companies have left Burma, including PepsiCo, which is mentioned in the book as having a bottling operation in Burma. However, other international projects, including the gas pipeline, continue.

At this time, there are still more than 110,000 refugees from Burma in camps along the Thai border, and many times more than that who are deemed to be economic migrants. More than a million people are displaced within Burma itself, and according to Amnesty International, there are still more than two thousand political prisoners being held in the country.

Most of the ethnic groups maintain fragile cease-fires with the government. The Mon signed a cease-fire agreement on July 29, 1995, feeling they had little choice, given pressure within Burma from the military, and pressure on refugees in Thailand from the Thai authorities. Despite the cease-fires, tension and skirmishes continue between ethnic forces and the Burmese army. There are also continued forced labor, human rights abuses, summary arrests, cultural suppression, and militarization of the country.

THE QUESTION OF OUR TIME

The situation of the Mon casts light on the struggle within Burma as well as the plight of refugees in Thailand. But it also points to a larger issue of our time, for in our day many of the world's smaller cultures face extinction. The Mon, like many other ethnic minorities, are poised between the twin dangers of annihilation through ethnic conflicts on the one hand, and assimilation on the other. In many ways the Mon are already being quietly assimilated, especially in Thailand.

All along the Chao Phraya River are Mon Buddhist temples that house ancient Mon manuscripts written on palm leaf. While I lived in Thailand, one of the monks traveled from temple to temple, trying to save the palm-leaf documents. Often, the manuscripts had already been ruined through improper storage. Sometimes the monks at a temple were third- or fourth-generation Thai-Mon, could not read the language, and had no idea of the significance of the text. On one occasion the traveling monk discovered that the manuscripts had actually been burned just days before he arrived.

The quest to save Mon texts became symbolic for me of what is happening to the Mon and other indigenous cultures in our world. Indigenous cultures are like palm-leaf manuscripts that are crumbling before we can read them. The threat to indigenous cultures in our time is not merely a matter of a people being lost, of songs that will be heard no more, of patterns of cloth woven and worn no more. This is a global crisis, an apocalyptic change. We are no longer facing only the endless shifting of migrating cultures overlaying and absorbing one another, which is the history of the world. We are also facing the possibility that most or all of these small ethnic groups could be absorbed and assimilated by a few dominant cultures, and any authentic uniqueness in the assimilated cultures could be lost.

And so we are left with two questions. First, how do we preserve ethnic and cultural identities without dissolving into a dangerous kind of tribalism that leads to "ethnic cleansing," religious intolerance, and war? And second, how do we develop a global human community that still nourishes and celebrates diversity? How do we recognize our unity across cultural borders without promoting the disintegration and assimilation of the world's smaller ethnic and cultural groups?

These global issues form the backdrop to an entirely human and personal story. During my years in Thailand I was swept up in events I could barely understand, let alone control. My presence among the Mon had no impact on the large political realities that affected the lives of the refugees. And that is not really what this book is about.

This is the story of a journey to the tropics, where I lived in another culture and among followers of a different religion, members of a different tribe. It is the story of how Buddhist monks from an indigenous people and an American Catholic became community to one another in a world so chaotic and dangerous it tested both our faiths. Ultimately, although I went overseas hoping to make some use of myself, the Mon had more of an effect on me than the other way around. The Mon monks exhibited a compassion that spanned orphaned children, mangy animals, torture victims they hid at the back of the temple, and their Catholic coworkers.

I wrote this book because the Mon entrusted me with their stories and their friendship. These are powerful gifts. I wrote this book because my friendship with the Mon changed me. And I believe that a changed heart is the first step in changing the world.

I wrote this book because I carry this story inside me like a seed.

Acknowledgments

There is a Hebrew word, *tzedaka*, that is alternately translated as "righteousness" or "charity." Both translations seem to fall short of the real meaning. I know, because this is a *tzedaka* book, by which I mean both that any proceeds I make from the sale of the book will be donated to charity and that the experiences I had in Asia were a gift that created in me gratitude as well as a sense of ongoing obligation.

I would like to thank all who helped concretely with the book itself: to Sue Silverman, first and foremost, for seeing something of worth in the manuscript and recommending it to the University of Georgia Press; to Malcolm Call and the people at the University of Georgia Press for saying yes, and to all who had a hand in turning the manuscript into a book, including Kelly Caudle, Sandra Hudson, Mary Koon, Emily Montjoy, and Jennifer Comeau Reichlin; to Michael Call and Kent Meyers for their suggestions and careful reading; to Tom Lansner for help with the political background; to my Mon friends for help clarifying Mon legends and history. Although I have sought to make sure my memory and impressions correspond to objective fact, when dealing with a cross-cultural setting, errors and misunderstandings are inevitable, and I am sorry in advance for any misrepresentations of Mon culture.

Thanks to my community, my friends, and my family for putting up with me both while I was living through the experiences in the book and later while I was writing.

Most of all, of course, I am grateful to the Mon, particularly my monk friends, for their friendship and for showing me how big the world really is. Names have been changed to protect privacy, but you all know who you are.

Finally, thanks to Buddha, God, and any other forces, visible or invisible, who may have had a hand in making the book what it is and in making me what I am.

Blessings in the Rain

So faith, hope, and love remain, these three;
but the greatest of these is love.

1 CORINTHIANS 13:13

None of the means employed to acquire religious merit,
O monks, has a sixteenth part of the value of loving-kindness.
Loving-kindness, which is freedom of heart,
absorbs them all; it glows, it shines, it blazes forth.

ADAPTED FROM THE ITIVUTTAKA,
TRANSLATED BY JUSTIN H. MOORE

Flying Buddha

One day the Lord Buddha was flying through the air with twenty of his disciples. It was a Wednesday, and the moon was waxing when he came upon a small patch of land just emerging from the mouth of the Sittang River. There he saw two sheldrakes, one male and one female. All around the sand where they sat was water, and there was only enough room for the female bird to rest on the back of the male. When the Lord Buddha saw the sheldrakes, he smiled.

His disciple, Ananda, asked, "Master, why are you smiling?"

"Do you see the sheldrakes?" asked the Buddha. Ananda looked and saw that the birds were the color of gold and each had a pearl in its crest. "Where these golden sheldrake rest will one day become a great nation. It will be a place of peace and harmony. There my teachings will flourish."

That is how the Lord Buddha predicted the founding of Hongsawatoi. *Hongsa* (sheldrake) and *watoi* (city) are Pali words that the Mon people adopted to speak of the city that would be the center of their kingdom and a symbol of their civilization.

Many years later Hongsawatoi was finally founded with the help of the god Indra. On the first day of the waxing moon in February, Indra measured the ground. Starting from the spot on which the golden sheldrakes had rested, Indra set a strong pillar. Then he took a string of pearls and measured out the boundaries of the great city. He used pearls to signify that the Mon people would have the treasure of freedom and whenever they were attacked they would return again to rule themselves.

The first of the seventeen kings of Hongsawatoi was Sammalakumma, who was so named because he was born during a lunar eclipse. The second king of Hongsawatoi was his younger brother, Wimalakumma, who was so named

3

because he was born just after the eclipse. The two of them were born of dragon blood, for one day a dragon princess went up a mountain, where she met a man, Wijadhe, and became pregnant with his child.

The dragon princess left one egg in a flower bush. Eventually, the egg hatched into a little girl. When the girl grew up, she married a king and gave birth to the two boys who would become the first kings of Hongsawatoi, Sammalakumma and Wimalakumma.

The first dynasty of Hongsawatoi lasted from 825 C.E. to 1043, when the last king of this dynasty betrayed the religion of Buddhism. The second dynasty started with King Banya U, who reestablished the kingdom in 1353. Hongsawatoi was the center of a great kingdom and the golden age for the Mon people, but again and again the Mon were attacked, and they fled into exile, taking refuge in the cities of Thailand, especially Chiang Mai and Ayuddhaya. They fled in 1584, in 1629, in 1659, in 1662, and in 1740.

Finally, on the eighth day of the waxing moon in the month of May in the year of 1757, just before midnight, the city of Hongsawatoi fell for the final time. Soldiers from the Burmese army overran the city, riding elephants and wielding knives and swords. They drove some of the people into nine huts and burned them alive. The total number of the dead was uncountable, but among the dead were three thousand monks, seven thousand pregnant women, five thousand school children, and six thousand babies; the bodies of the dead lay scattered in the forests and on the mountains and in the fields surrounding the city. The record of this suffering was written down on palm leaf and is told from generation to generation.

Today the Mon people live in exile, without a homeland. They flee again into the cities of Thailand, and even in their own land they are not free, for they are forbidden to teach their language and their ways; in their towns and forests they meet with enemy soldiers. So they look back and remember Hongsawatoi. Like children of the sheldrake, they fly over foreign territory, waiting to return to that small part of the earth that is truly theirs, where the teachings of the Lord Buddha will flourish, and peace and harmony will reign for them and their children.

Like most real adventures, mine has its roots in story. In this case, the stories come to me by way of Brother Matthew, a member of a Catholic mission community with projects throughout the world, including Thailand. He tells me stories of the past, the great golden age of the Mon people, stories of Lord Buddha flying through the air with his disciples, and stories of the golden sheldrake, whose children search in sorrow for the lost glory of the Mon kingdom.

He also tells contemporary stories, terrifying, compelling, and gruesome stories, about the indigenous people called the Mon, who come from just over the border in Burma. He tells stories about a little Buddhist monastery here in Bangkok, where Mon monks are sheltering orphans, torture victims, and war-wounded refugees.

One of my favorite stories is how he came to meet the Mon in the first place. During his first months in Bangkok, while he was studying the Thai language and exploring the possibilities for local ministries, Matthew was accustomed to taking long walks through the slum where he lived. One afternoon he wandered onto the compound of a nearby wat, or Buddhist temple, with the sole intention of seeing a monkey that was screeching in a cage.

From one balcony a monk watched him, then sent a younger monk down to greet Matthew in English. They exchanged pleasantries and chatted awhile. Before leaving, Matthew gave the monk his business card.

A few days later, while Matthew was at supper with the other members of the mission community, two monks from the wat came to the door of the house, politely took off their shoes, and approached the dining room table.

"Good evening, Brother Matthew," said one of the monks, as community members looked on, surprised. "I bring greetings from the Abbot. He has asked me to deliver to you these important papers."

From a small shoulder bag (worn by monks when they travel), he took out a thick stack of paper. "This is the schedule of the English classes you will teach each day at the wat. Here is the list of your students."

Matthew stared at the papers with his fork still halfway to his lips. "Sorry?" he said. "I think there must be some mistake."

"Ah," said the monk. "I see. A mistake has been made." His face did not look as though he believed there had been a mistake. He and the other monk continued to stand by the table, looking expectant.

Matthew picked up the papers that had been placed by his bowl. "Would you be so kind as to let your Abbot know I will not be able to teach English to his monks. I'm very sorry. I'm still in language school, studying Thai, and then I will be assigned to a ministry of my own."

"You can speak to the Abbot yourself when you come to the temple," said the monk cheerfully. With that, the two monks said good-night and disappeared into the street.

The next afternoon, after language school, Matthew dropped by the wat to give his regrets to the Abbot. As he approached, he found he was sorry to have to refuse the offer to teach. There was something compelling about the wat. And while teaching English wasn't his idea of the ideal ministry, he thought perhaps the encounter between two great faiths would be something worthwhile in our divided world.

He found the Abbot on the balcony overlooking the compound, and attempted to hand him the class schedule. "I am so sorry," he said. "I am not available to teach here at this time."

The Abbot made no move to take back the schedule. His smile did not waiver. "Come with me," he said. "There is something I must show you."

Matthew followed him across the compound, past a room filled with Buddha statues, under walls painted with scenes from the history of the Mon, across the dirty asphalt, over a heap of rubble from a construction area, and into the farthest and darkest building. Once inside, it took his eyes a minute to adjust to the darkness. It took another minute to believe what he was seeing.

On the floor around his feet, strange shapes were emerging out of the gloom. They were human shapes, but incomplete. There were men without arms, men without legs. There were bodies breathing shallowly on rush mats, open ulcers on their chests. There were women with dull faces suckling naked children. There were blind men leaning toward the voices of those who fed them.

"What on earth?" Matthew turned to the Abbot in amazement.

"We are not who you think we are," said the Abbot.

Before Matthew had fully digested that information, the Abbot continued. "You think you have found a Thai temple, yes? A Thai temple in a city in Thailand. But the birds on the gate of this wat are not a Thai symbol. They are the symbol of my people. They are the symbol of the Mon.

"We here in this wat are foreigners, just like you. But unlike you, we are refugees from our own land, and we are illegal in this one. The people you see in this room have been brought from Monland, in Burma, across the border into

Thailand. They are sick. Or they have been wounded in the war. Or they have been tortured.

"They are hiding here until we can get them to a doctor or bring them medicine. If they are caught by the police, they will be arrested and sent to prison.

"The children you see in our compound are war orphans. Their parents have been killed or maimed and cannot take care of them, so their families have asked the monks to take them to safety.

"Our own country is at war. The Burmese government does not only take away the rights of its people. It is trying to destroy the ethnic peoples altogether. The Mon are the oldest culture in Burma. Our language is the root of the Burmese language. But the Burmese government is trying to take our language away, undermine our culture, and kill those who resist.

"We are used as forced labor for the roads and the railways. Our villages are destroyed by the army. Our women are raped and our men are tortured, imprisoned, or killed.

"We need your help. We cannot go to our Thai neighbors. We cannot go to the Thai government. There are Mon people who are citizens of Thailand, and they help us when they can. But they have to live here, and to do some of the things we need would make trouble for them. But a foreigner could help us, a foreigner would be free to get us what we need.

"We need medicine for our sick. We need someone to help us safely see the wounded to the hospital without being stopped by the police. We need money to send these children to a Thai school. And we need someone to teach our monks, who are also refugees, so that we can live the life of true Buddhists, who study and pray together.

"Will you help us?" asked the Abbot. "Will you teach English to the monks? Will you work with us to find doctors and medicine for the sick and wounded?"

Matthew stood speechless.

"You said you are a Brother, yes?" asked the monk. "You are a man of faith? We also are men of faith, and we need you."

One afternoon, two years later, in the fall of 1992, I am sitting at a table in a sunny corner of a house in Bangkok, munching on toast and spilling buttery crumbs on the language books from which I am striving with limited success to learn Thai.

I am a Catholic lay missioner and a member of the same community Matthew belongs to. Some days I wake up, not completely sure how I got here. My childhood was not the usual ground in which a missionary mentality flourishes. There was no stable, solid Catholic family behind me, thinking that the highest achievement of parenting would be to send a child into service with the Catholic church.

This is not surprising, since, technically, I'm Jewish.

I was born to a Jewish mother and a Catholic father. As my mother says, I'm the only person she knows who was born a Jew, raised as a Quaker, educated in Catholic schools, employed as a Catholic missioner, and sent to Hong Kong to work with Evangelical Lutherans in a project to serve Vietnamese Buddhists.

Given the richness of my family background and my subsequent immersion in Buddhism, some people have remarked that if I only had a touch of Islam about me, I could engage in serious interreligious dialogue just by sitting alone in a room and talking to myself.

Ultimately, my choice to hook up with a Catholic community has as much to do with family structure as religion. I'm a city child of the 1960s, a time and place when it would have been as uncommon to have a single religious background as it would have been to have only one mother and one father. Certainly no one in my immediate circle was very focused, and my own background is sufficiently chaotic to meet the most exacting standards of my generation.

After I'd run through my initial set of parents, I went on to acquire a variety of foster, adoptive, and stepparents, and though I didn't have the worst childhood on record, I would have to say on the whole, life was a little rough. Which is pretty much par for the course for a kid born in the Bronx.

So when the chance for service came up with the Catholic church, the list of my potential coworkers looked like a menu of what I'd been hungry for all my life: Father, Sister, Brother. I joined up, singing. I was ravenous, sure I was now going to find what I longed for most and what had so far eluded me: a secure family. We would go out as a team to a world in turmoil, where we would both proclaim and exemplify the oneness of all people.

Plus, I might make some use of my otherwise lazy self. Usefulness is an especially attractive (and neurotic) calling, since all troubled children assume if they'd just been of some use when they were born, their family life would have gone more smoothly.

To sum it up, being part of a Catholic community offers me a potential sense of family and something useful to do. What could be better than that?

After three and a half years in Hong Kong, working with Vietnamese refugees, I have recently been reassigned to Thailand. I am still in my orientation phase, studying the language and waiting to see what project will most need my skills, or at least a warm body. Sooner or later someone will determine that I'm sufficiently prepared, or at least sufficiently underfoot, that it's time to make some use of me.

In the meantime, I spend my afternoons in the community house, drinking Cokes, eating *phad thai,* and pestering members of the community for information about what they do and what needs doing here in Thailand. Matthew is always obliging and tells intriguing, if horrifying, stories about a sleepy Buddhist wat on a busy street between the hawkers and the fish factory.

Suddenly this afternoon, Matthew's face appears over the rim of my language book. His eyes are red, and his clothes are rumpled. He tells me his work is exhausting. He has tried to get a doctor to come to the wat with treatments for ordinary medical problems that shouldn't require a trip to the hospital: a bottle of foul-smelling ointment for a skin rash, an inhaler for an asthmatic, some shampoo for little boys with lice. But no doctor has come for weeks.

On top of that, every day there is a new crisis: a new case of cerebral malaria, a new orphan from the border, another arrested refugee. He is plagued by calls from the United Nations High Commissioner for Refugees (UNHCR) and other NGOs asking to collaborate on difficult cases. Matthew is trying to teach English as well as attend to the refugees' health. He complains his classes are interrupted, he can't finish anything, and in short, he's losing his mind.

His solution to these problems is to invite me to the wat to assist him. I feel afraid. Matthew is always a little wild when he speaks of the place—of the Mon monks and their memories of carrying each other through the jungle, through the malarial passes, and across the border, fevered and starving. Into freedom, or what they hoped would be freedom but turned out to be only another kind of death.

I have often wondered how Bangkok must have appeared to the monks when they first saw it. I imagine them stumbling out from under banana leaves and coconuts, leaving the land and the legends of the golden sheldrake behind. In

the distance, they see the Thai capital city—a smog-covered, hideous convolu-
tion of metal and concrete. Bangkok is the only city I know of with traffic jams
twenty-four hours a day. Into this place the monks have come barefoot, illegal,
seeking a refuge they will be denied, watching their fellow refugees get arrested
and thrown into a detention center so crowded they cannot all lie down to sleep
at once.

So, yes, I am afraid. Of their memories, of their unlikely dreams, of their jus-
tified but frustrated sense of self-importance, of their unrelenting need. Their
pain and squalor overwhelm me with a sense of my own helplessness.

Today, Matthew's most immediate problem is simple: there are two refugees
with major injuries. One is a blind man with no arms, and the other is a young
boy who has been shot through the bladder. It is going to take awhile to figure
out what can be done for them. Matthew could send them to a hospital with
a monk, but what he really needs is someone who can delve into the details of
each case and find out options for treatment. He wants to know how much each
treatment will cost, and what will happen when the patient returns to jungle
villages, where health care is minimal.

The monks are happy to escort patients to the hospital, manage the funds
with scrupulous honesty, and bring back the small plastic bags of nameless
medicines. But asking questions and outlining various options for treatment
is culturally foreign to them.

"So," says Matthew, looking at me. "I could use some help. Are you game?"

It is important to understand that for the sort of person who volunteers for
overseas service with a religious community, usefulness is the ultimate quest
and the deepest temptation. Religious volunteers approach the world with a
curiosity so immense, it is a form of love. But many of us are also compelled
by a sense that we are incomplete and in need of redemption. The attempt to
make something useful of ourselves stems both from a joyful wish to engage
with life, and a conviction that we are lacking in some way and need to make
up for something we cannot quite remember doing wrong.

Driven by a mixture of faith, arrogance, and inadequacy, most of us will accept a challenge no matter how unrealistic and hang on with the tenacity of one
of those animals whose teeth are so constructed that they physiologically cannot
let go. Once they take the first bite, they keep going in the same direction until
the meal is devoured, or they die trying.

Perhaps all of this explains why when Matthew tells me our current projects include making the lame walk and the blind see, despite my fears I say, "Sure. I mean, why not?" I grab my backpack and follow him down hot streets, the air thick with the aroma of spices, to the wat.

To get to the wat from the community headquarters, Matthew and I decide to take a water taxi part of the way. We shove our way on board, and knowing that monks and women are not allowed to touch, I try to squeeze past a crowd of monks at the back of the boat without brushing up against them. The air is full of gas fumes, and the boat jogs and bobs over the water, making me nauseated, even as my eyes take in the glittering beauty of Thailand's largest city.

We glide down toward Wat Arun (the Temple of the Dawn), its spire piercing the skyline. In the distance is the royal palace. Its golden roofs rise above the stink of the river, which smells of dead fish and clogged sewers.

At each stop, the water taxi hovers near the bank, gunning its engines and jerking now nearer, now farther, from the landing platform. At our stop, Matthew and I leap off with the rest of the crowd, hoping we are close enough not to fall in the water and be crushed against the pier as the boat bounces against it. Not confident of how to maneuver off the moving boat, at the last minute, I just close my eyes and jump.

Once on land again, we find ourselves on Thailand's oldest paved street, ironically called New Road, and from there we travel into one of the tourist sections, up Silom Street. There is no place as full of contradictions as Bangkok. Along its crowded streets you can buy orchids in pink and white, symbols of delicacy and beauty, but you have to step over trash and globules of spit as you continue down the street. I trot behind Matthew, struggling to keep up on one of Bangkok's most crowded boulevards. Here the ultra-modern and the ancient meet. Skyscrapers and department stores made of glass reflect the tropical sun, turning the street into a blinding pool of light, while competing *garudas*, ancient spirit guardians, stare one another down from the front of the buildings.

Men and women in tight black suits and shiny shoes scurry to offices, where the work begins sharply at nine, but on their way they pause to leave a string of jasmine buds at small spirit houses, the shrines of whatever spirits may have been displaced from the land during construction of the modern buildings.

Finally, we duck down an alley and leave both the main thoroughfare and modernity behind. On a side street, just behind the skyscrapers, shacks of tin or wood lean precariously over cracked sidewalks and litter. Old men sit placidly on the stoops of their houses, chewing betel and emitting red plumes of spit.

As we proceed down the end of the street, it becomes quieter and quieter until at last the chanting of monks rises above the distant roar of taxis and tuk tuks (three-wheeled vehicles that resemble motorized rickshaws). Matthew turns in under the gate of the wat, and disappears.

My first impression of the wat is the glitter of gold above and behind a dirty outer wall that symbolizes the wall around the universe in Hindu cosmology. High concrete separates the wat from the street and ordinary life. At the end of the outer wall is an open gate. At the top of the gate are statues of two golden birds, the famed golden sheldrakes of Mon legend, their wings folded, looking watchfully over the street. Following Matthew, I step inside the protection of the sheldrakes' domain and enter the world of the Mon monks.

Inside the temple grounds, a jumble of impressions assaults the senses: traditional, wooden buildings with wide porches, mazes of concrete structures, construction going on in the back of the lot, garbage and rocks strewn on the asphalt just inside the gate. Monks stroll back and forth in their orange robes, leaning their bald heads toward each other in greeting. They have serious eyes and walk gracefully, but they are also mostly young, and sometimes stop to laugh or jab each other in the ribs.

Children of all sizes rattle around the compound. Some, the larger ones, wear novices' robes; littler ones wear tattered shirts and dirty shorts. A few women in sarongs, their T-shirts embossed with absurd advertisements in English, meander under the eaves. They nod at us and disappear into the dark mouths of doorways.

In a corner of the compound, Matthew shows me the wooden cage with the monkey in it, and we stop for a moment, while Matthew reminisces about his own first visit.

"It's funny how the important things in life sneak up on you," he says. "I mean, all this, my work, my life now—it all happened by accident. I was just trying to get a better look at the monkey."

Matthew and the monkey and I amuse ourselves for a while by making faces at one another. Then the monkey stuffs its entire penis into its mouth. I consider this to be a sign our visit is over.

To our right is a two-story building with stairs running from the courtyard to the upper level, which is open to the elements in traditional tropical style. There are no glass windows, no doors, just open sides where breezes provide natural air conditioning. At the top of the stairs a few monks gather to watch Matthew and me, two foreigners, enter their world. From various balconies monks' robes are hung out to dry, flapping like flags. They billow over the asphalt with other wet laundry. Three filthy little boys splash each other at a single spigot by the gate, while they wash out their shirts.

Matthew escorts me through the dark hallways of the inner buildings. "*Mii khon may sabay may?*" Are there any sick people here, he calls from room to room. I follow him, saluting each person we pass with a wai, the traditional Thai greeting. The *wai* is a gesture of respect formed by placing one's hands together as if praying and bowing slightly to the person being addressed.

In a large room off to the right, refugees squat and chat with monks, smoke, or lie sprawled on hard wooden floors, sleeping. Beyond that, in the "women's quarters," women lie with their children curled up beside them in a dank, mildewy room.

A small boy presents himself to Matthew for inspection. Matthew leads the child into a patch of light, or rather lesser darkness, and checks the boy's small, mottled, rash-infested legs and arms, shaking his head over this affliction that's never-ending when you have so many little children coming in from the border all the time. They pass the same infections back and forth among them as they sleep like spoons in the dark, moldy downstairs rooms.

"O.K.," says Matthew with a sigh. "Let's see what we can do for you." He takes the child's hand and leads him upstairs to the classroom where medicine for the children is kept. The mother follows and squats in the doorway while we get a green box of lotion to bring back to her.

The older children are in class. Or rather classes. There are four different lessons going on, one in each corner of the room. The head boy in each group points to various words on a blackboard, and the others huddle around, sitting neatly on their feet on the bare floor. Each group shouts to hear itself above the others. It is a counterpoint of lessons. The main teacher, a monk, is at another board writing sweeping sentences of Mon curlicues. A cacophony of Mon voices drifts out onto the balcony, repeating, reciting, chanting, as if at prayer.

We sit for a moment at the back of the cool room and feel the breezes drift through the open door. A shadow falls across my face, and I look up. Some of the monks are standing around in clumps, smiling. Matthew introduces us. "Phra Nantathara, tell her about your village. What did you see there when the SLORC came?" The monks are shy and struggle to speak in English so heavily accented I catch only a few words.

It seems horrible to hear of forced labor, torture, escape, these most urgent events, and not really to understand the words. To know a human being is telling you such intimate things, for pain is always intimate. To hear the events that repeat in their dreams at night, and to know you are not quite getting it right. They also seem to feel this strain, the obstacle of language, and so mostly mumble and look down at their bare feet. "Yes, I saw many things. Yes, I escaped in 1990. Yes, in my country, in Monland, there are many problems. But I must apologize for my English. Eez not very good."

Leaning against one post is a monk with a round face and kind, serious eyes. All the monks are bald, of course, their heads shaved as a gesture of humility, but because his head is so perfectly round, he looks balder. And very young. Probably in his early twenties. We smile. "Are you also a student of Matthew's?" I ask. "Are you studying English?"

"No." he says. "I do not study now. I already know some English. A little." His voice is high and nasal and young, but his accent is better than the others. There is a confidence and maybe a sadness about him that seems unusual for his age.

"What is your name?"

He says it twice, and I repeat it uncertainly. It sounds like Thomas without the final "s." "Like this?" I write it the way I hear it.

"No, this way." He takes a pad and writes, "Phra Dhamma." (*Phra* is the salutation for monks.)

"This is my monk's name," he says, immediately filling in for me a world where a person lives through more than one identity, and where for a little while, wearing the robes of holiness, one takes on a holy name.

We smile at each other awkwardly until Matthew pulls me out into the strong sunlight and leads me downstairs. "If you ever need help, if you need someone to translate for you or to answer questions, I recommend you go to him."

I look back once, trying to memorize the face. Phra Dhamma stands at the top of the stairs and waves down at me, casting a long shadow.

Back in the open courtyard, I am assaulted by the heat. In Thailand the weather is not a background detail. It is something palpable, something to maneuver through, a tactile medium like the sea. Some days, even breathing takes effort. It is like trying to inhale through a heavy towel soaked in scalding water.

Eager to get out of the direct sunlight, Matthew and I hurry across the grounds, to the darkest building, the dankest room, at the very back. Here the ill and injured wait on rush mats. Some chat quietly and share food left over from the monks' morning begging. Some have amputated arms or legs wrapped in gauze. Crutches and prostheses lean against the walls, casting eerie shadows, imitating the lost limbs they replace. Fretful children lie panting slightly in the hot, wet air. There are no beds, no chairs, no televisions, no refrigerators. No modern comforts to distract the refugees from their real lives. A blind man leans forward, his head to one side, in the attitude of one who is listening. From the rustling and whispers around him, he tries to decipher who has entered his sanctuary and what the significance of our presence might be.

Matthew and I stand in silence for a moment, staring at the human wreckage around us. "Will you help me help them?" Matthew asks, at last.

I am aware I am standing where he once stood, in this place both hideous and holy. I have no idea what I am getting myself into, but what else can I do?

I nod, not at all certain I am up to the task.

Florence Nightingale

An educated monk with good but nasal-sounding British English intercepts Matthew and me while we are in the refugee room. He introduces himself as Phra Banyaa. He calls Matthew "sir" and chides him over the rash on an old monk's back. "He is relying on you, sir. When are you going to come with an injection? When are you going to cure him? He has been waiting for your injection for six days now."

"Hmmph," mutters Matthew, "when am I going to heal him, indeed? When am I going to inject him? We don't even know what's wrong with him. Sir this, sir that. Next he'll be asking when I'm going to grow the amputees new arms."

I laugh, but he frowns at me and I stop.

"What we really need," he says, "is a doctor who will come to the wat regularly to check people out. I'm working on finding one, but without much luck. I'll send you to the monthly meetings of the border consortium where all the NGOs who work with refugees meet. There have got to be some Western doctors there who'd be willing to look in on these folks."

"O.K.," I say. "I'll see what I can do."

We spend several weeks trying to get a doctor, and in the meantime, I settle into a routine. Within a few days I am coming to the wat alone. Matthew checks in on me periodically by phone, and is available in emergencies, but his daily schedule and tasks are different from mine. Like some mythic figure standing at a crossroads, he points the way for me, but does not accompany me on the journey.

So every morning I make my way to the wat through Bangkok's clogged streets. I pass hawkers' carts, where you can buy a bowl of noodles for the equivalent of fifty cents, then peer into the department store windows behind the hawkers, where you can buy the latest electronics for hundreds of dollars.

Traffic zips by me, while monks walk single-file in a calm, measured line. Women and men bow before them for a blessing and place a bag of rice, a bit of cake, or a Coke in their begging bowls. The monks walk barefoot over the hot asphalt as motorcycles speed by them, making their orange robes flutter. Crowded buses belch black fumes, then stop to disgorge tourists in shorts, a few transvestites, and businessmen with briefcases.

I squeeze past tables of wares, which offer pirated videos, drawstring rayon pants, and fake Gucci bags. "You like? You like?" The hawkers hold up ankle bracelets and soapstone elephants and lacquer boxes for me to inspect. "How much you give me? Today I make special price, just for you."

I slip past them all, toward the alley, hearing them call after me in Thai and English the quintessential Thai greeting: "*Pai nai? Pai nai?* Where you go, lady, where you go?"

Suddenly, I am beyond the bustle of the main street. The air seems cooler without the noise and fumes of commerce. The same old men who sat on their porches yesterday and the day before are here today, as if they had never moved. They watch me silently while I make my way to the temple wall and pass under the wings of the golden sheldrakes.

The first thing I do when I arrive is sweep through the wat, getting an overview of who needs what. Then I wait for the monks to eat, and when they are finished, I take people to see doctors, or if there are no new cases, I swing by to visit refugees who are brooding in some hospital bed alone.

"You're a regular Florence Nightingale, sir," says Phra Banyaa to me one morning with his British accent. The "sir" comes out more like "suh."

I laugh. "Where on earth did you hear about Florence Nightingale?" We are coming down the wat's stairs, which are narrow, steep, and slick. I am concentrating on not breaking my neck.

Because Phra Banyaa speaks such good English, I have asked him whether he would be willing to translate for me whenever Phra Dhamma is busy. "Will you do me a favor? When I come to the wat, will you take me to the different rooms and tell me who is sick? Will you translate for me?"

At first Phra Banyaa treats this proposal as if I had unexpectedly asked him to marry me. "I shall have to think about it," he says, and turns away to stand silhouetted on the balcony, his chin on his fist, considering this grave matter.

When I come back the next morning, he is waiting for me in the room with the refugees. He proves to be an excellent and amusing guide.

Soon after Phra Banyaa and I begin working together, I learn something important about him. We are in the eye clinic, and the doctor tells Phra Banyaa that his current prescription is as good as his eyes are going to get. He has chronic conjunctivitis and is malnourished, as are many of the monks, but neither of these conditions is treatable with glasses. The doctor dispenses eye drops and multivitamins, but Phra Banyaa is deeply disappointed.

"I will explain to you," says Phra Banyaa, sitting on the barstool of the eyeglass shop in the back of the clinic. "I was tortured. This is how I lost the sight in my eyes."

I know it is a common belief that torture of any kind affects your eyesight, even if your injuries did not in any way involve your eyes. I resonate with the metaphor, of course. When you have seen what one human being will do to another, and when you have suffered, nothing ever looks quite the same again.

Now Phra Banyaa puts his head down and lapses into silence. I sit beside him but don't know what to say. Being a woman, I am not allowed to touch a monk. I cannot even put my hand on his shoulder for comfort.

I am new at this work and too inexperienced to ask for stories. I am still embarrassed by sudden and unearned intimacies. Besides, they usually happen at the least opportune moment, such as now, when two of the patients are having temper tantrums because they are frustrated with their prescriptions. In the midst of the melee, Phra Banyaa sits glumly, muttering to himself and reliving memories of torture. Given all there is to straighten out, I leave Phra Banyaa's side, without asking any questions, and take refuge in activity.

Later, I regret my lack of response but don't know quite how to retrieve the opportunity. I am too shy to ask Phra Banyaa his story. I am afraid of what I will hear and how it will make me feel.

Despite his pain and my failure to listen, Phra Banyaa continues over the next month or so to be a helpful companion. He is attentive to others, always knowing exactly where to point me to find those in need.

* * *

One day Phra Banyaa tells me there is someone I must see. He takes me out to the yard, where we come upon a decomposing overstuffed chair with the legs sawed off, lots of wadded rags, and an old man. It is hard to see where the furniture and cloth end and the man begins. The whole combination smells powerfully of urine. "He has been sick a long time," says Phra Banyaa.

"What is the matter with him?"

Phra Banyaa says a word in Mon, and the man lifts up his shirt. Under it are several sarongs, tied one on top of the other. He gingerly unties each layer. Beneath all this is an orange cloth wrapped tightly around him with something stiff in it to hold it in place. He peels this final wrap off slowly, and I peer inside. Just inside the orange cloth, his intestines are squashed into a pink, bulbous ball. He pulls the orange strap further out and his colon falls into his lap.

"Oh!" I say, jumping backward.

I'm not sure where to take a case like his, or what doctor to appeal to, so, callous as it may seem, I let the monks go off for their midday meal, and I myself go home for lunch.

After lunch I call Matthew. "So," I ask. "What's with the guy with his colon in his lap?"

"I beg your pardon?"

"There's an old man, crippled legs, sits in a sawed-off chair in the corner of the yard. His colon seems to have fallen out."

Matthew's tone of voice makes it clear he does not appreciate what he considers hyperbole. "I think I know who you mean. He had a colostomy a year or so ago. It is normal for an inch of the colon to stick out of his side."

"That was the longest inch I've ever seen," I say. "It was about six feet long. You'd better come to the wat and have a look."

I return to the wat, where I find that the old man has fallen asleep in the shade beneath one of the walkways. He is covered with flies that swirl around him at my approach. "What's his name?" I ask Phra Banyaa.

"Nai Han."

Hearing his name, the old man awakens. "Could I see again?" I ask. I have half decided that I must have made the whole thing up. How can it be that a man's colon has fallen into his lap? And if it were true, how could he be sitting here snoozing quietly in the shade?

Nai Han unties the many sarongs looped over his belly like a woven basket. He peels away the orange cloth. That's definitely not an inch of colon. A glossy tube entwines over itself in long, moist loops and spills onto the floor. "Thank you," I say. "Just checking."

Nai Han tucks himself back into his clothing. He grins and nods, completely unperturbed.

Half an hour later Matthew arrives with raised eyebrows. "Well?" he asks. Nai Han repeats his performance, peeling away his orange girdle. Out tumbles the pink mass of his colon. Matthew jumps backward and says "Oh!" reminding me of a replay of myself. "Hmm. Looks like you're going to the hospital," he adds, trying to be cheerful.

"Yes, but where?" I ask. The chronic question. Officially, these refugees are illegal in Bangkok.

The monks, themselves indigenous Mon refugees, visit the camps along the border regularly and cross over to the villages on the other side. When necessary they bring people back with them to Bangkok, if the medical help they require surpasses what is available at the border. Other refugees already in the city, and also illegal, make their way to the wat to find lost relatives, seek spiritual encouragement, or beg food and a damp place on the floor to lie down. The wat is the last refuge for the sick or for those whose money has run out. They head here when every other resource is exhausted and they find themselves alone and illegal on streets where their clothes, their accent, and the lost look in their eyes betray them as foreign.

When they need medical assistance, it often takes awhile to find a doctor or hospital willing to treat them. For small matters, there are various public hospitals, and if you space them out so that no one feels overburdened, you can usually find a doctor willing to help. Cases that require surgery are harder. There is a small, private hospital, but it is expensive. "Try the closest public hospital," Matthew advises.

One of the monks trots out to the main road to call a cab and when the taxi enters the grounds, the men lift Nai Han into a wicker wheelchair that looks like a throne from a strange fairy-tale palace. In addition to having his colon on the wrong side of his abdominal wall, Nai Han is crippled, his legs permanently akimbo and half-folded beneath him. He must move from the chair to the cab, and unable to stand, he scuttles like a crab, the monks holding him up by the arms, to keep him from collapsing like a folding chair onto the asphalt.

It takes awhile to get us all packed into the taxi bound for the hospital. In addition to Nai Han, we are taking Nai Hong Sa, who was shot through the abdomen twice at the age of fourteen, when he was serving as a soldier in Monland. He is nineteen now. One of the bullets went through his bladder. He was operated on several years ago, and some device was inserted to allow him to pee. Now the flesh is rotting away, and he is in pain. We have taken him to several other hospitals already but have been unsuccessful in finding a doctor who will treat him. Nai Hong Sa is the cause of the delay. He has the restlessness of wounded youth. He has disappeared, sulking, into the depths of the temple buildings, and no one can find him.

Once at the hospital, the monks drag Nai Han out of the taxi. Because he can't stand, they deposit him on the ground while one of them gets a wheelchair. At the registration desk, Phra Banyaa registers both patients as having "stomachache."

The next stop is the nurses' station, where their blood pressure is checked and they will be sent to an appropriate specialist. "Next!" calls the nurse. We wheel Nai Han before her and hand her the hospital card given to us at registration. "Stomachache?" she asks.

"Well not exactly," I say, realizing that I have no idea how to explain in Thai that his colon has fallen out. For some reason, "Doctor, this man's colon has fallen out" has been omitted as one of the standard conversational phrases taught at language school.

Determining that I am a foreigner and my language is inadequate, she goes straight for the patient, assuming she will get a more comprehensible response from him, but of course he speaks neither Thai nor English, only Mon. He gives her a polite but uncomprehending stare.

Thinking he may be feeble-minded or hard of hearing, she begins to mime a bellyache and shouts in very simple Thai, "Does your tummy hurt? Oooo, Oo." She moans, rubbing her abdomen to show him what she means. When this still meets with no response, she reaches for him, and it looks as if she intends to press down on his abdomen with her hand.

"Wait!" I say, waving at her to look. Nai Han catches on that all this fuss has something to do with him. He unties his many sarongs and lowers the flap of his orange girdle to reveal all the secret machinery we usually prefer to keep hidden inside us.

The nurses jump back with a few Thai curses I definitely haven't learned yet and put their hands over their mouths. We are ushered into the doctor's office without another word.

The doctor calmly enters the examining room, smiling good cheer to Nai Han, the monk, Nai Hong Sa, and me. He examines Nai Han first, behind a hideous green polyester curtain.

At first there is some darkly comic confusion about Nai Han's inability to straighten his legs. The doctor pushes on Nai Han's legs and his torso comes up to the sitting position. The doctor pushes his torso down onto the examining table and Nai Han's legs come up into the air, half-folded, like the legs of a mosquito.

The doctor laughs a little, shrugs, and begins his examination, which mostly consists of a lot of poking. He uses the most sophisticated equipment known: the human finger.

After a few minutes, Nai Han screams. It is a terrible, animal sound. It is unbearable. I'm all wound up and edging into fury before the doctor even finishes the exam and comes to sit at his little wooden desk to explain things. By the time he's through with his explanation, I'm ready to strangle him.

"The hospital policy is not to help aliens unless it is a real emergency. This man will not die today if he goes untreated. So this is not an emergency. You must take him to the Police Hospital. Shall I call the police for you from here?"

"No!" I gasp. "No police! If you won't help him, I'll take him somewhere else, but no police. Are you refusing to help him?"

"I would like to. It is an interesting case. But it is against the hospital rules. Why doesn't he go back to his own country? Surely they could help him there."

I laugh rudely. "He doesn't go back because he's Mon! He's from Burma." The doctor is completely amazed at this display of temper and clearly has no idea what Burma has to do with it. His eyes grow wide with bewilderment.

Phra Banyaa nods at Nai Hong Sa. "What about him?" he asks. But I stand up and say in a tone that is inexcusably rude that I imagine it will just be the same answer for Nai Hong Sa's case as it was for Nai Han's.

I am trying to be offensive, but the doctor does not take offense. He nods sadly. "Yes," he says. "I am sorry."

I feel rage and contempt and a growing embarrassment at my own bad manners, which I do not seem to be able to get quickly back under control. Exploding at doctors, no matter what the circumstances, is definitely not "culturally appropriate behavior," and as part of my training for overseas service, I have been groomed to be culturally appropriate above all else.

"What is the matter with him, anyway?" asks the doctor, nodding at Nai Hong Sa.

"He was shot," I say.

"Shot?!" I seem to have outdone myself at amazing the doctor. It is clear he never contemplated the possibility of such an answer.

"Shot!" I repeat angrily, as if it were the doctor's fault. As if this will tell him what happens to Mon people in Burma. I feel impatient with his ignorance. "How can you ask why he can't go home? Don't you read the newspaper?" I ask in exasperation.

"No," says the doctor, innocently, perplexed. "I don't."

I say a cold "thank you" and walk out, followed by my small entourage of wounded. When we get back to the wat, I tell Matthew the sad story, and he suggests we try the private hospital, never mind the expense. Sometimes, but not always, the private hospitals are more lenient with refugees. But they also cost more, so we try to use them sparingly.

We have recently gotten a grant for our medical work and should be able to cover Nai Han's treatment if we can find a doctor who will agree to take him. The whole trick of this work is to get past the institutional gatekeepers, the receptionists, accountants, nurses, and administrators, and go straight for the doctor. When physicians stand face-to-face with the ill and wounded, they either side with the institution and the law, as did the doctor at the public hospital, or they remember, in a moment of joy, what it was that brought them into medicine in the first place.

In some ways our position is frustrating. We have the will to help the Mon but not the competence. In their wisdom, the Mon asked Matthew for the community's help, recognizing that foreigners would be a good addition to the equation, reducing the danger to the refugees by providing someone to negotiate for them. Our job is to build a bridge between the Mon and those who have the power to heal them. We are neither the wounded nor the healers. We are the connection between the two, the smallest part of the interaction, the electrical current that unites them.

"Let's try to get Nai Han admitted tonight," says Matthew. We make arrangements to meet back at the wat at 7:45 P.M.

At night the wat is a lively place, lit like a carnival. I find Phra Banyaa standing on the wooden platform outside the main prayer room. Monks are beginning to gather. It is an ordinary night, but I feel excitement in the air. It is the same as I have felt on cold winter nights in the States, when as a student I used to go to the 10 P.M. mass. It was a simple thing, a routine thing. But prayer provided a break in the schedule, a rounding off of the sharp angles of the day, when I could exchange the harsh fluorescent lights of the library for the warm lights of the chapel.

"Have you eaten, sir?" asks Phra Banyaa. He squints out of rose-colored glasses he has pilfered from another monk, though they have no relationship whatsoever to his own visual requirements.

"Yes, and I guess you have not!" I say, thinking of the monks' meager diet of two meals a day, both before noon. He laughs. I wonder if he is hungry, with his two small, early meals, or whether he is merely amazed at our endless capacity for digestion.

"What are you doing tonight?" I ask. "What is all this?"

"Worship," he says. "It is almost 8 P.M., and at 8 P.M. we pray."

"Watch this. You'll like it," says Matthew, coming up beside me. The oldest monk unties two metal gongs from where they have rested, entwined by ropes around a pillar in the middle of the room. They are elaborately shaped at the edges with pyramids of curlicues sprouting out. But they are also disappointing somehow. Flat and small, not much larger than dinner plates. The real interest is a big drum outside the room, hanging over my head.

"That's just the dinner bell," laughs Matthew, noticing my interest. The superior size of the dinner drum intrigues me and in my own mind proves that all religions are really about food.

This is not dinnertime, so no one bangs the drum. Instead, the old monk clangs the gongs. They are hanging by ropes from the ceiling, so they spin when hit. He hits one, then the other, with a mallet. They twirl and vibrate. The bell resonates through the courtyard, and monks appear from everywhere. After a while he clangs them from the other side, and they spin backward. Again and again. Clang, clang, clang.

As the monks gather, they sit on the wooden floor, all facing the same way. Each monk has another at his shoulder whispering to him. "The equivalent of confession," explains Matthew. "They are telling each other any rules they have broken today." I watch the sloping backs, the leaning figures, the ritual, familiar and foreign at once. There is something archetypal about it, these pairs of faithful men. One is silent and still, the listener. The other leans forward, telling his sins.

Eventually, the monks begin the evening chant, and Matthew and I leave them to go back to the room of the wounded. The refugees are lying on the concrete floor, watching a small black-and-white TV Matthew has recently given them. Nai Han is lying there, too. Matthew donated his TV partly for Nai Han's sake, since he is immobile, and we imagine he must get bored, but it is the other refugees who watch the TV, while Nai Han watches them.

Matthew leans down and scoops Nai Han up tenderly like a baby and carries him through the doorway. Nai Han lies quietly in the cradle of Matthew's arms, his legs dangling at improbable angles.

Phra Dhamma comes with us, along with another monk, Phra Dala Non. We all pile into a tuk tuk. Because they look quaint and exotic, I always want to ride in one instead of a closed taxi, and I always regret the decision. Their sides and back are open to the air, and the fumes are so bad it's as if I'm drinking gasoline throughout the trip. Further, the noise of the other engines around and the vibrations from the tuk tuk's motor are overwhelming—somewhat like having a jackhammer stuck in your teeth.

Once we arrive at the hospital, our bones still rattling, Nai Han is placed on a stretcher and wheeled into the emergency room, while we sign the registration card and attempt to look for the records on his original surgery, which was performed at this hospital.

It seems his records are irretrievable. This is an unfortunate but frequent consequence of translation. Thai script is not the same as Mon script, and neither has anything to do with English. Sometimes they list the "Nai," which, like the Thai "Khun," is roughly the equivalent of "Mr.," and sometimes they don't. To top it off, because most Mon people don't have last names, sometimes they make up a last name that has absolutely no relationship to the individual, just in the spirit of creativity. Or they give the last name as "Mon," which is sort of like saying "This is Mr. Han, Mon person."

Matthew is attempting to be helpful, but he is getting excited, and when he is excited, his linguistic acumen deteriorates. Thai is a tonal language with a complicated vowel system. Many words sound similar and get mixed up in the mouths of foreigners, creating myriad opportunities to turn ordinary conversations into humiliation for ourselves and entertainment for others. In this case the receptionist asks what is wrong with the patient: "*Khon Khaay pen aray?*" "*Pen aray*" means both "what's the problem?" and "what is it?," and "*Khaay*," depending on the tone, means either "patient" or "pay." So the conversation between Matthew and the receptionist in Thai goes like this:

"What's the matter with this patient?"

"He's a Mon person."

"Yes, but what is the matter with the patient?"

"We'll pay, we'll pay."

The monks attempt to sort out the confusion, and to avoid disgracing myself by bursting into laughter, I go to see how Nai Han is faring in the emergency room. I find him behind a curtain, lying on a rolling cot with pretty blue and white sheets. His colon is standing absolutely upright like a charmed snake, and it is wearing a turban. A nurse is cleaning it off by wrapping it in a thin wet cloth. She is twisting it gently to get the grit off it. Nai Han doesn't seem in the least disturbed by all this. He is smiling broadly and watching the procedure when I come in.

At this point, Matthew also bursts into the emergency room, waving his arms and calling out in Thai, "The horse, the horse! We need to speak to the horse!"

He wants to speak to the doctor before any surgery is attempted so that he will have a general idea of how much all this is going to cost. Unfortunately, the word for "doctor" and the word for "horse" are maddeningly close and easy to confuse.

The entire emergency room staff gather around him in dismay. Just then, the doctor comes in.

"Ah, horse," says Matthew, with relief. "I'm so glad you're here."

Phra Dala Non, who speaks fluent Thai, steps forward and takes over communicating with the doctor, clarifying what our options for treatment are, and the cost. I lean over and whisper in Matthew's ear, "You called the doctor a horse."

He grimaces for a moment, trying to decide whether this is funny. Finally, he laughs. "Probably," he says.

Eventually, a nurse wheels Nai Han out of emergency, and in silence we ride up to the floor where they have made a bed for him in a makeshift room with other overflow patients, who are already tucked in for the night and drowsing off.

I step out onto the balcony for some fresh air. The hospital is ugly by day, composed of huge concrete boxes, but night softens it. The white walls gleam above the dark leaves of trees. A chapel in the courtyard spirals up to the sky like a shell.

Phra Dhamma, the monk with the round face, is resting against the balcony, his elbows propped up on the ledge, which is lit by the moon. Beside him is Phra Dala Non. I lean on the ledge beside them and listen to the trees sighing in the tropical night air.

I ask Phra Dhamma about when and how he came to Thailand. "I was actively involved in uprisings in 1988," he says. "For example, I was flag bearer when about seventy thousand Mon monks, students, and civilians marched from my village to Moulmein, and I spoke to the crowds about democracy.

"On 18 September 1988, a group of military officers called the SLORC seized state power. The SLORC cracked down on all demonstrators and strike camps throughout the country. Thousands of students, monks, and civilians were killed in the streets.

"On that night we called an urgent meeting. If we tried to remain at the strike camp anymore, we must be arrested surely. Early in the morning I and about 250 strikers fled from our villages to go to Three Pagoda Pass together.

"It was the rainy season, and very difficult to walk through the jungle. We had to cross streams on the way, and we had no boat. A student drowned in the water. Two or three students died of malaria. Many people were attacked by malaria, including me. I was sick for much time.

"We lived at Three Pagoda Pass then, and I became a monk again and taught Mon language to the children. But on 11 February 1990, Three Pagoda Pass was occupied by the SLORC, and I sneaked into Bangkok."

"That's a pretty sad story," I say.

We're all silent for some time. Then Phra Dhamma looks at me. "Wicki," he asks, "what other name do you have for me to call you? Is it Miss Wicki?"

"It's just Vicki." He looks unconvinced. "It's different in Monland, isn't it?" I ask. "If I were a Mon woman, what would you call me?"

He turns to look at me as if this is a very obvious question. "I would call you my sister."

I wonder what it feels like to live in a tribal reality where it is natural to make such an assumption: everyone is sister, brother, aunt, uncle. But in a way I am my country's gift of sisterhood to the Mon. I am here to say these are true names, these words that make us family.

Later, as I get ready for bed, I realize this has been a strangely typical day. I didn't appreciate how odd my life had become until much later, back in the United States, when I told the story of Nai Han, while picking my teeth, at dinner with family members. "You saw a man with his colon in his lap, covered in flies, and you just went home to eat lunch?" my family complained. "You think a colon standing on end is *funny*?" they asked. "You made fun of that wonderful man, Brother Matthew, for a language mistake, after all he tries to do? I don't get it," they said. "Isn't there a moral to this story?"

When you work where there is poverty, everything gets jumbled together: tragedy, stupidity, laughter, meanness, nobility, joy, reverence, tenderness. My life overseas was concerned with love, war, and body parts. That's a hard combination to make sense of. What's the moral of the story? Gee, I don't know. What was I feeling when I ate lunch after seeing a man with his colon in his lap? Lots, I guess, just don't ask me what. I think during the course of a day, I felt everything a human being can feel, though maybe two feelings emerged as foremost and never left me: admiration for the Mon, and a slightly sick feeling in the pit of my stomach.

One morning a few days after Nai Han went to the hospital, Khun Phat, the administrative assistant in the community office, tells me Matthew called while I was still at breakfast. "Something happened at the wat," she says. "Something bad. Matthew has left instructions. You are not to go there today. The police have come. They arrested many. A man named Nai Soh tried to escape when he saw the police coming. He jumped from the roof and broke his back."

I call Matthew. "What happened?"

"Everything," he says.

The police had waited until we were both out of the wat. Probably they did not want to do what they were going to do in front of foreign witnesses. Sixteen people were arrested. Two of them leapt off the roof and over the back fence into the Chinese graveyard. One injured his foot, and the other, Nai Soh, broke his wrist and his back. The police were frightened when they saw the injured men and hurried away, taking prisoners with them. But they would not touch the injured—they did not want to be held responsible for what had happened, and they thought taking care of the injured men in prison would be more trouble than it was worth.

Now the injured men lie in the hospital, which is asking for large sums of money for the necessary surgery. "Some of the monks want to abandon the injured," says Matthew, "in the hope that the hospital will take pity on them if they know there really is no money."

Matthew is adamant that the men not be abandoned. The price is actually very reasonable for back surgery, and if we delay to haggle over prices, it may be too late to keep Nai Soh from being permanently paralyzed. He is delirious and swelling up like a melon. He believes he is going to die.

When Matthew arrives at the hospital, Nai Soh begs to be sent back to Monland. He says that's all he wants: if he's going to die, he wants to be in his homeland, to die among his own people.

Matthew stands beside his hospital bed with his arms crossed. "No one is going to die," he says, stubbornly, asking a monk to translate. "Tell him that. No one is going to die, and no one is going back to Burma. Not today."

A few weeks later, Nai Soh has sufficiently recovered from his back surgery to be able to come back to the wat. I stop by to visit and find Nai Soh in the mood for talk. I ask Phra Banyaa to translate for me. Nai Soh explains that he was a monk in a monastery in Monland. One day he went out to visit someone. While he was gone the soldiers attacked. He came home to find everyone gone, the monks' hall empty.

There was silence in the courtyard. Soldiers surrounded the village. Nai Soh didn't dare go out. For two days he hid in the monastery alone, starving. At night he listened to the wind and wondered if it were the ghosts of friends who had been shot. Finally, the military came back and found him. Before throwing him in a prison cell, they dragged him out of the temple compound and beat him. They beat him with sticks, and they beat him with guns. Then they shot him. He lifts his shirt, and I see the jagged scar where the bullet pierced his chest.

It was more than a year before Nai Soh was released from prison. Afterward, he headed for the border, and from there on his story is the same as the hundreds of others we have heard. Life on the border was shabbier even than life in an oppressed Mon village, but for a while it was free. When the Burmese military took Three Pagoda Pass, even that malaria-infested refuge of near-starvation was closed to them, and they fled to Thailand by the thousands, Nai Soh among them.

That night I call Matthew and tell him Nai Soh's story. When Nai Soh broke his back, we had thought he was mad or stupid to jump off a roof to escape the police.

"Now I understand what the sight of those police uniforms meant to him," says Matthew. "Imagine, after what he's been through, what it must be like to have men with guns coming to get you."

For the next few days I feel sobered by Nai Soh's story. I try to cheer myself up by spending more time playing with the children. I especially enjoy tickling Kyang San, the small daughter of one of the refugees. She squeals, delighted.

Phra Banyaa watches and smiles. "You love the little children, I think."

"Yes. I do."

"And do you have the little children yourself?"

"No. None of my own."

"Ah. Then you stay alone?"

I nod. "Alone."

It has begun to rain. On my way out, Phra Banyaa stands in the rain and waves to me. "Many blessings on you, sir," he calls, waving. "Many blessings."

I wave back, my heart going out to him entirely.

Now it is raining in earnest, and by the time I get to the main road, everything is flooded. The stores are two feet under water. Shopkeepers stand in their doorways, bailing water off their floors in buckets, and splashing it out the door. The street is already calf-deep in black, swirling muck.

Within one block I am soaked head to toe from rain and accidental splashing from hasty store owners who don't stop to look when they toss the water out the front door. My leather sandals turn from beige to sodden gray. The sky is overcast, and the trees are shrouded in a gray coat of mist.

Soon after the rains begin, I come bursting into the wat with good news. For weeks Phra Banyaa has asked me to bring a doctor for the routine cases, and for weeks Matthew and I have searched for one. I have asked at the border consortium, where many medical groups offering services to refugees meet monthly. I have asked among other NGOs we know. Finally, a doctor has agreed to come every few weeks. I feel excited and heroic. I can hardly wait to see Phra Banyaa's face when I tell him a doctor is coming at last.

I run to the room where Phra Banyaa lives with the refugees. It is nearly empty. Nai Soh lies on his pallet in the corner. Nai Han is home from the hospital, sitting on a mat eating rice. He smiles in greeting. Nai Thondin, a recent arrival and land-mine victim, is outside and hops in on his one leg to get his crutches. The rest of the room is empty.

"Where is everyone?" I ask. "Where's Phra Banyaa?"

Nai Thondin's wife says, in Thai, "Phra Banyaa is in Sangkhlaburi."

"Sangkhlaburi!? But the doctor is coming!" Sangkhlaburi is five hours away on the Thailand-Burma border. I look down at my list of sick people. "What about the others?"

"Gone."

"Gone *where*?"

"Out."

"Will they be back?"

To this there is no answer, but the remaining refugees look at one another uncomfortably.

Soon after my discovery that Phra Banyaa and many others are gone, an explanation comes from Matthew. They have been sent back, all of them, to the border, or dispersed to various provinces, by order of the Abbot. Those who can't speak Thai well enough to pass for a Thai are a liability. They draw attention to the wat, and so have been banished. They were offered Thai lessons at a nearby, sympathetic Thai wat. Those who applied themselves and were successful are staying. Those whose Thai is still unconvincing and who do not need urgent medical attention must go.

It is a smart move by the Abbot, in response to increased pressure on the refugees by the Thai government. It is becoming more and more dangerous for a refugee to be in Bangkok. The police hunt them on every street, and the wat is adjusting accordingly. But for me there were no good-byes. No warning.

I think of all of us: the Thai government, police, hospitals, volunteers like myself. We all have our ways of not listening, of turning away. The police rush in on men so terrified they throw themselves off the roof and land wounded among old graves, where the police then leave them, too busy to be bothered or too ashamed to ask forgiveness. Doctors turn the wounded away and don't even read the papers to understand the situation that is driving people across the border.

And me, I am implicated, too. I get busy, so I won't have to hear the stories of people I have ostensibly come to serve. A man tells me he has been tortured, and I say, Excuse me, I need to pay a bill or call a cab or get a prescription. I walk away, and though part of my heart wants to say, "Tell me your story," another part wants to say, "Be silent. I'm too afraid to listen."

Most of us long for a kind of connectedness we rarely find. Probably it is available everywhere, even in our living rooms at home, with our silent or estranged families, or on the streets of our hometowns. But we don't quite have the courage to risk the kind of relationship we long for. So we search in exotic lands and in extraordinary circumstances for the story or event, the one face that will break through to us, engage us, make us feel. But when faced with the opportunity, we are as frightened and alone as we are in our living rooms, and we shrink from the very engagement we desire and have come so far to find. We hide in busy schedules because we don't know how to feel, and we don't know what to do about the suffering, and we don't know what it means.

My mind brushes over the image of Phra Banyaa standing outside the wat, blessing me. "Blessings on you, sir. Many blessings." Perhaps he knew we were to be separated. It is a moment I go back to again and again; there is something mythic about it. It is a moment that seems to mean more than itself. It creeps into my imagination as an unwanted symbol of the Mon, and perhaps of all the indigenous. The tortured man, the indigenous man, the man in danger, inquires after my state. He stands alone in the rain, waving, bestowing blessings. And then he disappears.

Mothers and Sons

One of the worst things about refugee work is seeing how lost the young are without their families and how the most innocent are often the most badly damaged in the course of armed conflict. Matthew and I begin with thirty-some temple boys at the wat, all orphans, or effectively orphaned. For many, the conflict within Burma means families are separated and no one knows if their parents are dead or alive.

More orphans come every month, and eventually, we have nearly seventy. The boys arrive wide-eyed, with a look that says never mind the monk at their side or the dozens like them sitting cross-legged on the floor. At heart they know they are alone now and always will be. Even some of the older refugees, those who pass for men, are young enough to have the nature of boys, at once resilient and easily wounded.

For example, Nai Hong Sa, the young man with the ruptured bladder, was sent to defend the Mon at the age of fourteen. Now nineteen, he has carried the wounds of this war through the last of his youth, into adulthood.

One day Phra Dhamma and I take Nai Hong Sa to see yet another doctor in an ongoing attempt to find treatment for him. I follow Phra Dhamma to the reception area, where he reports Nai Hong Sa's ailment to the receptionist as the usual complaint: "stomachache." Increasingly this is the explanation for everything. Colons dropping out, blindness, deafness, missing extremities, shattered urethras. All are listed blandly on the admittance form as "stomachache."

When we go into the examination room Phra Dhamma expands on the stomachache theory. "What exactly seems to be the problem with his stomach?" asks the doctor kindly.

"He was exploded," says Phra Dhamma, in Thai.

The doctor raises his eyebrows. One could infer this is not the usual answer. "He was . . . ?"

"Exploded," supplies Phra Dhamma. "You see, the explosion went in here and came out here." He shows the doctor the equivalent places in his own body.

"Exploded or shot?" I put in, trying to be helpful.

Phra Dhamma, ever scrupulous to let the patient know what is being discussed, translates this into Mon for Nai Hong Sa, and Nai Hong Sa immediately replies, "Shot."

The doctor looks interested. This is the most intriguing case of stomachache he has seen all morning. He takes Nai Hong Sa into the curtained area and examines the wound. He comes back looking serious. We all sit.

"What are his expectations?" asks the doctor, in English.

"Expectations?" To me the question seems unnecessarily abstract.

Seeing us look at one another in a clueless fashion, the doctor tries again. "I mean, there are two different problems here. He has an infection. And he has to urinate through tubes. If the expectation is that the infection is to be cleared up, that is easy. If you are expecting him to be normal again, that is another matter."

"We were hoping for normal," I say.

The doctor looks down thoughtfully at the boy before him, takes out a little pad and draws us a picture. "I will begin by cutting him here," he says, making us gasp. Phra Dhamma takes the drawings and explains them to Nai Hong Sa, who looks horrified. In the end we all nod and agree the doctor will call us when a hospital bed is available.

Finally, we get the call informing us Nai Hong Sa can be admitted. I have a full day of other patients scheduled, but Khun Phat, the secretary at the community office, urges me to drop everything and get Nai Hong Sa to the hospital right away. "They sounded like you'd better get there now or he'll lose his place," she says. Happy, blustering with success, I obey.

At the wat, I pester Nai Hong Sa as if I were his mother. "Quick, quick. Are you ready? The taxi is here. Let's go."

Phra Dhamma accompanies us, and I plop down on the hospital bench in front of the two men. "How do you feel?" I ask Nai Hong Sa.

Phra Dhamma translates for me. "Frightened. He says he's frightened."

"Of the pain?"

Phra Dhamma shakes his head. "Of dying."

I feel an upsurge of protectiveness. "Oh, Nai Hong Sa, I don't think you will die," I say. "There will be pain for a while. But the reason it took so long to get you into the hospital is that this is not emergency surgery. It is important, but it is not life-and-death."

Phra Dhamma explains, and Nai Hong Sa looks at me in a state of absolute and perfect misery. He is shrinking as we speak, sinking down into his seat. "He had three operations at Kanchanaburi already," says Phra Dhamma, while Nai Hong Sa squirms. "He thought he would die every time."

After all the hurry of the morning, we wait for more than an hour in the big, echoing amphitheater of the general waiting area. I go up to the receptionist's window three times, and we are sent to fill out papers at two different offices before we are finally allowed to accompany Nai Hong Sa upstairs to the surgical ward.

Once upstairs I sit in a small hallway, speaking my broken Thai to the nursing students, pretty young women barely out of their teens. They circle around me and giggle, asking me questions in delight. "What country do you come from?" they ask. "How is the traffic there? Do they eat Thai food?"

I quickly come to the limits of my Thai, and my brain goes into a fog of language exhaustion. While I am chatting, Nai Hong Sa waits glumly on a bench. He is very still. He is too anxious even to fidget.

At last someone takes him away, dresses him in huge peachy-pink hospital pajamas, and escorts him to his room. Phra Dhamma and I follow. Nai Hong Sa hugs himself to keep his pj's from flapping open. A nurse presents him with a form to sign, but when he writes his name, the nurses point and laugh. His Mon signature is meaningless to them, and he doesn't know how to write Thai script. They dip his thumb in ink and press his thumbprint on to the paper, a lonely blue swirl.

He climbs into bed and sits large-eyed and expectant, like a child. What we do not yet know is that he will sit there for days, with increasing resentment, before anything happens. Khun Phat had gotten the impression from the hospital that the surgeon was practically scrubbed, scalpel in hand, and that all he lacked was Nai Hong Sa on the table. But for reasons none of us can fathom, the doctor will not operate for more than a week. No wonder you have to wait six months for a hospital bed.

The night before his surgery, Nai Hong Sa looks thinner and smaller than ever. Dressed in his huge hospital pajamas he looks much younger than nineteen. The circles under his eyes are so dark they look like bruises. The skin on his face looks as if someone were pulling it from behind his head, stretching it tight over his bones. The rest of us move around him, talking, laughing, pushing papers in front of him, fiddling with the pens on the counter. He stands, fixed and silent, an unmoving point of unhappiness in the bright room.

A nurse hands him more forms to sign, and he takes them in slow motion. He makes his mark, but the nurse takes the forms back and tsks at us. "When was he born?" she asks. "He hasn't even filled out the date."

The monks huddle with Nai Hong Sa and discuss the question earnestly. Finally, Phra Dhamma announces they've sorted it out. "Friday," he says. "We're not too sure about the month or the year, but he was definitely born on a Friday."

The Mon cultural idiosyncrasy of placing infinite importance on the day of the week a person was born, and having total disinterest in the date, is meaningless to the nurse. She glowers at us. "He is too young," she says, clucking in disgust. "Look at this. He has no money, no address. Doesn't know when he was born. He is almost a child. He cannot sign for himself. Someone must take responsibility for him. Someone must pay. Has he no father, no mother?" She looks at me accusingly.

"I will take responsibility for him," I say. "Show me where to sign."

After Nai Hong Sa's surgery, Matthew checks in on him. "All right now? All set?" he asks, and in a fury Nai Hong Sa pulls back his robe to reveal that after months of waiting and more than a week in the hospital, after pain and expense and surgery, he now has two tubes instead of one.

I visit soon after to find him sleeping on his side like a baby, curled up, his face peaceful on his arm. I have brought him a cold Coke and cigarettes, which is probably not what you are supposed to bring someone in a hospital, but it is what I would want someone to bring me if I were restricted to a diet both tasteless and nutritionally sound. I don't know whether he will be allowed to indulge in either gift.

I don't want to awaken him. I wouldn't know what to say, him with no English, me with no Mon. The hospital assures us he speaks a little Thai and has been chatting with fellow patients, probably charming them with that orphaned look of his.

I leave the Coke on the table by Nai Hong Sa's bed and tiptoe out. Another patient shuffles over, smiling, and touches Nai Hong Sa's foot to wake him for me. But I gesture "No, don't," and keep going. I feel suddenly shy to be caught, wordless in my tenderness, with no displays of joviality to offer.

Back at the wat, later that morning, I meet the doctor who has begun coming to help the refugees. The children are squirting one another with water pistols someone has given them. Adults, many of whom are blind or missing legs and not too steady on their feet, are tripping over the kids. The doctor fights her way through the chaos and passes an experienced glance over the small rash-covered bodies of boys we bring before her.

A truck pulls up through the gates. Several women hop out of it and wave the boys and monks over. It's hair-cutting day. The monks must keep their heads shaved, and the devout among the Thai Mon community come monthly to provide this service.

Several of the doctor's patients escape for the promise of excitement downstairs, but to those who are left, the doctor calmly dispenses scabies medicine and vitamins, shampoos for lice and antibiotics.

I admire her placid exterior and wonder whether I will ever be able to satisfy the expectations that local people and experienced missioners have of projecting a calm demeanor. "*Cay yen, cay yen*," say the local people; have a cool heart.

The opposite is "*cay rawn*"—hothearted—which is what I am. My heart is so hot it is a little furnace, always bubbling over with energy, equally quick to frustration and to inappropriate raucous laughter. Both extremes are suspect in this land. Thai nationals often put additives in motorcycle engines to make them roar more obnoxiously, but they expect people, especially women, to be smooth as glass and quiet as silk.

Among the children who do not run off when the haircutters arrive is a recent arrival, Nai Oo. A scrawny eleven year old who looks as though he's starving, he is much smaller than the others his age, and when he breathes, the ribs stick out of his narrow chest as if they might burst through the skin. We almost miss him among the crowd of small boys who are still left, poking and squirting one another while they wait for the doctor. He hangs back as if he would like to make himself invisible. "What's the matter with this one?" asks the doctor, who sees no immediate signs of the usual minor maladies of scabies, rashes, or lice.

Nai Oo responds in a thin high voice, and his story is translated for us: he has been coughing blood for three years. We adults tower over him, handle him, and discuss his fate while the child looks up with the nervousness of the very young when they are surrounded by too many adults.

"I'm afraid this isn't something I can handle here at the wat," says the doctor. "You'll have to take him to the hospital and have him x-rayed for TB."

After lunch, I go back to the wat to collect Nai Oo for his chest x-ray. I find him upstairs with the other boys, who are wrestling and leaping like puppies. They all look sturdier than Nai Oo, and with some instinct for gentleness, they exclude him from the roughness of their play. Nai Oo watches the others with longing, his chest heaving.

I ask Phra Dhamma to come with us. As we head out of the wat, I see that Nai Oo is padding barefoot down the wooden steps and out onto the asphalt. This is the tropics, and in places the street is so hot the tar bubbles.

"Shoes!" I call down the stairs after Phra Dhamma and point at Nai Oo's feet. "Phra Dhamma, please stop. Where are Nai Oo's shoes?"

Phra Dhamma turns and mumbles something to Nai Oo, who looks down at his filthy toes as if he has just noticed he has them. He looks up at the monk and shakes his head.

"None," says Phra Dhamma, already turning toward the street. "This boy has no shoes."

Phra Dhamma is shuffling in brown plastic sandals. Slurp, slurp, his feel fall out of them, then catch up with them again, slipping in. I follow behind in my beige, fifty-dollar leather sandals, now black with dirt and soot. One side has broken free of the sole and drags on the ground like the wing of a wounded bird. Having only one pair, albeit originally of good quality, has made me feel I have been true to the call of simplicity. But behind me Nai Oo hobbles over the hot, broken ground on his tough, bare feet.

I am briefly tempted to pick the child up. But at his age he might resent the damage to his dignity more than the injury to his feet. The boy himself has made no sign of distress. If Phra Dhamma does not think to carry him, it seems unlikely Nai Oo would want to be carted around by a foreign woman, so I restrain myself.

At the hospital, Phra Dhamma registers Nai Oo. "What's wrong with this boy?" asks the nurse.

"He has a cough," says Phra Dhamma. The nurse pops a thermometer into the child's mouth and disappears.

"We should tell her he's coughing *blood* for three years," I say to Phra Dhamma. He returns to the counter and tries to tell a receptionist, but she waves him silent.

"Save it for the doctor," she says, slipping down in her chair as if she's about to settle in for a nap.

"What's wrong with this boy?" asks the doctor, when he comes.

"He's got a cough," says Phra Dhamma.

"Sometimes he coughs blood," I add, giving Phra Dhamma a look.

"Been treated before?" asks the doctor.

Phra Dhamma and I both shake our heads no. My Thai is improving, though slowly. This time I understand everything the doctor says in the ensuing conversation, except the word for TB, though I know that must be what he is saying. After this preliminary discussion, the doctor sends us upstairs for the x-ray.

One thing that amazes me about life in Thailand is the sudden silences even among the multitudes. Along a hallway in a crowded building, you may unexpectedly find yourself alone. Our footsteps echo through the hollow, endless, green-gray corridors. We find the x-ray room open but unattended. All that equipment, inviting tampering or theft, and there is no one around, no one to register us, no one to ask if we are in the right place. We shrug at each other, then start fiddling with the sensitive-looking equipment, to keep ourselves occupied.

When the technician comes in, he asks no questions, and registers no surprise at the three of us standing among the bones of his machines, so I guess someone has phoned up to him. There are no screens, no protective coverings, no curtains, no orders for Phra Dhamma and me to stand to one side or stay in the waiting room. We mill about, while Nai Oo holds the x-ray plate up to his chest. It is hard for him to get his spindly arms around it.

Watching these proceedings I think of how much I love the illusory clarity of medicine. True, life is usually murkier than it seems in the waters of science. There are many maybes, many invisible wounds, many simple causes of suffering we do not know how to undo. But there are also windows through which we can see into a child's lungs. The doctor holds the x-ray up against the light, and the three of us, foreigner, monk, and patient, crowd around to view the white web of his secret, scarred life.

When the x-ray is over, I follow Nai Oo, who follows Phra Dhamma back downstairs. The child's shoulders are thin, with sunken wells of flesh between the bones, the protruding knuckles of folded wings.

We collect a little bag of medicine for Nai Oo, then go out into the hot, bright air. "Now we visit Nai Hong Sa?" asks Phra Dhamma, once we are outside. We hurry across the street to the bus stop, dodging motorcycles with three or four passengers on them, and three-wheeled tuk tuks, which seem to be aiming for us. Nai Oo's bare feet scamper across the boiling tar. He must have the soles of a bear cub.

On the bus Phra Dhamma rides free, sitting in front by the door, a monk's custom and right. Nai Oo nestles in beside him, disappearing under the orange shade of Phra Dhamma's robe. Only his huge eyes show, gleaming and round, like a pet owl.

Back for the second time today, I encounter Nai Hong Sa out in the hall, leaning over a balcony, watching two pretty girls who are chatting in the court-yard below. He has tucked his enormous hospital gown neatly under one arm to hold it tight, like a monk's robe. He keeps his tubes and bag discreetly at his side. When he sees Phra Dhamma, there is an explosive and angry burst of Mon, ending in a plaintive whine.

Phra Dhamma laughs gently. "What's he saying?" I ask.

"He wants to leave."

The monk and I shake our heads simultaneously. "No," we say in two lan-guages.

There is another tirade in Mon from Nai Hong Sa. I lean over the balcony and try to appear disinterested. Phra Dhamma can handle this. Nai Hong Sa storms and pleads.

Nai Oo stays close to Phra Dhamma. There is something in the flick of Phra Dhamma's robe and the corresponding lift of his chin that speaks unmistakably of authority. It inspires trust in small boys, just as the stance and uniform of the priest was assuring and awesome in my Catholic school days.

Phra Dhamma explains that Nai Hong Sa wants to go home to get soap and a toothbrush. I refrain from asking why he didn't take these items with him in the first place. I also wonder why I never thought of them myself, remembering

Nai Hong Sa on the day of his hospital admission, changing from his habitual sarong into Western trousers and a blue knit top. He took such elaborate care to dress himself for the outside world, to be prepared, but perhaps it never occurred to him he would be here for days, and as it eventually turned out, for weeks.

"No," I say firmly. "We've waited months for this bed. I don't want to risk losing it. We'll buy him a toothbrush downstairs. This bed is as valuable as gold," I add, laughing. Phra Dhamma laughs, too, and translates. Nai Hong Sa glowers, evidently not amused.

"So what was that all about?" I ask Phra Dhamma on the way to the store downstairs.

"He wants his mother."

I look out of the side of my eye to study Phra Dhamma's face. I can't imagine how to respond to this announcement. I am wondering whether this is a difficult statement for a Mon man to make. Is it an unmanly admission? Does it elicit condescension from Phra Dhamma as he repeats it? His face is untroubled. It is a simple statement of fact. "So," I think, storing this information away with my small but growing stock of cultural impressions.

"Where is she?" I ask.

"At the border in Kanchanaburi. He wants to see her very much. He is very afraid."

"Still afraid?"

"He is sure he is going to die."

"Still?" I ask with mixed amounts of surprise and pity.

"Yes."

"So that's the problem? That's why he wants to go home? He's afraid he will die here?"

"Not exactly. The problem is if he dies, he won't see his mother anymore."

I marvel at the way the human mind works, how tangled things are in the heart, where dying and missing one's mother acquire equal significance.

We end up buying a toothbrush, toothpaste, toilet paper, powder, shampoo, soap, and a comb. I haul each item out of the vendor's cart and present it to Phra Dhamma. "How about this, Phra Dhamma? Oh, and what about that?" He looks at them all with equal indifference and stands by quietly while they are purchased and put in a bag. I buy more than Nai Hong Sa asked for. It's a bribe, and I know it. "Tell him I think he will see his mother again, no problem," I say.

"Yes," says Phra Dhamma. "No problem."

Upstairs again, Nai Hong Sa is sitting in the sun by a window, pouting. He chats with Phra Dhamma for a while. So long, in fact, that I begin fidgeting, and Nai Oo starts picking at an old scab on his leg for entertainment. "Go now?" asks Phra Dhamma at last.

I nod.

Nai Hong Sa looks down, hiding his big dark eyes. For a moment he can't speak, can't look up. He struggles with himself briefly, then the moment passes, and he nods, accepting that we must leave and he must remain.

Phra Dhamma, Nai Oo, and I part at the corner: Phra Dhamma and the child go one way, and I head for home. Nai Oo is momentarily confused and not sure whom to follow. He looks first at the monk and then at me, and his thin arms reach for me. My hand goes out to him, an automatic gesture, made of instinct and longing. At the last moment, I turn it into a wave. Then I point to the monk and turn away. All this talk of mothers and sons has left something aching deep inside me, I who have never been a mother.

That night after leaving Nai Hong Sa and Nai Oo, I find myself dreaming of the family I left behind. People I haven't thought of for years come unbidden and sometimes unwelcome into my imagination. Chiefly, I think of one of my stepfathers, the one who mostly raised me from the age of six on. He is a terrifying man I haven't spoken to in years. Even the memory of him inspires both fear and longing. In my dreams I turn and cry out and long to be reconciled. When I wake I think someday I will return and see him face-to-face and cross the boundaries between us, which are much more ominous than the boundaries between countries and cultures. I will sit with him and eke out some tale of ruined love he felt for us or meant to feel. I will hear his guilt and his sorrow, and I will forgive him and be whole.

I know some of the reason I am so moved by the refugees is that I identify with them, though it is largely an unearned identification. The human heart is selfish enough that it sees its own history everywhere and creates symbols of its own pain and its own journey in everyone it meets.

In the end, Nai Hong Sa returns to the wat, smiling and round-faced, the sharp look of pain gone from his features, the fear gone from his eyes.

He stays long enough to have a few follow-up appointments and get himself into minor mischief. Matthew reports on him to me, in one of our nearly daily check-ins over the phone.

"I have had the talk with Nai Hong Sa I should have had months ago," he tells me.

"What talk is that?"

"About women mostly. Women and drugs. Here he is, a young man, healthy for the first time. I was worried he'd be eager to discover the world here in Thailand. And you know how easy it is to find a prostitute here."

"And how cheap," I add. I think back to a day I visited the work of one of our community priests, who established one of the oldest AIDS education programs in the country. One of his staff members told me that outside the tourist section you can get a woman or a quick fix of heroin for the same price: about 80 cents. A good bottle of beer, on the other hand, costs more than a dollar. There are estimates that as many as 80 percent of Bangkok's prostitutes are HIV positive.

Matthew and I are silent for a moment, thinking of Nai Hong Sa. "Well," I say, "how did he take the talk?"

"He looked very sheepish," says Matthew, "which probably means it came a little too late. Let's just hope he's been lucky this time, and that he'll be too smart for there to be a next time."

For a while I see Nai Hong Sa at the wat now and then. He looks healthier, but as he gains weight and energy, he becomes more restless. He paces in the courtyard, as anxious as when he was waiting for surgery. He is alone in a foreign country and has neither the sense of home his village could give him nor the adventure a young man expects from his travels.

He is cooped up at the wat most of the time. Whenever he leaves, he risks arrest. The longer he stays, the greater the risk. In the past, the sight of his tubes was enough to convince police they did not really want to arrest him and take responsibility for him. Now they leave him alone only out of habit. But sooner or later someone will notice him and haul him off to detention.

One day I ask after him, to hear he has already left. I am sorry I did not get to say good-bye to him, but I am not surprised he is gone. The restlessness has suddenly taken shape in action. Probably the Abbot also urged him to go, for his own safety and the safety of the other refugees. Though what he goes to and whether there will be safety for him anywhere is unknown.

I walk into the refugee room and contemplate the feel of the room without him. The little pile of possessions he had was hardly noticeable when he was here, but when I search the shelf I notice it is gone. He had so little. An extra sarong. His cigarettes. A cassette player Matthew gave him. Apart from these few things there was nothing to show he was here at all. No special corner he occupied. No furniture. No bedroll. Nothing. I sit in the sun awhile to say good-bye, even though he is not here to see me wishing him well.

I imagine a mother at the border squinting into the sun in disbelief and hope as the shape of her long-lost son emerges out of the forest. In reality I know this is an unlikely end to the story. Perhaps he will reach her old village and it will be gone, or the house will be empty and he will search for her from camp to camp. Or maybe he will find her and at first it will seem as if their joy is so big it must be felt by the whole world. But then little by little he will become restless again and will chafe at the things of his childhood, at small words, at the way she looks at him without comprehension when he tells the stories of where he has been.

And probably in the end he will disappear again, discovering both that he is too much of a man to live under his mother's roof and that he is not yet man enough to suit himself, and there are still discoveries waiting to be made along his journey. His mother will pack him some food and hold him and listen without belief to his promises to return, or perhaps she will simply wake up one morning and find him gone. And like me, she will be sad, but she will not be surprised.

Beyond Risk

Do to others whatever you would have them
do to you. This is the law and the prophets.

MATTHEW 7:12

See yourself in others.
Then whom can you hurt?

FROM THE DHAMMAPADA,
TRANSLATED BY THOMAS BYROM

A Soldier in the Jungle

In the jungles of Burma, a Mon soldier hears the click under his foot just before the sound of the explosion. There is not enough time to panic—just enough to know with absolute certainty that even if he lives, it will not be the life he has known, and he will not be the man he has been.

The soldier wakes up minutes later, with a confused memory of the sound of shredding, the smell of burning flesh. Maybe, he thinks, this has not really happened to him. Maybe it is something he heard about a long time ago. Something that happened to someone else.

He feels himself lifted, carried in a makeshift hammock through the forest. He hears feet hurrying through the underbrush, the rustling of leaves. His arms seem to be on fire. He turns his head to look at his right hand, but his eyes are filled with blood. He sees nothing but deep, colorless darkness.

When he next comes to himself, he struggles to open his eyes, but continues to stare into emptiness. He lifts a hand to his head to feel for a bandage, but meets with air. This confuses him. He has misplaced his body somehow. The jungle has swallowed him up. He is invisible to himself.

When he finally understands what he has become, for a brief time he is glad he is blind and cannot be reminded by every casual glance of all he has lost. Both arms are gone, one just above the elbow, the other just below. One eye is destroyed completely. The other lets in a little milky light.

In time, however, his blindness and his amputations acquire equal weight in his list of losses. Even if there were prostheses available in the jungle, no one would give one to a blind man. The hook at the end of a wooden arm can be deadly for someone who can neither feel it nor see it.

So he begins a life in which his body doesn't belong to him. Someone else is in charge of getting him to the toilet, dressing him, bathing him, feeding him. Other soldiers who are wounded are put to work watching the roads, counting cars. But there is no work for a blind, armless man. The army supplies him with a subsistence-level existence, but his life promises to stretch out in endless uselessness, boredom, and darkness.

Ultimately, his uselessness becomes his salvation. There are not enough friends and family to take care of him. And so an idea begins to circulate: it is time to find the soldier a wife.

She is a petite woman with a sweet round face and a body both slim and voluptuous. She moves into his life quietly, taking over without complaint the duties necessary for his care. Two children are born to them. A lively, chatty girl, and a fat, serious boy.

His children fill him with surprised gratitude. He holds them to his chest each morning, wrapping them in what is left of his arms, sniffing the sweet smell of their hair.

Throughout all this, shadows continue to move in the darkness behind his eyelids. Why, the soldier wonders, has the light leaking in from his one good eye not blinked and gone out? He continues to strain, detecting street lamps and dawn, sunlight through trees, all a filmy brightness. Indistinct. Like the shape of a face seen through heavy curtains.

He thinks if he stares long enough, he might part the mists of his blindness and reenter the world of the ordinary. With one eye, he could get a prosthesis. He could be useful again. And so, with the help of the Mon monks, he takes an unbelievable journey, an incalculable risk. He leaves the jungle and the border lands. Illegal and foreign, blind and maimed, without the local language, the correct papers, or a baht to his name, he enters the busy, noisy city of Bangkok.

Nai Nya Naa, the blind double amputee, is one of the first refugees I meet, along with Nai Hong Sa and Nai Han. It is as much a mystery to us as it is to him that he is aware of changes in light. The sensation is not enough to enable him to see, just enough to make him wonder if more might be possible. Matthew asks me to check into possibilities—to talk to doctors about options, prognoses, costs. So Phra Dhamma and I lead the way into the hospital. Nai Hong Sa is still with us, and he follows slowly, leading Nai Nya Naa by his stumps. One of Nai Nya Naa's eyes is closed completely; the other is catarrhal, as if swimming in skim milk.

We spend an hour in a waiting room as big and echoing as a cathedral. All around us families are chattering, laughing, consulting, and eating while the four of us, foreigners, sit silently among the bustle of Thai life.

When we are finally let into a side room, a doctor smiles in greeting, then proceeds to shine a flashlight into Nai Nya Naa's face from different directions. She asks questions in Thai, which Phra Dhamma whispers to Nai Nya Naa in Mon, over Nai Nya Naa's shoulder. Nai Nya Naa points with what is left of his arms to show which direction the light comes from.

Nai Nya Naa's left eye is shut tight, and the doctor lifts the lid to reveal a knotted white ball, like a hard-boiled egg not peeled very well, with a small swirling gouge at the center and just a bit of yellow, as if the yolk were leaking out.

I feel moved and embarrassed. Nai Nya Naa is unperturbed, seemingly unaware I have intruded on his privacy by viewing his wounds at close range. He cocks his head to catch what is going on around him.

I admit to myself that after hearing Matthew's description of him, I half expected Nai Nya Naa to be a shell, a husk we could move around like a coat rack. This is a shameful thing to realize about myself. But as I watch him submit to this inspection, I realize he's all there; only his arms and eyes are missing. He has a strong voice and a handsome face. A lean, graceful body. You can feel his spirit, his personality, from the way he waits to hear what Phra Dhamma is translating for him. He waits attentively. He has the listening look of the blind.

When we're done, the woman in the white coat who has been conducting this examination announces she is not a doctor at all. She is the nurse who does a preliminary investigation and determines which specialist the patient should see. She sends us forty steps down the hall and again we find ourselves sitting and waiting.

We go through the whole thing again with a doctor who is young and has a lisp. A nurse leads Nai Nya Naa to a complicated contraption with a helmet and a scope and straps his head in place. It looks as if they are about to attempt brain surgery, but the doctor merely seats herself before him and looks through the scope. She sighs and explains something to the monk. I think I catch the sentence "There is nothing we can do."

I ask in English to confirm it. "Now," she explains, "he sees light and dark. Surgery is a great risk. It might mean he would see nothing. Complete darkness forever. You understand?"

I look so disappointed that she hastens to add, "Of course it may be too early to tell. You come back when the chief surgeon is here, yes? Then we will give you a final answer." She schedules a more elaborate procedure for our next visit, but warns us not to get our hopes up. I have the feeling the follow-up appointment is mostly for my benefit, and that Nai Nya Naa can expect little from it.

Nai Nya Naa has seemed hopeful all morning. Now he leans toward us and listens, though he understands neither Thai nor English. He senses that we are coming to some conclusion about him. He asks something of Phra Dhamma in Mon. It is the first time today that he has spoken, other than to answer a question. Phra Dhamma draws in close and speaks quietly, intensely. He is giving the bad news.

Nai Nya Naa says nothing, betrays nothing. Only the muscles along his jaw and cheek ripple. His mouth flinches. I look the same way when I am about to cry. But he does not cry. When we came in I had expected our problem to be raising funds to treat him. But the actual problem is simpler and more final. There is no treatment. We leave the doctor's office slowly, leading Nai Nya Naa back through the crowd of hopeful patients, a silent parade retracing our steps through the noisy corridor.

We have just heard momentous news, but we do not give ourselves time to sit with the weight of Nai Nya Naa's prognosis. We keep busy to keep from thinking too much. Granted, we are busy about important things: we need to get to the cafeteria before noon to keep Phra Dhamma from starving. A monk eats only twice a day, and both meals must be before noon. Those are the rules. If Phra Dhamma misses this meal, he will go hungry for the rest of the day.

I bustle us down to the cafeteria, where Phra Dhamma finds a table and seats himself with the unconscious poise of a cat. Expectant without being arrogant. He flicks his orange robe to make it tuck in aesthetically. Nai Hong Sa piles up dirty dishes left behind by the last customer, while I buy four incomprehensible dishes, all on rice. "You want #@$%, right?" the kitchen server asks in Thai, waving her serving spoon and wiping a stray strand of long black hair off her forehead with the back of her arm.

"Ka. Right," I say, having no idea what I've ordered. I dump the four dishes on the table and hope the men will sort them out while I buy drinks.

When I get back, Phra Dhamma is gulping his food, perhaps with an eye to the time. I put a little heap of my noodles on the two plates of food for the injured and try not to look too curious. But I am curious.

I am touched by the simplicity of the scene before me. Nai Hong Sa is seated next to Nai Nya Naa, who is leaning forward with great attention, as if trying to hear a word whispered by a lover. Nai Hong Sa holds up the spoon, says something in Mon, and Nai Nya Naa opens his mouth.

That night I sit on my bed in the dark for a long time. I think of Nai Nya Naa leaning toward Nai Hong Sa and opening his mouth to accept food. For ten years someone has done this. Fed and clothed Nai Nya Naa. Tied his sarong, washed him, combed his hair, led him. Without institutions, without grants from foundations, without fuss. In the helper, himself an injured man, there is no show of either pity or impatience. Nor is there the inordinate cheerfulness trained into many Western volunteers, who, in an attempt to cover our discomfort, often take refuge in false joviality. In Nai Nya Naa I see no embarrassment, no apologies, no thanks.

The Mon do not seem to feel the tear-welling sorrow that I feel for Nai Nya Naa's blindness, but neither do they exhibit signs of the aversion I would feel if I were to meet a man like this on the streets of New York. Of course, I would pretend not to feel sorrow or embarrassment, but I would feel them both.

The Mon seem to treat their maimed as if they were assessing a common problem, distributing a common responsibility. They tally what the individual brings to the group, whether strength or weakness, into a sum that is all that the Mon own and are in this generation. They are not a series of individuals. They are the monks and the warriors, the mothers and the farmers, the infants and the injured. Their compassion springs not from generosity but from the conviction of kinship. They are a people, a nation.

I envy them.

The next day at the wat, Phra Dhamma is waiting for me when I arrive.

"Ah, Wicki. We are so glad you came. We have a big problem and wait and wait for your help."

"What can I do for you?" I ask, feeling very smug that I'm so needed. He hurries me into a dark, moist room under the stairs, with several monks and novices at our heals. At first I think the room is absolutely devoid of furniture like all the other rooms. On the walls are a few tasteless calendars with women's faces overly made up. Beside the calendars are Buddhist scripture quotes in Pali and English, and photos of monks holding signs with such political slogans as "Free the Mon" and "End forced labor in Burma." Besides these few decorations there is nothing in the room except a well-swept floor that feels cool and slick beneath my feet.

"Here it is," says Phra Dhamma, walking past me into the corner. Then I realize this room is not as empty as I had thought. In the corner a large sheet covers something bulky and angular on a table. Phra Dhamma flips the sheet back and reveals a gleaming computer much bigger and newer than anything I've ever used.

"Someone gave this as a donation," explains Phra Dhamma. "We like very much, but we lost some files. Can you retrieve?"

My smugness instantly vanishes. I'm so untechnological I don't even own a watch. Not wanting to reveal the absolute naked depths of my ignorance all at once, I decide to fiddle with the computer for a minute as if I know what I'm doing.

"Ah, no, Wicki. I think you must go to autoexecbat first," says Phra Dhamma, looking over my shoulder. I push a few more keys while Phra Dhamma looks increasingly concerned and makes little gasps. "Um, Wicki, I think you should not . . . ah, too late." The screen has gone completely blank.

"Oops," I say sheepishly.

"*Mai pen rai,*" he says. "Never mind."

"Maybe I should I keep trying?" I ask.

"Ah, Wicki, you work very hard. Maybe you should take a little break now," he suggests gently. "I will call the man who gave us the computer. He will help later."

I allow as how, yes, maybe a break would be a good idea.

Phra Dhamma throws the sheet back over the computer and tucks in the edges tenderly, with a little pat.

"Come," he says, tactfully changing the subject. "We will drink a Coke together." I follow him, shaking my head. How completely like life among refugees in Bangkok—a first-class computer in an otherwise bare room, operated with a good degree of expertise by people with one change of clothes and bare feet.

After drinking our Cokes, we proceed to the darkest room at the back of the wat. There we find Nai Nya Naa sitting with his older child in his lap, his wife asleep beside him. Their son, a fat baby, swings in a large blue cloth tied to a beam. He is wearing a small shirt that comes to his waist. He is naked below that, and his little round legs hang out of the cloth, kicking at something in his dreams.

Phra Banyaa is still with us at this point, and he tells us Nai Nya Naa's daughter is feverish. I put my hand on her forehead. It is so hot, it's uncomfortable to touch her. Nai Nya Naa rocks her protectively, the stumps of his elbows wrapped around her.

A confusing discussion ensues about who will take the child to the doctor. "How can they go?" asks Phra Banyaa. "Surely the family will be arrested."

This is one of the biggest challenges of refugee work in Thailand. This country is not a party to the UN protocol that governs treatment of refugees. Thus, even if a family officially is under UN protection, as this family is, they are subject to arrest and detention. The threat of detention hounds Nai Nya Naa and families like his, and they live in constant fear.

"They will not be arrested," explains Matthew, who has stopped by to visit Nai Nya Naa. He fills in the details of our program's strategy. "If a foreigner is with them, the police will not want to be seen arresting them. If a monk and a foreigner both go, the police dare not interfere. Or if a monk goes only with a child, no one will notice them. We will send someone with them, and they will be safe."

"Ah!" Phra Banyaa is delighted. "This is highly convenient, sir," he says.

"Ask them who should go to the hospital with the little girl," asks Matthew. "Shall it be Vicki? Or how about you, Phra Banyaa?"

"Sir!" says Phra Banyaa, abashed. "I cannot hold her, sir. You see, I am a monk."

"Ah, very true," says Matthew. "You are a monk."

The taboo against monks touching females is definitely a logistical problem when it comes to the medical program. It is like trying to work a jigsaw puzzle to figure out who can sit by whom, carry whom, lead whom.

"Then ask the family if it is best that the wife go."

The family confers. Nai Nya Naa asks huskily, worriedly, how long it will take, and holds the child closer to him.

"Maybe one hour," Matthew lies.

This creates more discussion in Mon. Nai Nya Naa is unhappy about the suggestion that half his family disappear even for an hour. I refrain from saying that the prospect of going anywhere and back in Bangkok traffic within one hour is highly improbable. The family and the monks discuss the possibilities while someone goes out to the street to hail a cab.

While we are waiting for the taxi, a small group gathers at the entrance of the wat, ready for the trip to the hospital: a small boy and his mother, a novice with sores covering most of his head. Then I see Nai Nya Naa walking toward us, carrying his daughter. His wife and baby are beside him. They have decided they cannot be parted for so long. Not for an hour. If one must go, they will all go.

"What do they have?" Matthew asks. "Nothing. Each other. To ask to take his wife and child for an hour, after what they have been through, given the insecurity, the risk of arrest, is a big request even if it is for the child's good. What if the wife is arrested? It's unlikely with a monk accompanying her, but it could happen. To ask to take Nai Nya Naa's family is like saying to a man, 'Give me all your money for an hour. I promise I'll be right back.' "

The family sits on the bench and waits for the cab. The feverish child cuddles into her father's lap, her flushed face raised to his. His cheek rests against hers as he whispers soothing things to her, turning his ear to hear what she whispers back. Her little hand lies on the end of his left arm, which stops just below the elbow.

With the stump of his arm, Nai Nya Naa lifts his daughter's hand, tosses it lightly into the air, making her smile. Then he stops and enfolds her again, his arms so short they hardly reach each other as they cross over her little chest.

I say Nai Nya Naa's name, and he smiles. That small, quirky smile.

The baby is fat and alert and seems too big for the mother to carry, slight as she is, small as an American pre-teenager. I watch them get into the cab, the sick girl clinging to her father, his amputated arms trying to encircle her, the mother leading her blind husband, with her son on her hip, as they set out in the unknown and dangerous city.

Watching Nai Nya Naa with his family, I think this is a man whose soul has been burned clean. Whatever is left of a human being after you take everything extraneous away, that's what he is. A man stripped down to his essence. A presence like clear, deep water.

It has been several weeks since Nai Nya Naa's first appointment, and at last the day has come for his follow-up visit with the chief eye surgeon. I call Phra Dhamma to see if he can accompany us to the hospital. "How are you, Phra Dhamma?" I ask.

"I am in the pink," he says.

"Oh," I say. "That sounds very good indeed."

"Yes, I believe it is. And how about you? Are you fit as a fiddle?"

"Er . . ."

"Or perhaps you are just fine and dandy?"

"Phra Dhamma, have you been studying English again?"

"Yes," he says. "My friend Phra Dala Non is helping me. He knows many expressions."

"I can see that."

"Phra Dala Non is a good teacher. Maybe sometime when you come to the wat, Phra Dala Non and I can teach you to speak Mon."

"Good idea," I say. "In the meantime, would you like to come to the hospital with Nai Nya Naa and me?"

"Also very good idea," says Phra Dhamma.

An hour later we collect Nai Nya Naa from the refugee room. His good eye is red today. He lowers his head to be able to reach his face with his stumps. He wipes at his eyes, as if to brush away tears. But there are no tears. He has lost his quiet, his inner silence. His feet tap in the taxi. When we arrive in the hospital waiting room, he jiggles both knees and shuffles his feet up and down. He rubs his chin against his chest. He sniffles. I can't offer him a Kleenex, as he has nothing to hold it with, and I don't think he would appreciate a strange woman dabbing at his face. His knee jiggles over until it touches mine. Surprised, he jerks it back and is still for a moment.

The three of us sit in the waiting room for hours in silence. At last they call Nai Nya Naa's name, and I lead him down the hall. He maneuvers wonderfully despite my lack of expertise and language. With no language in common, I cannot say, "People sitting on both sides," "Narrow aisle," or "Bench to your right." I am conscious that my hands are sweaty where they fall below his sleeve line onto bare skin. He cannot wipe the moisture off, and probably he is too polite to do so, even if he could.

At the end of a long hall, we wait again. And wait. And wait. Through an open door I see a cart with a sheet and all sorts of tools. Sharp, gleaming scissors and needles. I think the room is empty, except for a nurse who is rummaging through the tool tray. Then I see a foot jerk up from just beyond the cart. Someone is lying there in the bright, otherwise empty room. The patient is covered by a white sheet, except for the feet, and so blends in with the furniture. The nurse is ministering to his head, invisible to us from this angle, in a way that surprises or pains. All we see is the quick twitch of one foot.

A woman with gauze as thick as a sock wadded over one eye is pacing the hall. She weeps out of her good eye and holds one hand over her mouth, as if to keep from saying something unforgivable.

On the door a sign in Thai script says, "Please take off your shoes before entering the operating room." It takes me a long time to make this out, and I find the message peculiar. I am a child again, learning to read, and learning the strange culture of the world. In this case both the world of Thailand and the world of medicine are strange to me. I am used to "Shoes and shirt required." What am I to make of "Please remove your shoes before entering"?

We are called again and sent to a room so small all of us barely fit. Two men scoop some clear glop onto Nai Nya Naa's eye, then pass a machine over it. The inside of his eye appears on a screen. It means nothing to me. The inside of an eye is foreign terrain.

A nurse instructs us to present our files to the surgeons, whose waiting area is on the other side of the building. The crowd of people waiting is daunting. Phra Dhamma and I deposit Nai Nya Naa in a line of waiting patients, then find seats nearby. A monk must not sit next to a woman, so Phra Dhamma finds an old man to slip in next to. He quickly falls asleep. I find a seat two rows back, and before I know it, my own head is on my chest.

I wake up with a start, and my eyes turn automatically to the seat where we left Nai Nya Naa. He is not there. I look around frantically. Where can he have gone?

I have not said anything, but all eyes in the waiting area are instantly on me, and simultaneously everyone points. I follow the direction of their fingers and find that Nai Nya Naa and Phra Dhamma are sitting in a line of patients just outside the door of the exam room.

I get up and sit in a space where I can keep a better eye on them, feeling shy. No one has said anything to us, but we have obviously attracted attention—the monk, the foreigner, and the blind man with no arms. The other patients have been watching over us, a fellowship formed from forced patience and long silences. They know when we sleep and what we want to know when we wake up.

Eventually, we are all three allowed inside the exam room. A row of patients, blind or gauzy, sits along one wall. Three doctors sit at desks along the opposite wall. It is like some sort of underworld: a mostly dark room with a long line of miserable people wearing heavy bandages over their eyes. When one of the doctors is free she waves to the next patient who sits before her and submits to scrutiny, followed by short barks of command. Occasionally, the doctors lean together to confer before prescribing treatment.

I can see why Matthew sends me or comes himself. The monks, patients, and Thai doctors are all of a piece. They have an infinite capacity for burying their own curiosity. The monks are reliable and fastidious with money, but they could shuffle Nai Nya Naa in and out all day and never ask anything more than "Which door?" The doctors aren't much better. They conduct their examinations in silence and issue orders but no explanations.

This lack of questioning reminds me of an experience I had in Hong Kong, where a similar cultural aversion to questions prevails. "Why did God love Adam?" the teacher in our Christian language school asked, coaxing us to what she thought was a simple truth. Mostly Westerners in the class, we sputtered out possibilities: "Because God made him?" "Because God loves us all?"

"No," the teacher proclaimed, amid some disappointed clucking. "God loved Adam because Adam never asked questions."

It is my capacity to ask questions that makes me useful to Matthew and such a deep source of irritation to everyone else.

After Nai Nya Naa is briefly examined in silence, I begin to fire questions at the young doctor with the lisp. The other doctors stare at me, as do all the patients. They gape for a moment, seemingly surprised that someone on the patients' side of the table is capable of speech. "So," I ask, "does today's test clarify anything? Is it possible to help this man?"

They pass his results down the row, where each doctor sits at her own scope and takes a look at Nai Nya Naa's chart. Then they stand up, consult with one another, and decide they need more tests. They wave us down the hall to test the pressure behind Nai Nya Naa's eye. This will tell us whether the corneal chamber has completely collapsed.

The doctor with the lisp accompanies us. She and an assistant help Nai Nya Naa lie down on a table, while one of them puts a metal clamp right on his open eye. She does this without warning, presumably because she has no words in his language to explain what is happening. He does not flinch.

They have made some error and so do it again and again. The clamp falls apart and a screw rolls across the floor, under a cart. The doctor gets down on her hands and knees, and crawls under the cart, searching for it, her hands roaming on the cold linoleum. She and her assistant are young. They giggle and cover their mouths with their hands.

As we lead Nai Nya Naa back to the surgeon's room, the doctor reverts to professional decorum and professional vocabulary, sharp and precise as surgical knives. The chief surgeon takes charge of us. "The prognosis is not good," she says. "The chamber under the cornea has collapsed."

While I do not particularly merit special attention, she has apparently decided to take me seriously. In fact, she seems intrigued that anyone might want more than a handful of pills or a quick cure under the knife. She unfurls a huge wall chart of the inner workings of the eye, through which she directs me with the help of a pointer.

"Still," she says, "it is not hopeless. We may be able to repair the eye. He has up to a 50 percent chance."

This statement, with its small room for hope, is like Nai Nya Naa's sight, which for now leaks in at least some light. There are, however, two catches even to our less than 50 percent chance of success. The first is that this surgeon feels the same as the first doctor. "If we succeed, he may see. Not perfectly, but better. But if we fail, he may lose even the little light that he has."

The eye is a delicate thing. And like much in science, precision in prognoses is more a happy delusion for amateurs than a reality. The doctors don't know exactly why Nai Nya Naa can still see light. In trying to heal him, they could ruin whatever is still functioning in his eye.

The second catch is that to repair the eye, they will need to do a cornea transplant. "You understand," she says, pointing to the chart on the wall. "We need one of these. We basically need a new eye."

But they have no eyes to give him, they complain. That is the problem. In all of Thailand there are no eyes to spare. There is a three- to four-year wait for Thai citizens, longer for refugees like Nai Nya Naa. "So," she says, giving me a challenging look. "We will do the surgery if we have an eye for him. Can you find him an eye?"

At this question the room falls silent. The other patients have been eavesdropping, those who speak English whispering translations to those who don't. There are no eyes in Thailand. No eyes to spare. Can the foreigner find an eye? They angle their good eyes to get a look at me. It is a room full of birds, blinking at me, out of one eye at a time.

I have no more idea how to go about getting an eye than I would know how to grow orchids in Siberia. But I am afraid that if I treat this as a ridiculous request I will lose the doctor's interest altogether. Besides, my usefulness nerve has been tweaked, pinging like the funny bone after a blow, and once awakened it will not let me rest. "Maybe," I say.

This perks them up. They all look at one another and begin speaking much too quickly for me to follow. Not just the doctors, the patients, too. "O.K.," says the doctor, hopefully. She is uncertain whether to take me at my word and not quite willing to give up the possibility that I may be able to produce. "When you have an eye, come back. If you can get more than one, that would be very good. We have a lot of people waiting. Try to get me as many as you can."

She then explains the eye must come through customs if I am planning to bring it from the United States. "This is a problem," she says. "Sometimes the eyes go bad while waiting to be inspected." I imagine an eye floating in its solution, in a box, surrounded by ice, rotting in the airport like an old grape, while yawning tourists look on and customs officials smoke cigarettes.

Back in the crowded waiting room I explain to Phra Dhamma what I have learned from the doctor, and I ask him to translate for me. "We still do not know, really," I confess. "Maybe they can help him, maybe not. We have to find him an eye first."

Nai Nya Naa smiles as this is translated. His quiet smile. It is an adventure too enormous to give up on and too silly to take very seriously. He seems at ease again.

On our way down to the pharmacy for some ointment the doctor has prescribed, I check out my own frame of mind and find that I am fascinated by this medical work. I appreciate the illusion of clarity, the percentages that try to put order to the unknown. The doctors have a language that measures out human misery in small doses, in 50 percent chances. I certainly prefer "less than a 50 percent chance" to "this man will never be able to look after himself." The latter may be true, but there is no harm in coming to the acceptance slowly. I have a feeling there will be disappointment at the end of this quest. But the investigation, the precise medical vocabulary, the probably useless medicines they portion out to Nai Nya Naa, unaccountably make me feel better.

I lead Nai Nya Naa to the pharmacy, holding him high up on what is left of his arm. I ease him down into a chair, edging him backward until he can feel its rim against the back of his knees. I hold him firmly under the armpit when he sits and slide my hand over his back to comfort him, though he no longer seems to need comforting. I pat his back. He laughs. I think he is amused by me.

I am falling in love with him, my usual response to disaster.

A Basket of Prayers

Life in Thailand is not all hospital work. Tonight is the night of the full moon, the twelfth month of the year 2563. Never mind that my Western calendar disagrees. I am no longer in the West.

It is the festival of Loy Kratong. Phra Dhamma and Phra Dala Non are accompanying me and other community members to a nearby wat where we can participate in the festivities. I have dressed in a nice black skirt and blouse for the occasion and am giving myself a last appreciative look in the mirror when one of the community members shouts up that the monks have arrived. I reach the bottom of the stairs to find the monks gaping at me in evident dismay.

"Hi, guys," I say. "What's the matter?"

They look at one another and at me in growing horror. "What are you wearing?" asks Phra Dala Non.

"What do you mean what am I wearing? It's a skirt."

"You can't go outside in that," he says.

I look down at myself expecting to find that I'm covered in bird shit or some other abomination, but all I see is my nice black outfit looking as coordinated and presentable as I'm likely to get.

"What's the matter with my outfit?" I ask.

"It's black!" they say at the same time.

"So?"

"Black, you know. Color of death," says Phra Dhamma.

"Very bad luck," says Phra Dala Non. "You wear that and the Phi will follow you."

Phi is the Thai word for spirits, who are reportedly both plentiful and very busy in Thailand. There are supposed to be more of them than there are people.

"Please go change," says Phra Dhamma.

"But . . ."

"We cannot go out with you like that," says Phra Dala Non.

"Not possible," adds Phra Dhamma.

"But . . ."

"We will wait here for you," says Phra Dala Non with finality. They both cross their arms and look completely unmovable.

I huff back upstairs, throw my clothes on the bed, and dress in my usual bedraggled and uncoordinated ensemble of baggy trousers and a loose blue rayon shirt. When I meet the men again at the bottom of the stairs, they both look very relieved.

Now the monks, the other community members, and I set out from our modern apartment to appeal to the spirits of water and moon. The streets are dirty and crowded. The usual melee of trucks, buses, and motorcycles with their deliberately noisy engines, distorted by some gadget in the gas, roar like giant mosquitoes. Up against the storefronts, their mouths darkened with corrugated tin, are table after rickety table of baskets (kratong) made from folded banana leaves. The baskets are full of flowers: orchids, storm-sky purple and white, and an occasional golden chrysanthemum. Incense sticks and candles rise from these gardens of petals.

We buy a cheap basket and hobble over the broken sidewalk with the crowds toward a local Thai wat. The wat is lit up with little fairy lights and large spotlights. Everywhere people are in a carnival spirit. On one side of the wat, vendors have set up their stalls. People buy flowers, toys, and ice cream bars, and squat to slurp soup. We pass a shadow-puppet show. The shadows are cast against a white cloth, edged with purple. Small children sigh, enraptured.

Statues of Buddhist patriarchs sit in a line along one side of the wat courtyard. They have been dressed up for the occasion in yellow robes, and the devout have stuck gold leaf haphazardly over their heads like strange cancers.

"Why do they allow cars in here?" one of the community members complains, as we try to weave through the throngs of people, down a narrow road, while cars creep against the grain of human traffic, blocking our path.

Once beyond the cars, the wat opens onto a courtyard by the river. Here we stand in line to light our small candles and incense from a large common candle.

Around us chaos reigns. Young girls kneel by the river, rocking, waiing, praying, lifting their baskets up. One steadies her basket in the air then lets it fall over the fence into the river, hoping it will land right-side-up. To one side of us, three little boys are lighting a spinning firework right in the middle of the crowd. It spins like a weapon in a sci-fi movie, sparkling as it goes, sputtering out under people's feet. The boys kick at it frantically to get it away from them, and it skitters across the ground and burns a girl's ankle.

Behind us an old woman is selling caged birds, live eel in sandwich bags, and turtles crowded into a plastic tub. "Can I buy a turtle as a pet?" I ask.

Phra Dhamma explains that people buy these creatures only to set them free, to make merit. I wonder if the turtles appreciate the thought as much as the merit-makers do. I imagine slinging those turtles into the river and wonder if they skip like stones. I hear people dropping them in. Their flat bellies make a cracking sound as they hit the hard ground of water. Unfortunately, this is a common mistake among merit-makers. We assume that others are better off simply because we intend to be helpful. Whether we really understand what they need, or, conversely, what will injure them, is another question.

We are to put money in our basket. Someone has already done this, but I want to put in five baht myself. I am afraid if there is nothing of mine in the basket, then my troubles won't float away as they are supposed to, and the candle, lit and shining beneath the moon, will bring me no luck. I wonder if this basket will help me to help Nai Nya Naa.

"What should we wish for?" someone asks. I close my eyes and give the river a long list. Someone else lowers our little basket down off the pier. Somewhere between the light in the water and the moon above, our troubles will leave us, and our prayers will return home to bless us for the coming year.

We decide to take the riverboat and float around for a while. I'm proud because I suggested the ride, after reading the sign in Thai. Not long ago the sign would have said *squiggle squiggle, 5 squiggle.* Now the squiggles say "*Loy kratong.* Boat trip on the river. 5 baht per person."

On the boat, people reverently hold their baskets until we are mid-river. They lean over the edge and let them drift downstream. "That one is well designed," says Phra Dala Non. A basket resembling a birthday cake floats by, many candles blazing and never tipping at all.

From the shore a crowd sets off firecrackers and shooting rockets that boom like canons and fall into the river like stars. We disembark and walk back through the temple garden, where dozens of old bathtubs sit in quiet, stolid lines, filled with greenery.

Back on the street, the city seems to be choking itself. With five hundred new cars a day, the last six months have seen the city go from crowded to unbelievable. The resulting tension has consequences. The bus drivers, who work fifteen hours a day and take "horse medicine" (amphetamines) to stay awake, all seem to have gone berserk. Last week two community members were traumatized on runaway buses. The driver of one bus wouldn't stop to let the frightened, shouting people on or off. He barreled down the road, block after block, and plowed into a taxi, which he then pushed ahead of the bus for another block.

I've had my bag slit open twice. The first time was a shock. I was getting off at a crowded stop. I got bumped a few times and had to squeeze through several people by the door. The fit was so tight that when I got off I realized all the buttons of my blouse had come undone. No kidding. And my wallet was gone. At first I thought I must have dropped it. Then I saw the gaping wound in the bag, the sharp line of the knife. Thieves slit open the sides of women's bags, reach in, and pinch the wallet. In my case they got a very full wallet but very little money. I had stuffed the wallet with tampons, expecting to be out and about all day. I'm sure the thieves were as surprised as I was.

The second time, I was wearing a bag my mother had bought me on a recent visit, and we outsmarted the crook. The bag had a lining and a secret pocket up high to keep my money in. The thief cut open the outer layer but did not pierce the lining, and the money was safe. But I mourn for the pretty bag, with a gash through its belly like a gutted fish.

One of the staff at the house also had her bag slashed on the bus. She says this is a rough route. The street out by the temple has lots of young boys who, she claims, steal in order to buy drugs.

Now it is late, and I walk home slowly with the rest of the community. We walk single-file to get through the crowds. Back in my room, outside my window, fireworks continue to flare. I turn out my lights to watch. Crack, crack, boom. Asia with its chaos and beauty continues to fascinate me in this, my fifth year here. I go to sleep thinking of all my friends in far-off lands—my distant homeland of America. I send them my good wishes. Out across the seas, I send my hopes and dreams. I say a little prayer that all of us will wake in the morning to find our anxieties have floated away and our dreams are coming to meet us, shining like candles on the river.

Searching for an eye for Nai Nya Naa takes a lot of time. But that's O.K. I'm determined, and I have nothing better to do with myself. In between contacting doctors and hospitals, I take up the offer for Phra Dhamma and Phra Dala Non to teach me Mon.

I understand that humility is good for the soul, in which case the study of Mon propelled me toward sainthood. I thought I was really bad at Thai until I tried Mon. My Mon is excruciating.

During my first lesson, I'm enjoying the breeze that blows softly through the open-sided rooms on the second floor of the wat. It is incredible to me that I am never comfortable in the community house, which has the Western convenience of air conditioning in the bedrooms, but I'm almost always comfortable at the wat, which has no such luxuries.

The community house is concrete and enclosed. If you do without the air conditioning, it's like sitting all day in a hot bath. Further, there is condensation everywhere—the walls sweat as much as the people do. But if you turn on the air conditioner, it's like having ice dumped down your back. When you first turn the system on, it makes the sound of an airplane engine getting ready for takeoff, and then shoots out a wall of frigid air that whips your hair back and freezes it in place.

The temple, on the other hand, is completely open to the elements, and most of the living quarters are off the ground on the second floor, but this means there is always a gentle breeze. The air moves and soothes and lulls. It is warm but gently so. It is breezy, but the air doesn't come at you with the force of water sprayed from a fire hose.

The result is that I get happily sleepy. Unfortunately, neither comfort nor sleepiness is conducive to good study habits. My first lesson is not promising. The monks attempt to get me to say a particular sound correctly. The letter it corresponds to looks like a dot within a circle and it sounds something like a "B," but it kind of starts in the throat in a way no English letter does.

They say it, I repeat it wrong; they say it over, I repeat it wrong again. Over and over, like a scene from *Pygmalion*. I'm wondering when they're going to start popping marbles in my mouth.

"Wicki," says Phra Dala Non very seriously. "I will tell you a story about this letter. This is a letter in the Mon alphabet but not in the Burmese alphabet. The Burmese have big trouble when they try to say this sound. Sometimes when a Burmese soldier comes into Mon State, and he is caught by Mon soldiers, he tries to pretend he is Mon. So the Mon soldiers tell him to say this sound, and if he says it right, we think maybe he is Mon, but if he can't say it . . ."

"What?"

"Then we shoot him."

"Oh," I say. "That sounds very serious."

"Yes. This is a very serious letter."

They go back to repeating it, and I repeat it after them, badly, like a Burmese soldier about to be shot. Then all of a sudden they stop, shout with elation, and begin to clap.

"What? What?" I ask, sleepily.

"You did it," says Phra Dala Non.

"You mean I did it right?" I ask, very surprised. It had felt like I accidentally swallowed my tongue.

"Excellent! Now do it again."

Smiling, really confident now, I try it again. They look uncertain. I attempt it again, and they shake their heads and look disappointed.

"Where did it go?" asks Phra Dala Non. "It was there and now it's gone."

"I'm sorry," I say. "Do you think we could take a rest now? Maybe have a Coke?"

They both look relieved. "Good idea," they say together. "We rest now, try again some other day." But somehow some other day never comes, and my first lesson is also my last.

Meanwhile, since Nai Nya Naa's last appointment, I have been writing to everyone, talking to everyone, practically stopping people in the street to ask, "Do you know where I can get an eye?"

I bump into Nancy, one of our community members from the Northeast. I explain Nai Nya Naa's story to her, and ask if she might know a doctor who will give us a clearer idea whether it's useful to continue this wild goose chase—someone who might have some rough guess as to where to find an eye if we do proceed. "You wouldn't happen to know anyone like that offhand, would you?" I ask her.

"I might."

"You're kidding."

Nancy is the single-most resourceful person I have ever met. She not only has an idea, she has his card. In her purse, no less. Now, why she carries the card of a famous Thai eye surgeon around with her when she travels is beyond me. There are people who can imagine all sorts of contingencies, and who carry all their contact addresses with them everywhere just in case they run into someone looking for a cornea and they have to come up with something on the spur of the moment.

"Here it is." She digs the card out from her purse. "The nurse is an American. She's the one you'll want to talk to first, to get the scoop. Here are the hours. No need to make an appointment."

"You wouldn't happen to have their fee schedule sliding around in that purse of yours, would you? We're a little low on cash."

"Sliding scale," she assures me, as she whisks out of the office, humming and perusing her mail.

I rush over to the wat in great excitement and find Nai Nya Naa sitting in the shade of an overhang outside the refugee room. Phra Dhamma sits opposite him in the sunshine, his feet up on a chair. On Nai Nya Naa's lap is his daughter. "Nai Nya Naa, hello," I call. He smiles.

I briefly explain to the monk that there is a new doctor who wants to see Nai Nya Naa, and Phra Dhamma translates. Nai Nya Naa lifts his daughter off his lap, stands, and declares himself ready.

"Where are your shoes?" I ask in English, which no one understands. I point to his feet and lead him inside. "Shoes," I say.

He can't see me pointing, and the others don't understand what I'm saying, so this is not the most efficient communication. But Kyang San, his little daughter, understands the gesture, shouts "shoes" in Mon, and goes running off to get his thongs.

I lead him back outside to put them on, but his feet find my shoes where I have left them outside the door, as is Thai custom. He begins to slip my sandals on, to the surprise of the monks who are watching and to my own silent consternation.

At this, his daughter squeals, the monks wave and yell, and all the refugees laugh. Finally, we get my feet in my sandals and Nai Nya Naa's in his, and we walk slowly toward the front of the wat.

Nai Nya Naa has memorized the compound with his toes. He slows automatically before steps and water pipes, feeling his way with one delicate foot. His daughter cries and hangs on him, unwilling to part with him.

When I get Nai Nya Naa to the bench in front of the wat, there is his wife. His daughter climbs back into her papa's lap. He lifts her under the arms and swings her. She looks funny dangling from his cut-off elbows.

His wife is suckling their fat son, slapping his round thighs lightly for the pleasure of making them jiggle and hearing the sweet sound of her cupped hand on his smooth skin. It is like spanking Jell-O. He is a placid child and not easily distracted from the business of breakfast.

Phra Dhamma has agreed to accompany us to translate for Nai Nya Naa and has succeeded in coaxing a taxi into the wat compound. By now, several other refugees have decided they want their eyes checked, too. Phra Dhamma has decided that Phra Dala Non is a better Thai translator than he is, and we now have four men trying to climb over one another in the backseat while the taxi driver looks around frantically in evident confusion.

The taxi driver is as exasperated by the traffic as we are. He takes the back road onto Satthorn Street, where we discover ourselves in the middle of the noon rush hour, which is increasingly extending to blend into the tail end of the morning rush hour on one side, and the beginning of the evening rush hour on the other side, until the whole day is one long gridlock.

We drive around for an hour, arguing about where we're going. The driver is impatient and mumbles to himself. He has a cataract like a veil over his right eye. I am surrounded by the visually impaired.

I, the fat American, sit in front, as I cannot sit by a monk. In the back are three dignified, orange-robed monks. The many folds of their robes are pleated over their arms, and they sit with the upright dignity of kings, despite being crunched. In the midst of them sits Nai Nya Naa, blind, armless, and slightly nervous. He has slouched down and his right knee is tapping. Next to him an old monk stares without seeing, from behind glasses that obviously do no good.

We drive around in circles for another half hour, past the endless stores divided from the street only by tin garage doors, past steam curling up from unknown hollows beneath the gutter; past signs in Chinese characters and Thai script; past shops that sell all useful things, including Coke, laundry soap, comic books, and dried squid; past crowds looking in on some activity, people packed in so tight that all we see is a carpet of black hair; past blaring Western music and blaring Thai music so loud it is mostly fuzz and crackling static. We are hopelessly lost, each of us offering an opinion on where the clinic we're headed for might be located.

The driver is as frustrated as I am and eventually invites us to disembark in the middle of nowhere, never mind the lost revenue, thank you very much. I rush into the nearest building and frantically call the clinic for more specific instructions. When I return, I find the monks flapping their orange wings in the hospital parking lot, trying to get some air into their nylon shrouds. With their billowing robes and their shiny, hot faces they look as if they are about to dissolve into shapelessness. Meanwhile, Nai Nya Naa squats and sweats in resigned silence, his face turned up into the sun, the only one of us who can look straight into the burning sky without pain.

I wave down another taxi, which brings us to the clinic, where the receptionist tries to sort out who are the patients among us. When each of them has a little card with his name and a number on it, we are escorted into a room so dark we are all stumbling. Patients sit around in the dark, letting their pupils dilate naturally.

The doctor sits in one corner with a variety of scopes and soft lights. He calls the old monk first and declares nothing can be done: he has a degenerative disease, and glasses won't help him.

Discouraged, the monk returns to the line of waiting patients. He and the other monks sit together in a row and lean back against the wall, a line of semi-recumbent monks. Other patients sit in complete silence in the dark. I know they're there, because I can hear their breathing, but they are as hard to make out as shadowy figures from the dead. It's so dark that patients need someone to lead them from the bench to the examination table, where the doctor sees one person at a time, looking through a scope into each dilated eye, and from there presumably straight into their souls.

An old woman stumbles into the room after us and is completely blinded by the darkness. She teeters toward the back, and proceeds to sit on a monk. This is a serious taboo. No sitting on monks allowed. A monk is forbidden to even touch a woman, let alone to have one in his lap. There is a horrified silence in the room and then everyone begins shouting at once, "A monk, a monk! That's a monk you're sitting on."

The old woman shoots up into the air like a firecracker and begins a profusion of apologies. The monks are stunned into silence. Their Thai is not good enough for them to want to speak much in public or draw attention to themselves, as to do so would be to risk revealing they are foreign and illegal. They wish for her to stop apologizing and sit down but don't want to make a fuss either way.

The woman sits briefly in a spot beside the wall, where others have called her, then thinks better of it, throws herself down on the ground in front of the monks. They are so embarrassed they don't know where to look. She kowtows three times and asks forgiveness.

"*Mai pen rai*," they say. "It's not important. We understand. Never mind."

"Never mind, never mind," says the doctor in his most reassuring voice, looking up at last from his work at his waiting room, which, since our arrival, has deteriorated into something of a circus. "It's not a sin," he adds, which I understand only because "sin" is one of the vocabulary words I learned from my language tutor this week.

When the doctor calls Nai Nya Naa to the examination table, I accompany him, though for him this dark room is no more of a handicap than most rooms. He seats himself in the chair, and the doctor takes a good look at him, a surprised kind of look, before asking him to place his chin on the strap of the diagnostic machine.

"A land mine?" the doctor asks, looking up at me.

"Yes."

"These mines, these mines," he says in English. "These terrible weapons. Whoever invented them is a bad person. Such maiming. Such suffering. And for what? No one deserves this."

For no reason at all my heart lightens. No reason, perhaps, except to find that there is still goodness in the world, and mercy among men who have no natural bond to the ones who come to claim it of them. No bond except humanity.

This doctor agrees with the first surgeon that it is a long shot for Nai Nya Naa to see well again. "It is difficult to assess the extent of the internal damage," he says. "If we operate, there is a chance he will see. Not perfectly, but better than he does now. It's a risk. But look at him. Look at the way he is now. Don't you think it's worth a try? I suggest you explain the risks to him, and if he agrees, we'll do the surgery. We have some eyes coming in from Sri Lanka. It's a wait but not an interminable one. I'll put you on the list."

Once we're dismissed, I stand in the waiting room for a minute, adjusting to the news, while the monks collect themselves. Andrea, the chatty American nurse, is holding her four-month-old grandchild over one shoulder. She stands next to me, sees my face, and laughs. "It's true," she says. "Sometimes miracles do happen."

Yes, I think. They do. Even in the midst of wars, even when humans do their best to destroy one another. Even in the midst of poverty and powerlessness, there is a small current going in the opposite direction, a current of gentleness and generosity. Once you get in the middle of that current you are lifted, buoyant, swept along in the midst of wonder, carried like a leaf.

"Personally, I would rather lose my legs than my arms," says Andrea, breaking through my mystical reverie and shifting the baby's weight to the other shoulder.

"What?"

She nods at Nai Nya Naa, who is sitting calmly in a red plastic chair, waiting for the monks and me to come claim him. "I've thought about it, you know."

"But it would be good to be able to walk," I say, "so I think I'd rather lose my arms."

"But then how could you read or eat or bathe or dress yourself?" she asks. "If you lose your legs, you can use a crutch or a prosthesis or a wheelchair. There are ways to be mobile. But if you lose both arms, what do you have? Nothing. What can you do? Nothing. You're helpless."

How odd, I think, to be having this conversation so casually, we who just met a few minutes ago. We know. Somewhere deep in the heart, all of us understand how tenuous our privilege is. How relative it is to say natural, or normal, or entitled, or forever, or whole. Or even to say "me," and think it will always mean the same thing.

On the way out, I bash into Phra Dhamma. We are trying to go through the same narrow passage at the same time from different directions, and we are both distracted. Neither notices the other. I apologize and feel sheepish. I do not kowtow like the old woman, but I wonder briefly what secret or public rites these monks will have to perform after all these clumsy women have sat on them and tried to knock them down. Phra Dhamma says nothing, but his face says eloquently that this is the perfect end to a terrible day. Looking at him makes me want to burst out laughing.

This is social action and interreligious dialogue at its most fundamental. The chaste and pure may remain so. But as they enter the world as healers, teachers, fellow travelers, there is little chance they will remain untouched.

And despite the monks' encounters with women, this is not by any means a terrible day. The task is not complete yet. It will likely be a long wait until surgery can actually be performed. And there is the whole matter of the risk involved. Nai Nya Naa must understand what is at stake. We must sit down with him and make sure he understands. He must choose for himself and not be swept along on the tide of activity, or swayed by my determination to believe I am having an impact on the world.

But for me, for now, I am happy. We are making progress. I am making myself useful. There are real possibilities in Nai Nya Naa's life that we hardly dared imagine a month ago.

I find myself in tears as we leave. I put on my dark glasses to hide what I am feeling. Nai Nya Naa has never seen his children. He has held them, yes, and loved them, but never seen them. "Just think," I lean around toward the backseat and ask Phra Dhamma to translate for me. "Nai Nya Naa, if this works, in a few months you will see the faces of your children for the first time."

Dancing with the Hurricane

In the end, it takes more than a year before a cornea for Nai Nya Naa arrives from Sri Lanka. The eye clinic calls, saying we should make final arrangements for the surgery.

Although I should have done it a year ago, I have not yet had the courage to discuss with Nai Nya Naa the risks of a cornea transplant. I have no excuse for not having done so. Instead, I have discussed the matter with Matthew, and I have thought about the possible implications of this surgery alone in my room at night. But I have not even asked if, given the risks, this is really what Nai Nya Naa wants.

It is much simpler to keep working at the clearly defined task of "arranging things" than to sit down and actually have a conversation. I prefer the concrete endeavor that can be easily checked off my "to do" list, the job that brings with it the fastest illusion of progress.

Also, I shy away from thinking of the risk itself. I am an American and a person of faith. I want desperately to believe that if we work hard enough and do good things, everything will work out all right. Of course I know better, or I am beginning to. Life with the refugees has taught me the terrible fragility of the things of this world, and most fragile of all is human happiness.

There's a nagging fear in the back of my mind that the surgery may not work, that I have offered Nai Nya Naa false hope and a dangerous sense of security when he ought to have been less trusting. Also, I have put my whole effort into trying to be useful, and if it should turn out that what I have done is not useful at all—that I have made myself busy but not busy at anything that is really needed—I will lose my sense of purpose.

Given all this, when the clinic asks us to come in for a final checkup, I collect

Nai Nya Naa, gratefully putting off for one more day the discussion I realize we must have soon.

At the clinic we are sent upstairs to the surgical unit, to test Nai Nya Naa's urine and blood, give him an EKG, and in general determine that he is in sufficient health to withstand surgery. Phra Dhamma is leading Nai Nya Naa by the arm, while conferring with me. We are both so absorbed in our conversation, we don't notice the narrow door ahead of us. Phra Dhamma and I issue no warning to our charge, and Nai Nya Naa, walking beside us, smacks into the wall beside the door, then bounces backward. Phra Dhamma and I stop short and clap our hands over our mouths, unsure whether to laugh, until Nai Nya Naa shakes his head and smiles.

To go upstairs we must go outside the building, up the stairs, then back inside again. At the upstairs door, Nai Nya Naa politely but unnecessarily steps out of his shoes. Everyone smiles and shouts at him in three languages.

I love to watch him put on his shoes. His toes grope their way into the rubber sandals slowly, cautiously, the way children feel around a blind corner, afraid of spiders.

"We'll have to prick his finger for some blood," says the nurse, then stops short, looking first puzzled, then embarrassed. "How can I prick his fingers? He doesn't have fingers."

"We haven't run into this particular problem before," admits Andrea, the American, looking thoughtful and pulling on her ear—which gives her an idea. What about pricking his ear?

"That's for babies," says the nurse in disdain.

"Well," says Andrea, "in this case . . ." But in the end, the nurse cannot bear to do what she assumes would offend his dignity, so she decides to dispense with the blood test altogether. After a cursory examination Nai Nya Naa is pronounced fit for surgery; now, there is no further excuse for putting off the discussion of the risks involved.

The next day I collect Phra Dhamma and Phra Dala Non, and ask them to accompany me to the refugee room. Nai Nya Naa's wife places a chair for me in the middle of the room. It looks mighty lonely there, so I wave to her to bring more. One for me, one for each of the monks. But then there's Nai Nya Naa, waiting patiently on the floor. I don't want us to seem like the three kings coming to bestow wisdom, so I slide down to the linoleum and sit across from Nai Nya Naa. The monks follow suit.

There is little privacy in Asia, and none among the poor. Refugees begin to gather, a silent flock, hunkering down to listen, knowing through instinct that something of importance is going to happen. Nai Nya Naa's children perch in the hollows of his lap like birds. His wife begins to leave, but I ask the monks to call her back. This concerns her, too.

Normally, I say several sentences and have the monks translate the gist. But today is too important. Today Nai Nya Naa must understand everything, every phrase, every nuance. I speak a phrase at a time, and the monks translate.

"Nai Nya Naa, the doctor wants you to understand something," I say. "He's not sure this operation will be successful. He has looked in your eye many times, but he is still not sure how bad the damage is. If the operation succeeds, you will see better than you do now. You will not see perfectly, but you may see enough to take better care of yourself. If you see well enough, we can get you an arm. Maybe two arms." Everyone laughs.

"But the operation may not be successful. You have a fifty-fifty chance. If the operation doesn't work, or if something goes wrong later, you could lose your sight completely. The little light that comes to you now will be gone, and you will live in permanent, complete darkness."

All the air goes out of Phra Dhamma's lungs when he hears this. Phra Dala Non shakes his head in sympathy. As the news is translated, the whole room lets out a great sigh. It is too terrible to think about. To have so little and lose it all. To risk everything and come away with nothing.

Only Nai Nya Naa's face is unmoved. There is no great sigh from him, no sign of nervousness or self-pity. He sits cross-legged, and listens, his head cocked in concentration. His children and wife join him in stillness. They could be a snapshot or a statue. Even the baby stops sucking. They are a picture of a family waiting for something momentous, some word of blessing or despair.

"So now you must choose," I say to Nai Nya Naa, "to take the risk or not. To have the operation or not. What do you want to do?"

"I understand what you have told me," Nai Nya Naa says with dignity, after a small silence. Phra Dhamma and Phra Dala Non translate for him: "I understand what I may lose. I also know the life I have been living. I choose to take the risk."

That day, walking home in the rain, I feel sure I am in the presence of Spirit. For what is the Spirit but that which keeps alive the seed of hope at the heart of humanity? That's supposed to be my job, too. I am supposed to bring hope, to hang onto hope above all else. But hope is ultimately a product of courage and of faith. I seem to lack both. How do you learn to have hope in a world where everything, even the things of goodness and innocence, are at risk?

The night before Nai Nya Naa is admitted to the hospital, I do not sleep. This journey has been so long. There is much uncertainty still ahead, and the stakes are high. Every fifteen minutes I wake and think of Nai Nya Naa lying in the darkness of the temple, locked in the deeper darkness of his blindness. He, who has so much to lose, is the hopeful one. The faithful one. For he is willing, without blame or resentment, and even in the midst of his poverty of choices, to take up the small power that is his. Nai Nya Naa claims responsibility for the risks most likely to bring him life. And faith, whatever else it may be, is always the walk toward life.

As I toss in my bed, images of a tropical typhoon play through my dreams. I experienced my first typhoon when I was living in Hong Kong, where sea hurricanes can close all public ground and water transportation, and big engines bellow out a warning cry over the city. During that first storm, we went through the house closing blinds and shutters to keep glass from shattering in or out.

I remember watching from an upper window as a priest friend left the house against all better judgment. He said he couldn't help it; he had work to do. From the second story, he looked very small and easily broken, one arm raised protectively to keep the flying dust out of his eyes. He leaned into the wind and walked in slow motion, sometimes not so much seeming to battle with or through the elements as to be resting, supported by a shelf of air.

Trees were yanked out of the ground by their roots and flung across roads by the wind. Accidents abounded. The airport shut down. In our house a window exploded inward, scattering glass through the blinds onto the well-polished wood floor.

In my dreams, I see my friend again, his arms outstretched in the wind. You can't tell whether he's falling or flying. Then it's Nai Nya Naa out there in the storm, and finally it's me. I feel afraid and calm at once. As if my heart doesn't quite know how to keep its balance, but I have to go out there, because there's work to do. And suddenly I think this *is* the work: this willingness to engage with the uncertainty of life, this willingness to dance with the hurricane.

* * *

Morning comes slowly, and I rise sluggish and anxious at once. Everything seems to be in slow motion today. The traffic, the wat, my brain. I bring a little present for Kyang San: a bell from Japan, the kind worn by those who climb Mount Fuji. It was given to me by a friend who climbed to the top of the sacred mountain, in the rain, in the middle of the night. Perhaps it will bring luck.

Only the children are up to speed this morning. Kyang San rattles the bell, leaps in the air, throws the bell toward the sky, attempts to catch it with her mouth and eat it.

I go to the computer room, and Phra Dhamma invites me to sit, but I'm eager to get going. Nai Nya Naa knocks on the door, dressed in his best clothes. He has packed a bag with extra garments and other needs for a week or ten days. His bag is smaller than my purse.

We pile into the taxi, Phra Dhamma, Nai Nya Naa, a twelve-year-old temple boy named Joakhim, and I. There are no displays of tenderness or concern by the other refugees. Nai Nya Naa's wife does not weep and cling to him, though she does try to come with us, and is gently asked by the monks to stay behind. Kyang San does not beg for extra kisses. She runs on the pavement, tossing the bell.

I am beginning to think I'm the only one who's nervous, until we arrive. Watching Nai Nya Naa disembark, I notice that the foot coming out of the taxi is bare. Nai Nya Naa feels for the curb with his naked toes. "His shoes!" I cry. Such a constant refrain during my life with refugees: "Where are his shoes?"

Phra Dhamma asks a question in Mon, then laughs. "He got excited," he explains. "He forgot them."

We deposit Nai Nya Naa and the temple boy in the hospital room. Then Phra Dhamma and I poke around, fiddle with the air conditioner, the mattress, and the bell to ring for the nurse.

"Is nice," pronounces Phra Dhamma, satisfied.

Nai Nya Naa sits on the bed, digging his thighs with the stumps of his arms, as he does sometimes when he's nervous.

Phra Dhamma stands calmly, looking down at the temple boy who has undertaken the awesome duty of looking after Nai Nya Naa, translating for him, taking him to the bathroom, feeding him. The boy looks up solemnly, nodding at instructions. Phra Dhamma, standing with his arms wrapped inside his robe, kindly and stern at once, is a figure of immense authority.

The room has turquoise walls. If this works, I think, if Nai Nya Naa's sight is restored, the first thing he will see is the color of the sea.

I think surgery is imminent, but really we are settling in for a week of observation. One morning Khun Phat tells me the hospital has called. Nai Nya Naa had his operation at four in the morning. He's up and awake, but lonely. He wants a visitor, and could we could come by this afternoon?

On entering his hospital room, I expect to see him laid out, in pain, incoherent, but when we walk in, Nai Nya Naa is sitting up and smiling, his head hidden in a cloud of bandages. Sitting beside him on the floor is Nai Soh, the man who leapt from the roof to avoid the police. His back has sufficiently recovered that he can hobble around, limping. But here, confronted with the injuries of a friend, he seems to take on new strength. He looks fondly at Nai Nya Naa, sitting bolt upright, with his broad chest and his handsome face.

"Hello," I say, giving a wai to Nai Soh and saying Nai Nya Naa's name. They both smile. "So, Nai Nya Naa, how are you? I'm surprised to see you up so soon. How was the operation?"

Phra Dhamma translates and Nai Nya Naa waves the stump of his elbow at a small jar on the table. In it floats the dirty remains of a cornea. Strange souvenir. I wonder if Nai Nya Naa requested it himself or whether it comes automatically, a standard gift of transplant procedures. Nai Nya Naa's eye is heavily bandaged, so he does not know yet what this operation will mean for him. He only says there was little pain. He is hopeful. In fact, he is more talkative and cheerful than I have ever seen him.

A week later, the call comes that it is time for Nai Nya Naa to go home, and Phra Dhamma and Phra Dala Non go with me to collect him from the hospital. We arrive to find that his family is helping him prepare to leave. The three of us settle in for a while to chat.

Nai Nya Naa is still bandaged and doesn't know what the world will look like when he is allowed to open his eyes. He is subdued and says there is pain now and heat. Still all he sees when they change the bandage is light, though it is a sharper, more focused light than before surgery.

He sits very still on the bed, his stumps curled inward. Sometimes he digs them into his knee. I am as ignorant as he is about what his future holds. I ask to speak with the doctor and wait in the semi-darkness of his examination room for my turn. A stream of the sighted and the blind stumble up to his table, put their chins in the strap, and submit to inspection.

When my turn comes, I stand silently beside his desk, waiting for acknowledgment. He looks up at me kindly.

"I am surprised," he says.

"What is it?"

"Under the old cornea the eye is clear. I see no damage to the retina. It will take two or three months before we will know for sure. He will have to wear a bandage during that time. The body will have to adjust to the eye, and the eye will have to adjust to the light. But in the end he has a good chance."

"He will see?"

"I believe he will."

I go whooping up the stairs, startling the other patients in Nai Nya Naa's room by bursting upon them with this news. Everyone begins to laugh and talk at once.

We watch his daughter, Kyang San, as she leaps around the room, much-loved child, at home in her body. The girl gets down on her knees to greet me with a wai, but when I laugh and hold out my arms she leaps into them. "Did you have breakfast yet?" she asks seriously, a monk translating for me.

"I did."

Her face lights up with approval and curiosity. "What kind of curry did you have?" she asks.

This momentarily stumps me. "It wasn't curry," I explain. "It was bread."

Hearing this translated, she bursts into laughter. The monks also laugh. Phra Dala Non rocks back and bumps his head on the windowsill. At the clunk of head on wood, the child's laughter increases. She throws herself down, face first on the bed, and abandons herself to great belly laughs. Phra Dala Non looks insulted and pretends to swat at her but laughs in spite of himself.

Before we leave, we take pictures of the family; the family and the monks; the family and me; and the monks and me. We ask a fellow patient to take some of the pictures. In many Nai Nya Naa's feet loom large and most of our heads are cut off, but you can still see the smiles.

When we have used up most of a roll of film, we pack up Nai Nya Naa's small pile of belongings and go out to the street for a taxi. The car is so full, I send them back without me, the mother and kids in front, monks and Nai Nya Naa in back. I carry Kyang San down the stairs, her bare feet dangling, her little hands gripping my shirt. I hand her to her mother, holding her out in the air, suspended like a puppet. The mother shifts to take her onto her lap with the little boy. I hand her some money for the taxi and shut the door. Then I head for the nearest bus stand and travel back to the wat, squeezed in among Bangkok's multitudes.

When I arrive at the wat, Nai Nya Naa is sleeping in the shade of the porch, his bandage covering one eye like a pirate. Beside him his son sprawls, naked from the fat baby belly down, also asleep. Even in sleep, and despite his own future uncertainty, Nai Nya Naa has flung a maimed arm protectively around the child, cradling his head.

Death Railway

He makes his sun rise on the bad and on the good,
and causes rain to fall on the just and the unjust.

MATTHEW 5:45

That great cloud rains down on all whether their
nature is superior or inferior. The light of the
sun and the moon illuminates the whole world,
both him who does well and him who does ill,
both him who stands high and him who stands low.

SADHARMAPUNDARIKA SUTRA 5

A Letter from Prison

One evening, during my first year in Thailand, long before Nai Nya Naa has his operation, Matthew calls to tell me we have a crisis on our hands. The police have raided the headquarters of the Mon student leadership in Bangkok. Sixteen Mon have been arrested and imprisoned. While this is regrettable, mass arrests are common. The circumstances surrounding the arrest, however, make the event significant.

A letter has arrived for Matthew from the Immigration Detention Center (IDC), where illegal immigrants, including refugees, are kept. The note, which has been smuggled out by a sympathetic visitor, begs for help. The student leaders have been told that they and the other detainees from Burma are not going to be delivered to the border after their period of confinement, as is usual practice. They will be rounded up and handed directly into the custody of the Burmese military at Three Pagoda Pass.

Nothing could have prepared us for this news. It could mean a slow death for most refugees, who we fear would be put to work building the railway or the roads or used as porters in the army until they died of malaria, starvation, or assault by land mines or gunfire. There are also stories of sick porters lagging, unable to carry on at full speed, and of the army shooting them where they stand, taking up their packs, and moving on.

Women refugees also work on road and railway crews, and as army porters. But for them, especially the young, the army finds additional uses.

And for the student leaders? What is reserved for them? For those known to be supplying information on Burmese military atrocities to the international community, special treatment is expected: torture, imprisonment, execution.

The letter from the prisoners reports this repatriation plan as a new policy Thailand is preparing to implement. But it is still essentially a rumor. The imprisoned student leaders beg for our help in finding out the truth. If the rumor is true, the students hope that calling public attention to the threat will stop Thailand from actually implementing the policy. But there have been no public announcements of such a policy change, nothing in the news. The lack of official corroboration puts us in a difficult position. If the rumor is true and we do nothing, the students could be repatriated, and it would be too late for the international community to intervene. But if we go public and the rumor turns out to be false, we will create unnecessary panic among the refugees, and we will lose our credibility with international agencies. What's more, we might lose our visas.

Matthew calls an immediate meeting of the monks to pool our information. Phra Dhamma and Phra Dala Non attend. Like many who belong to the Overseas Mon Young Monks Union, Phra Dala Non periodically crosses the border to bring information back and forth.

Recently on such a trip, he visited his family in a village in Monland and found his nineteen-year-old brother on the verge of collapse, barely able to walk. The boy had been forced to work for the Burmese military building the Ye-to-Tavoy railway.

Phra Dala Non, at the risk of his life, brought back pictures of a camp where political prisoners are kept. He takes out the pictures of the prison camp and lays them on the table. We lean over to see them. Everyone is silent. The pictures have been taken at a distance and are not very clear. But there is enough in them of bleakness and suffering that no one speaks for a long time.

Phra Dala Non sits on Matthew's wicker chair and looks solemnly at us, with his sorrowful large brown eyes. "I will explain to you," he says. "In upper Mon State, twenty miles outside of Moulmein, there are five hundred political prisoners. Another seven hundred are nearby. They are breaking stone for the railway. Somewhere between ten thousand and thirty thousand people in this area are forced into hard labor, with one out of every ten people in a village required to work for ten days without pay. People from the monk's home village travel by train two hours to the work site, where they sleep under the trees. They carry their own food, and they must pay for all the expenses of the journey.

"If the food is gone, they starve," explains Phra Dala Non. "If they are sick, there is no help. Male and female must work. Young and old must work. Pregnant and not pregnant must work. Every house must give one person. The workers go into the heart of the jungle to do this work, and they have no rest. If they stop working, they are beaten. Some people run away, escaping to the border, where the ethnic armed forces protect them. Some flee across into Thailand. But, if they are caught trying to escape, they are beaten. Some are killed. Some die of exhaustion anyway.

"The railway is 110 miles long, from Ye to Tavoy. They say they will destroy a mountain to make it. They will lower the mountain twelve feet. And beside the mountain there is a field. They will make the field higher. It is terrible, hard work."

To make matters worse, the villagers are forced to build not only the railway itself but also the military outposts and barracks of the army, so that the soldiers will have places to stay when keeping an eye on the railroad—and when keeping an eye on the Mon.

Matthew unfolds the letter he has received from the imprisoned student leaders. He reads it to us aloud. The silence deepens. It is a confusing letter, as messages sent from the prison often are. It has more fear in it than information. But it is clear the imprisoned refugees have been told they will be handed into the custody of the Burmese military.

I look again at the picture on the table and think of all the possible futures of the imprisoned student leaders. Prolonged detention in Thailand. Torture and imprisonment in Burma. Portering for the army or serving as human minesweeps until their limbs are blown off or they are shot in a skirmish or they die of starvation, of abuse, or of exhaustion. Working as slave labor on the railroad.

The latter may sound like the least of these evils, but then I think of the POWs in World War II who were made to work for the Japanese on the Death Railway in exactly the same territory and under the same conditions. Cerebral malaria still makes its deadly sweep through the population during the rainy season. Modern workers are still forced into this labor by the enemy with whom they are at war. They are still inching their way through jungle and marsh and thick, knotty undergrowth, without proper equipment, using little or no machinery, the bulk of the work done by their own hands, and the heaviest of loads carried on their own bent backs. They are still made to work long hours, way past their endurance, with unreasonable deadlines for finishing each task. They are still used by brutal captors who, in both periods of history, have only one goal: to build a railroad through inhospitable terrain in order to carry the supplies and the army that will make their power over the native population unbreakable.

For the POWs there was worldwide clamor and sympathy when the story was told. There are, even now, monuments to their suffering and museums displaying gruesome pictures taken near the river Kwai in Kanchanaburi—the Thai town just this side of Burma's Monland. The pictures show their thin bodies, their ribs protruding. They show the chronic infections, the weeping ulcers of untreated wounds that do not heal in the wet heat of the tropics. They show the flushed cheeks of those dying from fever, and the dull expressions of those trying to live on their daily dose of watery rice.

Europeans, Americans, and even Japanese come to pay homage to the place of so much human misery. They come in sorrow and in shame to remember what human beings will do to one another in the quest for power. They come to look at what is left of their work, what is known everywhere only as the Death Railway.

While sleeping on a raft on the Kwai River, I myself have seen old men come to the river's edge to remember and weep. But the same story, happening today, with indigenous Mon, goes unknown and ungrieved. The world has not changed in the amount of cruelty human beings are willing to inflict on one another. And perhaps the world has not changed in other ways, either. Sixteen thousand Allied prisoners died while working on the Death Railway. While this is tragic, their number is minuscule compared with the more than one hundred thousand Southeast Asians who suffered and died as coolies beside them. Museums and other records list the names of Allied POWs, remembering them as individuals. The Asians remain nameless. When we remember them at all, it is en masse, their deaths recorded as a single appallingly high number in a footnote in the museums.

Now the Mon people are captive again, dying again, forced to the same labor the world considered a crime against humanity fifty years ago. But I have been to the river, and I tell you, there is no one who stands at its edge to weep for the Mon.

It is late now, and I see Phra Dala Non is beginning to nod off, emotionally worn out from telling the story of a fate from which he has so recently escaped. I realize that I, too, am exhausted.

There is not much we can do for those laboring on the other side of the border, except to get their story out to the world. But for those now in the Thai detention center and afraid of being sent into forced labor, perhaps there is something we can do. "What happens now?" I ask.

"We must find out if it is true, this terrible thing," says Phra Dhamma. "We must find out if Thailand is really going to hand refugees over to their enemies. Someone must go right inside the prison itself. Someone must speak with Nai Tangay, who sent the letter to Matthew. Someone must hear the story and tell it to the world. I will go there tomorrow. Will you come with me?"

Darkness.

I stand in a corridor just outside the bars of a detention cell where more than two hundred sixty men are crammed into a room six by sixteen meters. Within the cell there are no windows to speak of, only a murky line of daylight seeping in from a two-foot strip of translucent, frosted glass, high up on the far wall.

I step up to the cell, Phra Dhamma beside me. I whisper that I want to speak to Nai Tangay. The whisper is carried back, prisoner to prisoner, and a small aisle is made for someone to move through. Their movement stirs up the smell of must and rusty metal.

Behind the metal grille, a man's face appears, like a moon in the darkness, quartered by prison bars. The face is waxen, the color of ashes. It is a handsome face. A worried face. A pale hand emerges through the grille, and I take it. We smile weakly at each other.

I am startled when the man speaks English. I move in close and speak softly with him, my fingers curled around the prison bars.

"The police came here to talk to us," Nai Tangay says. "They say that the Thai law is changing. In two weeks we will all be handed over to the Burmese military. The policeman laughed when he told us. 'Don't you like it here?' he asked us. 'Are you bored here? Did you come to Bangkok because you like to work? I know where you can find work. We will be handing you over to the Burmese command at Three Pagoda Pass. They'll have work for you!'"

A guard walks by, and Nai Tangay stops speaking. He backs away into the shadows. When the guard is gone, he comes forward again. "Don't let them see that I speak English," he explains. "They are looking for me. When they arrested all the Mon in the office, they questioned us. They want to find the leaders among us. We have switched our prison cards with others in this detention center. We are trying to hide. If we are asked, we say we are construction workers. If they know I speak Thai and English, they will be suspicious."

So, I think. They have pretended they are construction workers, that they know little. I wonder how far that got them. Police raid the Mon office, and no one in it is a Mon leader? Further, there is a kind of dignity about Nai Tangay that is not easily hidden. His voice, his posture, his alert eyes all tell what he does not want to say—that he is a man used to leading others.

"What can we do?" I ask.

"Please help us find out if it is true that we are all in danger. I have a friend at the Australian embassy. Call the embassy and ask for Mary. Tell her I'm here. Ask her to help. Ask her to find out from the Thai government what they are planning to do with us."

I write this down in my notebook and tell him I will come back when I have word. "How did you end up in here, anyway?" I ask.

He tells me he was accepted for resettlement in the United States some time ago but had the bad timing to fall in love and get married while waiting to resettle. The resettlement acceptance did not include his wife, as they had not been married at the time of his original interview. To stay was to continue in danger of arrest. To go was to leave her behind. "What could I do?" he asks. "I stayed. It was not safe, but I stayed.

"My wife got an interview for resettlement, too, but by then she was pregnant. She had to get from the refugee camp to the embassy in Bangkok. She miscarried on the road. She never got to the city, and missed her appointment.

"I went to the refugee camp to visit her and on the way back to Bangkok, I was arrested for the first time. When the police arrested us, they beat one man. They kicked him in the stomach until blood came out of his mouth. Later, they burned a prisoner's arm with a cigarette.

"I was in the detention center here in Bangkok for two months. Then they sent me to another detention center in Kanchanaburi for one week. The IDC in Kanchanaburi is even worse than the one here. If a prisoner cannot pay a bribe there, the police leave him in a cell downstairs. When I was there, they shut off the fan and the lights and set dogs loose in the cell with the prisoners. Later, police threw buckets of water into the cell to clean off some of the stink.

"It was filthy, and by the end, my body was itching like everyone else's. Everyone has skin disease. I was very pale, too. When I tried to walk I could hardly move, I was so tired. They feed you a little food twice a day at 9 A.M. and between 3 and 4 P.M. If you have extra money, you can bribe the cook to get extra rice.

"Finally, it was the day to be set free at the border. A truck came to take us to the border camp, but it was like something for cattle. There were two hundred fifty people in the truck. We left early in the morning and arrived at the border at 3 P.M. Normally we would arrive by noon or one, but on the way, the truck broke down. The police provided a little rice and one egg. You have to find an empty plastic bag and fill it with water yourself, or you have nothing to drink all day in a hot truck crowded with men.

"The truck let us out about eight kilometers from the border, at the checkpoint. The man tells you, 'You are free now.' But you are standing in the middle of a road, very tired, very hot, thirsty and hungry, and now you must walk up a hill, on a dirt road, eight kilometers, with no more food or water, to get to a refugee camp.

"If you have money, when you get to the camp you can pay to go back to Bangkok the same day. Motorcycles wait at the camp to take you to the nearest town for five hundred baht [about twenty U.S. dollars]. The drivers share the money with the police so that they can take you right past the police checkpoint. There are also employers who will loan you the money, so long as you pay them back twice what they loaned you.

"All of that happened to me," says Nai Tangay. "I returned to Bangkok. I was free for exactly one week. Then I was caught again and now I am back in prison."

Hearing Nai Tangay's story has tired me out. I want to go home, but then I think, I have a visitor's card. I might as well explore the other cells. I walk down the corridor as if I know where I am going, stopping only to ask questions of other friendly looking visitors and volunteers. I introduce them to Phra Dhamma and tell them he is translating for me.

Out in the hallway Phra Dhamma draws me aside and says, "Wicki, be careful for me. Be careful." He says it the way a parent would tell a child to use caution around a delicate vase, trying to be gentle, but with a voice full of worry.

"Do not let them know. If they know I am from Burma, if they know I am Mon . . ."

He does not finish. He doesn't have to. I feel my face flush. Here we are, right inside the detention center. He is surrounded by police, and I have been casually telling NGO workers, possibly within the hearing of the authorities, that Phra Dhamma speaks Mon and that he is translating for me. There is only one explanation for his ability to translate, one it would not take long for police to recognize: he is Mon. He is a refugee. And like the men in the prison cells behind us, he is illegal here.

What a patient man Phra Dhamma is. We are looking at one of his possible futures, and I'm chatting to people in a way that could endanger him. Yet his response to me is quiet, polite: "Be careful." That's it. As if he doesn't want to hurt my feelings.

There are eight cells like the one where Nai Tangay is kept. I am shocked to find out the prisoners do not move from the cells, not for exercise, not for meals, not for anything. Here they stay, in one room, packed in tight as commuters on a five o'clock train, week after week, month after month.

There are no cots for them to lie down on, no carpet or mats for the floor. No tables, no lamps, no chairs. Not a stick of furniture. There are no closets to put belongings in, and in many cases, no belongings to put in a closet if there were one.

It is so crowded they can't all lie down to sleep at once, so they sleep in shifts, or squat for hours in a daze, their knees drawn up close to their chests. They claim that two men who squatted in that position for long hours every day have temporarily lost the use of their legs and can no longer stand up.

This is in the steaming heat of the tropics, and sometimes there is no water. The stench is overwhelming. Matthew has warned me not to be tempted to intervene in these small injustices. Some years ago two foreigners tried to protest against detention conditions, and the police responded by cutting off the water supply entirely, until the prisoners begged the foreigners to stop.

Upstairs, women, children, and infants are held. At night there are reports that police come for some of the women and take them out, to use them or sell them, putting them back into the cell by morning. Children are born here. Infants and toddlers stare at me through the prison bars.

These people are not criminals in the ordinary sense. They have not stolen or killed. Their crime is to have escaped oppression and poverty in their own countries. Most of them, the vast majority of them, are fleeing forced labor, imprisonment, or death in Burma. Many are officially categorized as "persons of concern" by the UNHCR and are supposed to be guaranteed international protection.

The conditions are appalling; they make me nauseated. I have to get outside, into the light, the fresh air, but then I hear a voice calling out from the darkness. "Miss Wicki. Is it you?"

I turn and at first see only the fingers of a prisoner, sticking out from chicken wire that covers the bars in some of the cells. Drawing closer I see the face of Nai Nyanika, a young Mon student who was in the community house just a few weeks ago, sitting neatly on the carpet in the living room, his legs tucked up underneath him, while he explained the situation in Burma.

Sitting in our house, he had been animated, and his face was strikingly beautiful. I had sketched him in my notebook while I listened. As he spoke of the land he loved and of his people, his face was luminous. Now his skin looks gray. Only the eyes shine out, full of fear or fever. "Help me," he says. "Can you please help me?"

For a moment I have an awful thought that perhaps he was arrested on his way home from our house. He had been invited mostly for my benefit. Still relatively new to the story of the Mon, I and others in the community had wanted to hear more about their situation. Now I feel guilty. Has he lost his freedom to satisfy my curiosity?

I ask about this, and he shakes his head. I get out of him a confused story about how he was picked up on the street, not far from where he lived. Although I am relieved I was not the direct cause of his imprisonment, the guilt does not leave me. Every time we invite someone to our house, we endanger them. Every time a refugee steps out of the shelter of his own room—and even sometimes within his room—if his whereabouts are known, he is in danger. Phra Dhamma, at my side, quiet, composed, brave, is in danger, too.

"How can I help?" I ask.

His needs are so simple, they shame me: an egg for protein, a pencil to replace his broken one, something to read. Slowly a crowd gathers around him, adding their own requests. One man is a poet and begs for a scrap of paper. He has written smaller and smaller lines between old words on the paper he had with him when he was arrested, and now there is no space left.

I cannot help with every request. I do not, for example, have a boiled egg in my pocket, or the aspirin one man asks of me. I dig in my purse, however, and find one pen. And my own poetry notebook. I am almost at the end of it, and there are only a few blank pages left to give the imprisoned poet. I am not sure what the rules are about handing things through the bars, so I look around quickly to see if we are being observed by the guards. Then I open my notebook and rip out the final pages.

There is something intimate about this. The furtive glances. The notebook of private thoughts, which I hold in the folds of my voluminous skirt, muffling the sound of paper tearing. I roll the sheets of paper and slip them through the coin-sized opening of the chicken wire. The prisoner gives me a sad smile and a brief nod, then pulls the gift gently out from between my fingers.

Now I think I am done for the day, at last. I have been here only a few hours, but I feel I could sleep where I stand. As I turn to go, my young friend asks me to hear one more request. A man steps up to the wire and looks at me with a mixture of suspicion and hope. "Go ahead," the young Mon man nods at him.

When the man is still silent, someone else breaks in. "This man is a Shan. He comes from the northern border, from around Mae Sot. He came over from Burma a year and half ago. He was arrested almost a year ago. He was supposed to be released from this prison nine months ago. He is still here."

"You've been in this prison for almost a year?" I ask, surprised. As bleak as the conditions are, I had understood that what made this life bearable was the brevity of the typical sentence. People can live on watery rice and a few vegetables in a filthy, overcrowded room for a few months. But for a year?

He nods and hands a little yellow card through the chicken wire. I unroll it and try to make out the Thai script. "His prison ID," someone explains. I have barely learned the abbreviations for the months in Thai. It takes me a few minutes to decipher the script, and a few more to believe what I'm reading.

"This says you were arrested last January. You should have been released last March. Why are you still here?"

"There are many of us like this," the man says. "Many, many. When your time is finished, you must pay to be deported. The nearest border camps are close to Kanchanaburi. If you come from that area, you can pay two hundred baht to begin the trip. You have to stay in Kanchanaburi detention center for a week, and you will have to pay again from there. And you will have to pay bribes to the police along the way. With maybe six hundred baht, you can get to the border, where you will be released. But if you come from the northern border, the police will ask you for more than three thousand baht, even before bribes. Even if you had three thousand baht when you came into the detention center, you would not have it when it is time to leave. You must pay bribes inside here for everything."

I think about these figures. The two hundred baht to get to Kanchanaburi is only about eight dollars, which sounds reasonable to an American but is often more than a refugee can scrape together. The three thousand baht is equivalent to one hundred twenty dollars and clearly beyond the capacity of most of these men, many of whom work illegally for construction companies that pay them with a place to sleep, a little food, and maybe some pocket money if they're lucky.

"So what's going to happen to you?" I ask.

"If someone can't help us, I don't know what will happen. There are many who can't afford even to go to Kanchanaburi, but there are more who can't afford to go to Mae Sae and Mae Sot in the north. So we live in this prison, month after month. We heard that before us there were some Chinese in this detention center, and they could not get home. Maybe they could not pay. Maybe China did not want them. I'm not sure. But they lived in this prison, crowded like this, little food, just like now. Year after year." He sweeps his arm to take in the room behind him, the grim faces of the prisoners. "Here they grew old. Here they died."

I look at Nai Nyanika, and he looks at me. "Can you prove that all this is true?" I ask them.

"We can."

"O.K.," I say, making up my mind that I will do what I can, even if it comes to nothing. "I will come back next week. I will bring paper and pens. You will write the ID numbers of all the prisoners who have been kept beyond their time."

Visiting time is over; the guards stride through the corridors, saying, "Time over, time over."

"Anything else?" I ask the crowd of faces behind the bars.

"Come back," they say. "Come back next week."

"I will," I promise. I turn quickly and walk down the hall with Phra Dhamma, out of the darkness of the detention center, out into the parking lot where even the smoggy air of Bangkok seems refreshing and wholesome compared with where I've been. I stand there, just breathing for a moment, trying not to think, just looking around, blinking, blinded by the light of the tropical sun.

Selling Death

On my next trip to the detention center I visit the women's cells. One of the prisoners thrusts her naked infant son at the bars and shouts, "I laaaawv you." She laughs and laughs.

I have come back for the list of names of those incarcerated beyond the terms of their sentences. My interpreter in this particular room, a prisoner herself, is showering when I come through the first time, and even when I come back ten minutes later they are disorganized. She keeps saying, "Five minutes, five minutes." She has lost the paper I gave her. I am not sure if she means that they are just beginning to draw up their list or whether they have really made one up and lost it. "Is Thai O.K.?" she asks.

"Yes, but only if it's neat." I have seen the Thai script on their official documents, and it is hopeless. If the other records are as hard to read as the awful scrawls on the police identity cards they all carry, it is no wonder that many prisoners are kept so long past their sentences.

In one corner of the cell a young girl lies on the floor while others coax her to get up and speak to me. All I can see are her legs and her dark hair. Her face is turned into her arm, which acts as a pillow as she nestles into the near wall.

"That one is Maria. She is one of the ones from Mae Sot area. She says she has no mother and no father. She has been here for six months. You should talk to her." They call for her to come to the grille and speak to me, but she mutters into her arm, and refuses even to turn her head.

"What's she saying?" I ask.

"She says, 'No. I don't want to be released. Leave me here. Just leave me.'"

They are terrible words. What can this mean? Is she simply a sullen teenager who will change her mind in the night and put her name down with the others on the list of prisoners who want help? Or is there some deeper mystery here?

Before leaving, I go to the office that coordinates the volunteers who visit prisoners. The volunteer organization also takes care of special cases and negotiates with police when there is a conflict. The organization is headed by a woman named Theresa, and I have come to give her the initial lists of people asking for intervention. As she routinely deals with police and they know and trust her, I have decided my job is to persuade her to bring the matter up with the authorities. She has been here many years; her Thai is perfect. If anyone can handle this with political acumen, she can.

She promises to look at the lists, but her face says she is not convinced this is a worthwhile pursuit. The pile of other papers on her desk is daunting. Before I have spoken two sentences, we are interrupted three times by other volunteers, each with an emergency bigger than the last.

"There's been a rape," one volunteer announces. He alternately rubs his thinning hair and wrings his hands. "A young girl." Mala, he calls her. I wonder if this is the same girl, the one introduced to me by the English name Maria.

He proceeds to the back room with Theresa to discuss the problem. Left alone, I stand in the suddenly empty office, the bundles of papers from prisoners still in my arms. I look down at the many names, the long list. There are more than thirty people who can prove they have been detained for longer than six months, although their sentences were only eight weeks.

It is a strange thing with which to be entrusted, a strange thing to hold against my chest, these names of people locked away, forgotten, disappeared. They themselves cannot leave the rooms of their confinement, so they send their names out into my care. These papers include no letter of protest, no speech by an activist, no endorsement by a politician. Their names are their only statement, raw as they are, pared down to the barest of facts. This is who I am. This is when you promised to release me. My signature on this paper shows, as you can see, I am still here.

I have heard many fine speeches; I have read many letters of appeal. I have myself on occasion been startled out of the underbrush of my solitude to speak on behalf of people in trouble. But nothing has been more eloquent than the simplicity of these lists, this perfect poverty of argument. Devoid of poetry or diatribe, nothing has moved me more, or been as compelling a cry for justice.

I lay the papers on the desk for Theresa, and turn to leave. Before I get out the door, another volunteer rushes in to report that a woman refugee is being held not in IDC but in a local police station. News has leaked from one of her fellow prisoners that she is being harassed by the police for sexual favors.

It is hard to tell what the truth is in either of these cases. Maybe someone has been raped. Maybe it is the girl lying upstairs with her face to the wall. Maybe someone is trapped in a nearby police station, with the man who wants to sleep with her standing between her and the rest of the legal process that will lead her through imprisonment and eventual deportation.

The veracity of these statements is not in question, but the details are. Given the situation in Thailand, the unthinkable is the norm. It is certain that women and young girls are taken from detention cells, maybe even from the room two floors up from where I now stand, and that they are sometimes raped. It is certain that somewhere, perhaps nearby, perhaps at the station just down the street, a woman refugee is being harassed by the police into whose care she has been placed.

What is in question is only whether it is this girl, this cell, this day. And what to do about it. If the girl upstairs is one of those appalling statistics, it is unlikely it's the first time she has been sexually abused.

The selling of young women into forced prostitution is one of the worst aspects of the trade between Burma and Thailand. More than twenty thousand young women from Burma have been sold and brought to Thailand, many against their will. When they arrive in Thailand, they are told that they are now in debt to those who have paid for them and that they must work to pay off that debt. In most cases they are never told the exact amount of what they owe, or how much will be subtracted from their account for each customer, or how much added for each meal, or how much interest they will pay, or any other detail regarding the arrangement with the brothel owners.

The northern border through Mae Sae is notorious for such trafficking. That means the girl upstairs, young, alone in a foreign country, and coming from the north, may be working in Thailand's booming sex trade. Convinced that younger girls will be more pleasing to customers, and certainly more controllable, brothel owners pay higher prices to agents who procure them, and in turn, charge higher prices to customers, particularly if the girl is a virgin, or can be passed off as one.

Many of the girls aren't allowed to leave the brothel at all. They are kept in small rooms, sometimes six by eight feet, where they both live and serve their "customers." If they refuse a man, they may be beaten. To such girls, the police are no refuge. The trafficking happens with the explicit consent of the police, who round up ordinary refugees each day but somehow fail to notice the twenty thousand girls who slip by police checkpoints into Thailand. The connections between officials (military, police, politicians) and criminals (pimps, brothel owners) are so deeply entwined, it is sometimes hard to tell them apart. Unfortunately, this is a characteristic not limited to life in Thailand, though it seems there are fewer efforts to put up pretenses here.

Frequently, women who have been arrested report that a police station was just down the street from the brothel and that the owner threatened that the police themselves would beat the women and bring them back, should they try to escape. Women also report that it's common for the man who requests their services to enter their little concrete room still wearing his police uniform, a gun at his side.

Ultimately, there is no future for a girl from Burma who has been sold in Thailand. The transaction is likely to be fatal. Those engaged in this trade are really selling death. According to some studies, as many as 80 percent of Thailand's prostitutes are estimated to be HIV-positive. The men who visit these women are frequently as ignorant as they are cruel, and refuse to wear condoms, thereby making it possible with each contact that they will either contract the disease or spread it. The fear of HIV contributes to the demand for very young girls. Customers assume the younger a girl is, the less likely she is to be infected with HIV. Younger girls, however, are the most physically susceptible, and within six months of beginning work in Thailand, they are often infected.

A young girl might be sold by her family, or be lured by the promise of a "good job" in Thailand, or simply see no other future for herself and so volunteers to a recruiter, venturing forth into the world beyond her village and thinking she's on the road to economic freedom. Many girls are tricked into believing that some menial job as a cook or a nanny or a maid awaits them. Some are simply taken, with no explanation at all.

I think again of Maria. Why did she lie there so still, so unwilling to speak? Is she one of the twenty thousand? If so, the police will likely continue to bother

her, assuming there is no other use for her and that she should be accustomed to it by now. Why did Maria turn her face against the wall? Maybe she has AIDS. Maybe she's pregnant. Maybe the police, seeing she is already damaged, continue the abuse. If she's lucky, when they take her out of her cell at night, maybe they feed her before they rape her.

There is no private place for her to tell her story, even if she were willing. If she comes to the grille to speak with me, there will be a hundred ears listening, including those of the room leaders, who, though prisoners themselves, help the police by controlling the other women.

Because she comes from the north, Maria's options are fewer than if she had come from Kanchanaburi, in mid-Thailand. The northern border is tricky for all the prisoners from Burma. Kanchanaburi is bad enough, fraught with its own trials, including its oppressive detention center and the almost impossible task of getting a girl home to her village, should she arrive alone, frightened and young, at the winding dirt road that leads between the two countries.

Even for the men, it would be a hard journey. To call it freedom would glorify it. Those who are deported to Kanchanaburi may stay indefinitely in the no-man's-land of the refugee camps, but life there is neither safe nor comfortable. Possibilities for advancement, for work, and for a future don't exist. Always strapped for funds, the relief agencies can only manage to provide refugees with some rice and a little fish paste. On the Thai side of the border, refugees are forbidden to plant crops, so they subsist on these handouts. Some of the refugees have beriberi and general malnutrition in addition to malaria.

For a young woman trying to get home to her family in Burma, the problems multiply. Right across the border, the ethnic militias and the Burmese army clash. How can a young girl, unarmed and without money, find her way through a war zone to her parents' home in her native village? If she did make it back, would her family welcome her, returning to them just as she left, poor and uneducated, but now also "used" and with a burden of shame to match her burden of poverty?

What can she do? Where can she go? There are no solutions for such a girl, given the present situation in Thailand and Burma. If Maria is one of these girls, she can rot in the detention center. If she is released, the Kanchanaburi border is not an option, as her papers say she is from the north, and the law determines that if she is released at all, she must be sent home.

In the north, the territory immediately on the Burmese side of the border is controlled by the SLORC. Those who cross may be arrested by the SLORC authorities. As there is no monitoring international presence inside the border, it is uncertain what happens to such prisoners. Are they eventually released and sent home? Or are they prosecuted for illegal exit from Burma? The arrest may carry with it further rape, and perhaps a stint portering for the army, which will most likely be the last work she ever undertakes.

If she is suspected to be a prostitute, options are bleaker still. And how can a young girl not be suspected if she arrives alone with that unmistakable look of furtiveness and fear? The SLORC may sell her right back into bondage with a new brothel owner.

And there are other stories, darker yet. I have not been to that world across the border. How would I know what is true, what is reasonable to believe? Like the refugees, I exist in a realm where our opinions are formed as much by rumors as by the observation of impartial witnesses. All I can say is that stories filter back to us of the SLORC testing the girls for AIDS and if the test is positive, taking them out, putting a gun to their heads, and shooting them.

If it is true, what must a girl think, as she is led out the door of the local military headquarters by an armed man in uniform? As she stands back where she started, with her bare feet or flip-flops on the soil of her homeland, does she think of the men who raped her, beat her, sold her, infected her? As she stands there, not yet twenty years old, does she think this is as far as she got, this is all her life brought her, this is all she will ever know, until the soldier pulls the trigger, and she drops like a stone?

Even a few days of seeing life in this prison has altered me irreparably, and sometimes I wonder how it is we all go on. These girls whose futures possibly include slavery, rape, imprisonment, torture, slow death by AIDS, or quick death by a bullet, these women familiar with pain, betrayal, and terror—how do they get up in the morning? And why does a human being fear death when, in a strange way, death seems the least terrible option? And yet they do get up in the morning, they do go on, and yes, they are afraid of dying.

Maria turns to the wall for a little while, retreats into silence for a few days, a week. But eventually she will turn back toward her cellmates, she will pick herself up, she will eat the bowl of watery curry someone puts in her hands. And if it should happen that she finds herself in front of a soldier, with a gun to her head, it is possible, it is even likely, that her last thought will not be bitterness at what her life brought her but regret for all that she will never live.

The next day I return to IDC. I take a bus up Silom Street, passing Swenson's, Pizza Hut, Burger King, McDonald's, and A&W, all within a block of each other. Across from them is the entrance to Patpong, a narrow street that features a legitimate night market as well as one of Bangkok's most famous red-light districts. Last night I was there picking up cheap gifts to send home to friends and family. At night, row after row of tables with awnings sell fake Rolex watches, pirated rock-and-roll tapes for a dollar, and shiny polyester shirts labeled as Thai silk.

Jostling among the marketers, hawkers entice customers into the bars that line the road with "menus" of the entertainment that can be enjoyed inside. Most of the menus are simply lists of foreign objects, like Coke bottles, that the women are going to insert into orifices other than their mouths. Open doors to the bars along the road show young women in high heels and bathing suits, dancing listlessly in rooms with black walls. Both the women and the hawkers look drugged to me, half-asleep, as if they might wake up any moment and ask how they got there.

Now, in the morning, as the bus creeps along the congested street, I stare down at Patpong. It has the empty calm of a war zone after battle. Beer bottles lie in the gutters, along with trash, vomit, lost change, and a few used condoms. Clinics advertising treatment for venereal disease are judiciously spaced throughout the lane, in between the bars, for convenience. You can stop at the bar at night and pick up a disease and stumble next door for treatment in the morning.

As the bus revs its engine and rumbles down the road, I think, not for the first time, that Thailand is a mass of contradictions. Part of Bangkok's official name in Thai means "city of angels." And yet here in the city of angels women dance at night like zombies for a room full of men on barstools, while outside people haggle over the prices of cheap merchandise. The street is awash in red neon lights and steaming sewers, like some kind of displaced underworld. Bangkok is a mix of the sublime and the rancid. The many spires of temples throughout the city remind me to look up, but when I do, I invariably trip over a beggar or step in a gaping fissure in the sidewalk and sprain my ankle.

I set aside these philosophical musings when I reach IDC. I attempt to speak to Maria, but I don't know how to ask the things I want to know. I don't know the words in Thai, and I don't know enough about the culture to be sure how to approach this subject, even in English with a translator. "Is she having any trouble with the men?" I ask. "Are any of you having that kind of trouble?"

"No," says the saucy, curly-haired Mae Sae prisoner who translates. "No. She just has trouble here in this room. With us women." She laughs at this and goes on to explain. "Last week there was a fight." She tosses her hair and looks at me, unconcerned.

I scan the room. I imagine this chaos erupting into violence. And I feel disloyal for preferring the musky darkness of the men's rooms, their quiet, serious faces pressed against the bars, the weight of war and their people's future pressing down on their thin young shoulders. War and poverty also press down on the women, but the weight is crushing. The suffering doesn't seem to lead to anything beyond itself. There is nothing redemptive about it. Their suffering is so unrelenting it takes me to a place in the human soul I would rather not go. Their vulnerability embarrasses me.

"Maria!" the interpreter calls again and laughs and sighs and slaps her pretty leg. "Maria, come!" To me, she says, "She is very young. Only fifteen." She says it as though that explains everything. Perhaps it does.

Maria picks herself up and emerges over the edge of the top bunk. She is very pretty, a pouty, sullen teenager with chin-length hair, well-cut and thick. Prison has worn down her hair's natural gleam, but it is full and soft and frames her round face, her heart-shaped chin. She looks at me suspiciously out of eyes squinting and hard. Perhaps she means to be offensive. But there is too much child in her for it to be a successful affront. Her eyes flash up at me, and despite the attempt at disinterest, they indicate curiosity, longing. Perhaps hope.

Maria, I think, where is your mother? Your family? Is there someone who waits for you in a little village across the border and wonders where you've gone? Or did they sell you, your parents, spreading out the few hundred dollars they got for you, to look at each bill on the table and touch it and think this is the most they will ever own in their lives? Or did they die long ago, and are you, as you claim, an orphan, who at the prompting of some distant, uninterested relative, or your own desperation, took your life in your hands and crossed the border into the unknown?

And, most difficult question of all, what can I do for you? What can anyone do? I ask none of these things but watch as she gracefully takes a seat on the bed and looks first at me and then at her fellow inmates with disdain, maintaining to the last her inviolable silence.

That afternoon, I am sitting in the office of the community house when the phone rings. An unknown voice introduces himself and asks, "Has there been a rape in IDC?"

"I don't know," I say. "I can't figure it out." And then, even though I don't know this man, even though we have never met, I tell him everything.

He is a sympathetic listener. Then he tells me an amazing story. "We have a friend on the border," he says. "There are others, too. I will call our friend, and she will speak to the girl. If the girl is in trouble, we can pay all her legal fees and get her out of the prison. There are people on the border who will take care of her after that."

He calls others who have visited IDC, pieces together what he can. Later he calls back. "Well," he says, "it looks as if something may have happened after all. A Shan prisoner translated for the girl. She says the police 'used Mala as a wife' in the station, before she was sent to IDC, and they're doing the same thing now. I will call our friend on the border. She'll come on Monday. Don't worry. We'll get the girl someplace safe."

Safe, I think. Is there such a thing? I think of the language he used to shield the identity of those involved, in case someone was listening in on the conversation. "Our friend on the border." It strikes me that there must be a kind of underground railway. A few of the twenty thousand who were sold into prostitution may have a way home. Or at least a way out of the labyrinth of abuse and suffering in which they are caught. Maybe just a few. Just the lucky ones. But it's a start.

"Our friend at the border" has been elevated into a different realm. Like the gods, she cannot be spoken of by name. There are heroes all over the place these days. War produces them as surely as it produces casualties.

I go to bed deep in thought. The situation of women refugees fills me with horror but also hope. There is a net of human hands, reaching out, ringing the city, stretching all the way into the jungle. The hands reach out, but the faces are hidden, an anonymous circle. I am not really involved, or I am only the smallest link in this chain. Still, I am glad to be here. In my prayers I whisper my hopes to the universe. What I can do, let me do. Together let us hold up the light that guides a lost child home through the dark.

Misunderstandings

One morning when I arrive at the wat, Phra Dhamma treats me to a Coke, then leans forward in his chair. There is something on his mind, something he has been thinking about for a while, I can tell.

He begins in the Asian way. "Wicki, do you have free time?"

This is the ritual Asian opening to an invitation. If I say yes, it will not necessarily commit me to anything specific. But if I say no, I will never hear what adventure I was about to be invited into.

"Yes," I say. "Yes, I have free time."

He tells me two of his friends were arrested. He is very worried. They were in Bangkok for months, but only a few days after visiting the wat, they were seized by police. "They are not in IDC but in a different detention center in Nontaburi," says Phra Dhamma. He wants to visit them. Will I go with him?

I say yes, but it is a hesitant yes. I tell him that another Westerner tried to get into IDC last week and was not allowed in. I have an ID card that lets me into IDC but am not sure it will work for other detention centers, and the police seem to be getting stricter. So I will go, but maybe I won't be able to get in.

"O.K.," he says, "you don't have to go." He looks at the ground.

Clearly, it is not O.K. I am afraid I have offended him. He thinks the qualifiers I have tagged onto my yes are a way of saying I don't want to go. I'm not sure myself whether I want to go. I am curious and a little afraid, though I am not sure why. Maybe I'm not sure I can cope with one more awful story, one more discovery of the depths of human suffering.

Also, I am confused. Why does he want me to go, what is he hoping for? Does he just want company, or do they need money, or does he hope the presence of a foreigner will be useful in some way?

I want to apologize, to get it straightened out, but before I can think of what to say, life intervenes. There is a new refugee at the temple, and Matthew comes in to ask us to speak with him. Phra Dhamma and I put our attempts at mutual understanding on hold to deal with more pressing concerns.

In the refugee room I find Nai Lon, who is twenty-nine and looks forty-five. He sits on a mat, a crippled leg outstretched to one side. He massages it while he speaks. He tells us the worst first-person story of torture I have heard so far. He was interrogated by Burmese soldiers who suspected him of supporting Mon rebels. They wanted to know the names of Mon rebels and supporters, and they wanted to know where he was keeping his gun. He told them nothing. "They took what they could get," he says, his chin set in defiance. "They took my body. But I didn't give them anything important. Not my gun. Not one name."

The soldiers repaid Nai Lon's silence with terrible inventiveness. "They rolled a three-foot piece of wood up and down my leg, tearing the skin off my shin. Then four men stood on the wood on my leg. I heard the leg break.

"Then soldiers put my head under water, dipping it in again and again, until I couldn't breathe. Then they tied a rope under my arms, and they strung me up in a tree with my feet just above the ground.

"When they took me down they kicked me. I was bleeding everywhere, and blood was coming out of my mouth. Finally, they put a plastic bag over my head, tied it, and poured water over the bag. After that I lost consciousness. I don't remember any more."

After torturing him, they put him in jail, without treating his injuries. His broken leg set by itself, twisted and more or less useless. He was released two years later and escaped Burma immediately, making his way to the wat to see if anything could be done to heal his leg. "I can walk a little, but I have to hold the leg this way to do it," he says, demonstrating a crooked hobble that propels him across the floor. "The pain is terrible."

After a trip to the hospital, we stare at his x-rays in disbelief. The top of Nai Lon's leg is splintered, shattered, like the tip of an old broom, straw-thin fragments poking every which way, jammed up into what is left of the joint socket.

We talk to surgeons in Thailand, and we call surgeons in the United States, but they all agree nothing can be done. At first Nai Lon doesn't believe this prognosis, and neither do we. He is angry with us, and we are angry with the doctors. But as the consensus grows among doctors we trust, we come to terms with the truth. No treatment will help Nai Lon's leg.

Nai Lon hobbles around the wat compound, holding his leg and grimacing. The torturers took less than a day to do this to him. He will never recover. Eventually, he regains his peace. He takes to sitting on a mat in the shade, his face calm, his leg splayed out at an odd angle. "I gave them nothing," he says again, when we ask how he's feeling. "Nothing important. Not one name."

For the next few days I am subdued, and spend time contemplating my failures and uncertainties: Nai Lon's ruined leg; Phra Dhamma's concern for his imprisoned friends, which seems to require some response that eludes me.

The next time I go with Phra Dhamma and Phra Dala Non to the hospital, I return to the question of Phra Dhamma's friends. "So, are you going to the jail soon to visit your two friends?"

Phra Dhamma looks uncomfortable. "No. Tomorrow or the next day, I go to Ratchaburi."

"Ratchaburi! So far! Is that where your friends are in jail?"

"No," he says, looking at the back of the seat and turning red.

I have a terrible habit of continuing to poke, when common sense would indicate it's time to back off. "What's in Ratchaburi?" I ask. "Are you going to visit someone?"

Phra Dhamma is embarrassed and doesn't answer. He spends the rest of the trip looking at his sandals. I notice that even in his own embarrassment, Phra Dhamma keeps a kind hand on the patient's knee.

"Very mysterious," I say, still unable to let go, and winking at Phra Dala Non in the rearview mirror, trying to make light of my lack of understanding, when in fact I feel that my inability to grasp the situation is a kind of betrayal, and it makes me ashamed. It is as if every failure to respond leaves the Mon more alone in a world that seems bent on their destruction.

I twist back around in my front seat to look woodenly out the front window while we chug down the back road to the hospital in silence. The only sounds come from the tuk tuks and motorcycles screeching along beside us, and the sigh of air conditioning inside the taxi. We lurch through heavy traffic to the main street, passing blue glass office buildings interspersed with exotic temples and little spirit houses. I hold my silence, if not my peace, for the rest of the way.

At the hospital, I fill out the forms with the usual prevarications. The patient is ushered into the emergency room, and the rest of us settle into the waiting area. By this time I'm ready to bite my tongue to keep from asking about Ratchaburi. I don't bite it, and before I know it the question is out of my mouth. "Can't you tell me why you're going to Ratchaburi?" Now I've said it, and I hate myself for the intrusion. It occurs to me that if I ever have children, I will make a terrible, bossy, meddling mother.

"I go to borrow money," Phra Dhamma says glumly, resigned to my persistence.

"Borrow money?"

"Yes, for my friends in jail."

"Do you need me to give you some money? How much do you need?"

He shakes his head and goes back to staring at his sandals. Shortly, he gets up to check on the patient, leaving me with Phra Dala Non. While he's gone I ask Phra Dala Non what he knows about all this. "Is he borrowing to get his friends out, or to get food for them or, what?"

"Food, probably, and other expenses," he says. "It is too late to bribe them out, unless we have much, much money."

"Phra Dala Non," I ask, "what should I do to help Phra Dhamma? I feel like I'm making a mess of things."

"Wicki," Phra Dala Non says gently, "you have done nothing wrong, but life here is very complicated. Not doing wrong and knowing how to do right are different things. And I cannot tell you what to do. If you want to help Phra Dhamma, you must talk to Phra Dhamma."

That night at home I begin to fret when I think of Phra Dhamma. It is hard to understand what he needs, and what my role should be. Money is a sensitive issue in most cultures; even children raised in the same house manage to misunderstand one another over it. How can I navigate such a complex question across cultural boundaries? Our relative economic inequality in what is at its best a friendship of equals further complicates the issue. Should I just get some money and give it to Phra Dhamma? Will that insult him or break some rule of our relationship? In his culture is he allowed to ask? Allowed to accept? Am I allowed to ask what he needs? To offer? To insist? Is there something that is so clear to him he cannot understand why it is opaque to me?

I explain my mystification to community members the next morning at the kitchen table, over toast and tea. In fact, anyone who sits down hears the whole story. "Isn't there anyone you can go to for help in interpreting their culture?" asks Sister Martha. "Someone who understands both them and you?"

"Maybe Robert Halliday," I say forlornly.

"So can you ask him?"

"He died before I was born." He was the British man who wrote a book about the Mon in 1917. The title of the book is *The Talaings*, which shows that even he did not understand the Mon well enough to know he chose an insulting title for his book. The word is what the Burmese call the Mon, meaning orphans, with overtones of illegitimate children, or perhaps the children of conquered and murdered fathers—a weak people. Halliday is one of the few outsiders qualified to call himself an expert on the Mon, but he still got the nuances wrong. Besides, he knew the Mon of the early twentieth century, which may or may not be the same as knowing the Mon now.

That night, Phra Dhamma calls. He tells me he is definitely going to Ratchaburi. I sigh, afraid that in the present political climate it is not a safe trip. If he goes to ask for money I could have given him in relative safety here, and if he is arrested on the way, I will never forgive myself.

In the morning I am dry-eyed and suddenly clear. Phra Dala Non is right. There is no one to help us sort this out. We must do it ourselves. I find Phra Dhamma by the computer room, preparing for his journey. "Will you go to Ratchaburi today?" I ask.

He nods.

I look at the ground, at his broad feet in their flip-flops. "Phra Dhamma," I say softly, "do you need money? Have you been trying to tell me you need something?" Before he can answer I go on. "I know there is a lot I don't understand. A lot. But I want to understand. You must help me. There are so many things I want to know. If you are in trouble, I want to help you. But I don't know what you need. You must tell me what you need."

He looks at me and nods seriously.

"I have just received a small donation for the prison project, only about twelve hundred baht [50 dollars]. If you need it for your imprisoned friends, you can use it. Do you need it?"

He thinks for a moment. "I will go to Ratchaburi first," he says. "I have friends there who are also friends of the men in jail. I will try to get money. But if I cannot get it, when I come back I will borrow from you. O.K.?"

"O.K." I feel a mixture of relief and fear. His independence and self-reliance are wonderful things. The erosion of a people's belief that they can take care of themselves is one of the worst side effects of international relief work. Ultimately, prolonged inequality destroys both personal friendships and cultural integrity. Phra Dhamma's insistence on first relying on Mon internal resources, his honesty, his willingness to take risks that will make him self-sufficient are his only defense against the natural tendency toward dependence. But is he safe, alone on his way to Ratchaburi?

The next evening Phra Dhamma calls at 9:30 P.M., and I shuffle out into the hall half-dressed to get the phone. He has been to Ratchaburi. He has come back to us tired, and empty-handed, but safe. He waited and waited, but his friends did not come, so he has nothing to give the men in prison.

"All right," I say. "I have some donation money for prison work, don't worry."

"O.K.," he says. "Tomorrow we go to the jail. You come, too?"

"Fine," I say quickly, without hesitation or qualifiers. "I'll see you in the morning."

Bangkok is subject to the worst kind of urban sprawl. In the morning Phra Dhamma and I, accompanied by Phra Dala Non, take a taxi and two busses through two hours of urban landscape, without ever breaking free of the grip of the city. Technically, the town we're headed to is not within Bangkok, but you'd never know it by the scenery, which is one concrete box after another, many of them built with drug money and serving no useful purpose. It is like traveling through a landscape created by Dr. Seuss. Crazy, blinding white squares of concrete stretch for miles and miles, reflecting heat and light, with the occasional stubborn fern or palm tree imposing itself on the otherwise barren scene.

In the taxi Phra Dhamma tells the story of his two friends. "We knew each other back before, back in Burma." They have been working in Thailand for four months near the border. "Hard work," he says. "Digging work and making buildings with bricks. But at the end of the four months, they did not get paid one baht. So they paid a thousand-baht bribe to police to let them get to Bangkok, and they came to see me.

"They stayed with me four days and three nights. Then one morning, very early, the police came. I was still asleep, but my friend got up to go to the toilet. On the way, the police caught him. If I had six thousand baht that day, my friends would go free. I went to Brother Matthew, but he had no money to give me. I came back to talk to the police, but by then the police took them away, very far, to a jail in Nontaburi, where we will go today. If they had money, they would not have to go. If I had money, I could have saved them. I went to Ratchaburi to borrow money from some friends we have there. I waited and waited. But my friend never came."

Boarding the bus for the next leg of the journey, Phra Dhamma fans himself. "I do not like the hot season," he says. "Never."

"Is it this hot in Burma?" I ask.

He looks around quickly to see if the mention of his homeland has raised or turned any heads; if anyone will know from this question where he comes from and who he is; if anyone will rise from the front seat, present a badge and carry him away.

Guiltily, my eyes follow his. When no head lifts, we settle in and wait in silence while the bus starts up.

After a while Phra Dhamma leans forward from the backseat, where he and Phra Dala Non are sitting in the cross breeze of two open windows. Smoke from another passenger's cigarette drifts back and whisks out the window like a full skirt hurrying out a doorway, a second behind the girl who wears it.

"Uh, Wicki," Phra Dhamma shouts suddenly over the traffic, "did I mention to you that my father is in prison?"

"Your father is in prison," I repeat stupidly.

"Yes. Four years now. And my friend who we will see today, his father is in prison, too."

"Why is he in prison?"

Phra Dhamma looks at me blankly as if, given Burma's present political situation, the assumption of reason behind a prison sentence is incomprehensible.

"Is it something he did?" I ask. "Or something you did? Or is it because you left?"

"It is many things. Where I came from, there are three townships near each other. Fifty men were arrested in these townships in June 1990 on the same day. Some had joined demonstrations. Some had sons who joined demonstrations. Some had sons who escaped from Burma. All these things mean prison."

"These fifty men, are they all still in prison?"

"Many, yes. At least thirty-seven still there."

"And . . ." I do not know how to ask what comes next, thinking of Nai Lon sitting in the shade with his ruined leg. "The ones who have been released, had they been, you know, hurt? Did they hurt them in prison? Beat them? Torture them?"

Phra Dhamma closes his eyes. "Hurt bad," he says. "Hurt very bad."

"And," I am almost whispering now, "your father? Was your father hurt like this, too?"

"My father, too. When I think about him, I feel very sad. He is in prison because I was in the demonstrations and because I escaped from Burma. He is in prison because of me."

I want to know more, but now we have arrived in Nontaburi. We are deposited on the side of the highway, which we cross, finding ourselves on a quiet dirt road. We walk to the jail, succumbing to the pleasure of the first bit of countryside we have encountered this long morning. On the way in, Phra Dhamma pauses. "Wicki, I would like to explain to you something. When we are at the jail, you must not say to them we are Mon or from Burma. You understand?"

I feel serious and contrite, thinking of my mistake on the bus, and my earlier mistakes in the Immigration Detention Center, where I often announced he spoke Mon without thinking of the implications. "I understand."

The outer room of the jail is filled with ugly furniture, which seems to be for sale. We make our way to the reception desk, a small table on one side of the room, where a guard sits, going over some accounting books. I slap my ID card down on the desk, though I have no idea whether it is sufficient to let me visit at this jail. The guard stares at it a long time, then picks it up gingerly, as if it is only pretending to be inanimate and may any minute spring to life and bite him. I am not sure whether my ID card is sufficient to let me visit, and given how long he takes to inspect it, perhaps the guard isn't certain, either. Eventually he shrugs and lets me through.

I follow Phra Dhamma and Phra Dala Non over to bars covered with chicken wire, separating the visitors from the holding cell where prisoners are brought to see them. The guards bring out several of the detained before they eventually find one of the prisoners Phra Dhamma has asked to see. Those brought out by mistake reluctantly return to the darkness of the building.

The monks begin to talk with their friend, and the guard retreats to his desk to watch over their conversation. A moment later the guard yells, "Hey, no letters."

Phra Dhamma and Phra Dala Non ignore him, chatting, writing, and rolling notes into long strips, which they slide through the chicken wire.

When the guard shouts, it happens that Phra Dhamma is writing a note for me, telling prisoners that if they are refugees, accepted as such by the UNHCR, they should identify themselves, and the UNHCR officer will get them some of their money. I have been asked to spread this information by a UNHCR officer in Bangkok who believes there is not enough flow of information in detention centers, especially for prisoners outside of Bangkok, who may not even know what they're entitled to. The guard stomps over and demands that the prisoner pass the note back through the wire. He confronts Phra Dhamma. "This isn't Thai," he says in disgust, unrolling the wad of paper the length of a cigarette. "I can't understand it at all."

Phra Dhamma points at me with his chin and explains the note is about the UNHCR and that the foreigner has requested it. The guard does not look at me, though I am sitting near Phra Dhamma, with only the minimal required distance between us. I stare off into the distance, looking innocent, picking the scabs of my mosquito bites. If I were Thai, or worse, Mon, perhaps he might harass me. But I am foreign and the UNHCR is still something to contend with, so he probably isn't sure what to make of me. He stares at me for a minute, then shrugs and walks away. I glance over at him occasionally and catch him looking at Phra Dhamma with hostility. My heart sinks a little, wondering whether my transgressions will be taken out on the monks.

Phra Dhamma continues to write notes to his prisoner friend, sliding glances over his shoulder at the guard, who alternately pretends to be engrossed in his accounts and looks up now and then to intercept an infraction. Behind his back, Phra Dhamma makes a face.

The guard cuts the visiting time short. On the wall a sign in Thai promises a thirty-minute visiting period. They give us twenty, including the ten minutes spent calling different prisoners out, none of whom are the people the monks have come to see. The monks submit to the indignity of the shorter period, and we go to the office at the front of the building, where Phra Dhamma registers that he is leaving gifts for the prisoners, including five hundred baht. It is all very official looking, a neat, if simple office, where young women write down what is being left, and the name of the prisoner. Despite the apparent legitimacy of the procedure, I am not entirely surprised, when, weeks later, Phra Dhamma reports that the money never reached his friends.

We leave the jail and walk the long quiet road back to the highway. It is disconcerting how a ten-minute walk can remove you so completely from the feel of the city. Half the time I forget there are such things as fields or crickets, or that the city does not take up the whole planet. Although I am reluctant to break the silence, I also don't want to waste this rare opportunity to speak to Phra Dhamma in relative privacy, uninterrupted by either the roar of traffic or the demands of life at the temple. Phra Dhamma was able to see only one of his friends at the jail. "How is he?" I ask. "Is he sick?"

"Not too bad."

"And the other friend, is he well, too?"

"Yes. They are sick now and then but not too sick. This jail is bigger than IDC. They can all lie down at the same time, there is enough room for that. So they get a little sleep. That is good. But my friend says our other friend cries at night."

I look at him sideways, always surprised by these impassive announcements indicating deep emotion. His face doesn't reveal anything more than that this is a simple statement of fact.

After a moment of silence, I ask, "How long did it take us to get here?"

Phra Dhamma consults a watch he keeps in his shoulder bag. "Maybe two hours."

And two hours to go back, I think. And we only got to see him for ten minutes.

"In the end," says Phra Dhamma, reading my mind, "I told him I do not think I can come again."

"So which friend was this one?" I ask. "Is it his father who is in prison?"

"Yes."

"Phra Dhamma, I know one time you had an interview with Amnesty International. When they interviewed you, did you tell them about your father? About the prisoners?"

He shakes his head. "I think, but I do not tell."

"Can I tell them?" I ask, my feet crunching in the gravel. He shakes his head no.

"Wicki, I would like to explain to you about something," he says for the second time today. "There was a monk in Burma. He was very active in the demonstrations. He was arrested. He was sentenced to one year in prison. Many people heard about this monk. Other monks heard about him, and people in other countries heard about him. People wrote letters and asked that he be set free. When they saw all these letters, the Burmese sentenced him to eight years because he had contacted the international groups."

"Oh," I say. "So you do not want me to contact Amnesty."

"I do not."

"It is dangerous?"

"Yes. Dangerous."

Noise from the highway has begun to reach us. The world is almost upon us. I sigh. "It is a problem," I explain. "If you speak, it is dangerous for your family. If you do not speak, there is no record, no proof, and no one from the outside can help you. Our oil companies in the United States go into Burma and say, 'I see no human rights abuses here.' You understand the problem?"

"I understand."

We have reached the street. Phra Dala Non, who has been walking quietly behind us now leads the way. He finds a lull in the traffic, and we rustle across, trample a hedge, and stand illegally in the middle of the grass and shrub island, with cars and trucks threatening our lives in both directions. Once we get to the Sala on the other side, where the buses stop, I think of a final question. "How do you get news of your family?" I ask.

"My mother visits my father. Then she writes me."

"But isn't it dangerous?"

"Why dangerous?"

"There was another refugee we knew. His father was in prison. We helped him to resettle in the United States or Canada, I'm not sure which. And he wrote to his family to tell them, but the Burmese military took the letter. They killed his father in prison, and took his mother and put her in prison."

"Yes," he says. "It is true. It happens many times."

"So how do you write to your mother without endangering the family?"

"Ah," he says, giving me a shy smile. "I do not put my name or address on the envelope. I use another name for myself. And I write in Mon."

We decide to take a taxi to a bus station where we can catch an air-conditioned bus home. In the taxi, Phra Dhamma, still concerned about his economic responsibilities, slides forward three bills. "I gave my friend five hundred baht," he says. "But I am only borrowing. On the twenty-seventh, I get some money from the UN, and I will give back to you."

"Perhaps you can keep this," I suggest. "In case they need it when they get out of prison."

Phra Dhamma shakes his head. "If they need it, I can get some other money by then." He follows the seven hundred baht with another twenty. "The other day coming you gave me three hundred baht to take a refugee to the hospital and buy him medicine, but I had some change."

Arriving at the bus station, all debts paid, we climb into a big blue bus for the next stage of the journey home. Phra Dhamma and Phra Dala Non sit in their monks' seats by the door. I slide over to the next aisle. Soon the bus is crowded. A schoolgirl sits beside me and in minutes is sound asleep, her head resting on my arm just below the shoulder. I look over at the monks. Phra Dhamma, too, is asleep, his head on the orange pillow of Phra Dala Non's shoulder. Phra Dala Non is staring out the window.

I turn back to my own window, wondering. It was a long journey, and I accomplished little. But Phra Dhamma has confided new depths: his imprisoned father, his beleaguered village. Did he really want me to come on this trip? Or did he think I needed to come? Was he hoping we would have enough money to pay his friends' fines and release them? In the circle of misunderstandings of the last few days, what was required of me? The only thing I have been sure I could offer is to say I am here. I close my eyes and nod off, knowing that is not always enough.

Where Our Sympathies Lie

I have not been successful at finding out whether it's true that the refugees will be handed over to the SLORC. I try, I worry, I scheme, but I don't accomplish much. To top it off, Matthew and I have been arguing. I have a vague sense it is my fault but can't figure out what I should do about it. And I'm much too proud to apologize.

Matthew has suggested we publish the rumors the Mon have heard—that we get the question into the hands of other NGOs, the United States government, maybe the newspapers. I recognize we have been unsuccessful at getting any real information on our own, but I am afraid of making the community name so public, and tying it to an unsubstantiated claim.

Given the depth of the refugees' fear and the uncertainty that surrounds this story, I am reluctant to cause further panic among refugee circles or to open ourselves to ridicule by the authorities with a story that may be false. Still, given how difficult it is to prove such a rumor until it has become fact and lives have been lost, Matthew sees no other solution than to appeal to the public. Even if the government denies the plan, as long as the refugees are safe, what does it matter if we have embarrassed ourselves in the process?

By the end of our third conversation on the subject Matthew and I are both close to shouting. "Everyone always wants to keep quiet about these things," Matthew complains. "Even the monks. Even the prisoners. Where does that get us? We do nothing, and the situation gets worse and worse."

I grudgingly concede I will try to write up a possible public statement. I promise to finish it by Mass that afternoon, and I set to work. Thirty-three drafts later, I have something rough sketched out. Matthew comes in after teaching an English class and takes a seat in the community house's air-conditioned office.

He wipes his forehead and peels his shirt from his damp back to let a little of the cool air circulate. I hand him the draft and sit down nervously.

He reads it silently, then looks up in amazement. "But this is no good without the community letterhead," he says, astonished that I could have missed this point. "It doesn't mention who we are or how we know what we know. It's no good without that. We've got to take some risks if we're going to be effective."

I squirm in my chair. He is right, of course. There is no way to ask for help publicly on this issue unless we are willing as a group to take responsibility for what we know or think we know. But in my inner struggle between courage and fear, fear has won out.

On the desk where I have been working is the original letter that came from the prisoners. "Give that to me," says Matthew in disgust. "I'll have to do this myself." He stands and walks angrily through the office door and stomps up the stairs. "They came to me," he mutters to himself on the way out. "To me. I should have taken care of this on my own in the first place."

I sit for a long time in the office, red-faced, guilty, embarrassed, and slightly baffled. I feel simultaneously defensive and self-critical of my own position. When Matthew gets going, he is as insistent as an Old Testament prophet. I find his certainty annoying, especially when I suspect he's right, but I'm too afraid to do what he asks. I have a new appreciation for why so many Old Testament prophets got killed.

Later, I call a mutual friend to complain about the situation. "Matthew is always so passionate about everything," I complain. "I don't get a chance to calm down and think through what I should do. It makes me mad."

"How could you not misunderstand each other, how could you not be mad?" asks my friend. "You are so much alike."

After the quarrel with Matthew, I renew my determination to do something about the rumor of repatriation. If I can get an answer from the Thai government without exposing the community, I figure I will have fulfilled my obligation to the refugees and all will be forgiven with Matthew.

The problem is that I have no idea where to turn for verifiable information on what the immigration department and police propose to do with the prisoners, and I don't know how to attract the right kind of political attention without risking our entire operation here, or our reputation, should it turn out we have overreacted.

The strain is beginning to show. It has been days since I've slept through the night. Several days ago I ceased to be a rational human being at all. I have abandoned myself to moodiness and panic. I fidget through conversations and weep at music, even grocery-store Muzak. At night, I hide in my room and sulk. By day I go to the wat to torture myself with thoughts that any of the people I see here could end up in the detention center tomorrow, and from there on, who knows what will be done to them unless Matthew and I succeed at finding out what the government really intends.

Meanwhile, despite the deteriorating political situation, life goes on as usual in the city. Bangkok is absorbed in its own troubles and does not think about the Mon one way or the other. The city is growing—every day new cars appear, the traffic is worse, the crowds are worse, the pollution is worse. The city is splitting at the seams. I go out to rediscover it each morning. Sometimes I take the water taxi to avoid the crowds. On the way I see what one of our community members has named "the bloated dog of death," which becomes for me a metaphor for everything.

The "bloated dog of death" is an old dog who has been lying in the same spot in an alley on the way to the river for what seems like weeks. He is alive, but he never seems to move. He has lost most of his hair, though in places it still grows in scraggly tufts. Worms have chewed through most of his intestines, carving tracks and tunnels in once-smooth muscle. Gasses leak through these passages. Day by day his belly grows bigger, though he can't have eaten. He just lies there on his side, gray, swelling, and silent. An occasional blink of his eye lets us know he's still alive.

Every day as part of a fast-paced crowd intent on our own business, I step over him or around him. People hurry by, laughing, spitting on the sidewalk, sipping sodas out of plastic bags secured with rubber bands, leaving an opening just big enough for a straw. We chat about the weather, the traffic, the departure time of the next boat.

One day I walk to the water taxi, and he's gone. No more bloated dog of death blocking the path like a reminder, an omen. Where did he go? Did he die and get carted off to be burned or buried—whatever they do with dog carcasses? Or did someone haul him off to a temple where he could suffer more discretely? Or was he rolled still alive into the river, while people on the dock watched him float away, tip, and sink?

I board the taxi thinking of all that we walk by daily without seeing. Problems too difficult for us become accepted parts of the path to work and then disappear from consciousness altogether, become invisible. The taxi fills up, and I pay my few baht to the *grapaw* (literally, "money bag," the Thai term for money collector). The boat lurches forward on the shining water, spraying back a glistening plume. I think it is beautiful, even though I know the water is polluted, and I can smell its acrid essence: dumped fuel, exhaust, dead fish, and garbage. Along the way children splash each other under decaying wooden porches. They jump in, naked, brown, and gleeful.

It is all mixed up here, beauty, joy, filth, poverty. I have taken this route a thousand times but only occasionally really look around me. Who among us can say that they have truly seen what is in front of them? Who can claim really to be awake in this world?

I haven't been able to get through to the person Nai Tangay asked me to contact at the Australian embassy. After fretting, useless philosophizing, and equally useless self-blame, after the disappearance of the bloated dog of death and a certain amount of procrastination, I call again. Eventually, I get through to the right person.

I hope Mary will tell me this is being handled at a diplomatic level, that it is all taken care of, that I need not get involved but can continue to step around the ugliness of life the way I have stepped day after day over the dying dog. Unfortunately, Mary merely says her office has heard the rumor, too, that they have been unable to determine the truth of it, and that they are deeply concerned. She has a soothing voice, and the fact that her concern seems to go straight through to the center of her only makes me feel worse, proving that, after all, this is a threat that warrants worrying over.

"Some IDC volunteers will meet with the Police High Command next week. Should we bring it up with the police then?" I ask, crossing all my fingers in the fervent hope she will say no, that these matters are best left in the hands of people higher up, people who wear suits and have chauffeurs. In reality I cannot imagine myself in a room full of police, especially high-level police, eking out anything more coherent than a long, low whine.

But she thinks speaking with the police is a good idea. "What should I say?" I ask, wishing there were somewhere to take a short course in diplomacy, or an intensive one in courage.

"Say the embassy is concerned," she says. "Ask for assurances that no one will be handed over to the SLORC."

On Sunday I go to church. It's Easter. I think it is unreasonable to ask me to celebrate Easter Sunday when I seem to be stuck somewhere around Good Friday. Or maybe I'm somewhere in between. Maybe I'm a Holy Saturday sort of person. The murder of the innocent is real to me. I believe in it. I hear resurrection is just around the corner, and I will experience it in the morning, but in my heart of hearts, I'm not convinced.

Still, on Sunday, every activity seems equally useless, and I'm tired of myself. Church is not foremost on my list of priorities at the moment, but it is something to do and is more or less expected of me. In a way I hope that being obedient to the rhythm of the church year, even if I go through it without enthusiasm, will restore some sense of normalcy.

Today, the congregation is engaged in, of all things, a dedication of our new air conditioner. We will also unveil the new rose window and consecrate some new glass doors, the money for which has been donated by half a dozen groups. As part of the morning's ritual, each group who offered a donation will open the door they paid for. The name of the donor is prominently, if tastelessly, engraved on the handle of each door.

I sing listlessly in the choir under the new, almost silent air conditioner, admitting to myself that the machine is much less threatening than the old fans that used to whirl over our heads, jerking, squeaking, and occasionally crashing down among the pews. I am attempting to appreciate, simultaneously, the goodness of the Creator and modern technology when I hear the list of donors who contributed to our new doors. The donors are lined up in a special alcove behind me, and I crane my neck to see those ancient people crammed into pews hip to hip.

They are the prisoners of war.

The real ones. The originals. The survivors. The ones who worked on the Death Railway.

All through the typically terrible and lengthy sermon I can hardly breathe. I weep through several of the songs I'm supposed to be singing. I sit down at the wrong time, stand up when no one else is standing, and wonder if this constitutes an emergency sufficient to justify crawling over the back of the choir pew and dragging some seventy-year-old man out on the lawn to hear my saga.

And my idea.

Which is, of course, that salvation has arrived. That God has arranged this visit of war heroes to coincide with the dedication of our air conditioner. That both have been designed to save a new generation of forced laborers building a railroad through the Burmese jungle.

It is important to understand that this is not at all the picture of God I was brought up to believe in. I was not raised in the school of "ask and it shall be given unto you." I was raised in another truth, also orthodox: "The sun shines equally on the good and the evil."

My prayer, therefore, has never been a list of requests. It would not occur to me that the universe was so mechanical that prayer could be a coin you slipped into the appropriate slot of a vending machine to get the item you wanted. My prayer has largely consisted of listening. To what? To silence, I guess, though not an empty silence. I have assumed that while the sun is shining on the good and the bad, there is still a Spirit accessible to all, integral to all, connecting all. The spiritual life consists not in manipulating that Spirit to act on our behalf but in living what comes to us with courage. My view of God is sort of like Kennedy's attitude toward the country: "Ask not what the Spirit can do for you, but what you can do for the Spirit."

But the POWs at our church at the very time that new prisoners are being threatened with return to forced labor! It is too much! How can it be a coincidence?

After church I head for the lawn, which, like the church building itself, is a little piece of America or Europe. For this moment on a Sunday, you can almost pretend you never left your homeland, if you ignore the thick sounds of Thai city life drifting in over the hedge. Everyone wanders around with ghastly bonnets and ugly flowered dresses, chatting about the weather.

I plow into the crowd and grab the hand of the nearest veteran. He is a kind-eyed Welshman who can't possibly be seventy, can he? Despite his white hair and hunched back, his skin is smooth, and his eyes are bright. I intend to impress him with my dignity, to say, "Sir, I must approach you about a matter of the utmost urgency." Instead, I shake his hand and begin to cry. Not all at once. It is not a burst of tears. It is more like a building falling down in slow motion, a crumpling kind of coming-to-pieces.

Astonished, he listens while I pour out my story. "The prisoners are afraid they'll be handed over to the SLORC, their enemies. They will be forced to work on the railway, just as you were forced to work on the Death Railway fifty years ago." The man nods and listens, listens and nods, then directs me to their tour leader, saying he's sure something can be done.

The tour leader, on the other hand, clearly wants to get rid of me as soon as possible. I am talking too fast. I am hysterical. The tears in my eyes embarrass him. This crisis was over fifty years ago. The confetti, sympathy, and medals are long forgotten. Why is this woman babbling under the awning on the church lawn, while civilized people are saying polite things about the air conditioning and drinking iced tea? He says, "Very fine work, very fine. Good luck now." He shakes my hand with absolute finality. He means, "Good God, go blow your nose, for heaven's sake."

I try again with another veteran, this time retelling the story with less sniffling. He tells me many of them have already set up radio spots for when they return to the United Kingdom, Australia, wherever. It's perfect, I think. They don't even need to make a fuss here in Thailand. They can wait till they are home and then inform the world of what is going on. This is the safest way to go public. The monks can speak for themselves to the veterans, who can raise the question publicly overseas, probably eliciting some sort of response from Thailand. The kind old man tells me the name of their hotel and says I should contact another leader of their group, not a tour leader, but a member of their veterans' group, a Mr. James Beetle. "I think you'll find a lot of sympathy here in this crowd," he says.

I go home in a fog of achievement and a confused crisis of spirituality. Could God really operate like this, after all? Does the Creator arrange for air conditioners that were scheduled to be installed months ago to arrive belatedly in order to bring aging prisoners of war to the rescue of the Mon?

I can't wait to get home and call Matthew, who has called me every night recently to tell me new horrors—more people escaping from Burma rather than working on the railroad, SLORC burning their villages, so they flee across the border, their fields in flames behind them.

I sit at the typewriter and compose what I consider to be a compelling letter to the POWs, care of Mr. Beetle. I reread it to myself over and over. Wow, I think, powerful stuff. I invite them to come and hear the monks, no more, and if they are moved, to speak about what they have heard when they return to their own countries.

Matthew approves of this plan and talks to the monks, who offer to speak and be videotaped for showings in other countries, despite the potential danger to themselves personally or to their families in Burma if these tapes should fall into the wrong hands. This opportunity is too important, the possibility of getting the news out to the few people in the world who could turn it into a media event, people who will be able to speak with authority about what forced labor in the jungle means, about how atrocious it would be to hand over the refugees to that kind of life. The prisoners of war are people who will be admired, listened to, believed.

I fax my letter over to the hotel and ask Mr. Beetle to call me back. Then I wait.

A few hours later, worried that they may have gone out for the day, I call the hotel. Mr. Beetle picks up the extension in his room, and answers cautiously. "Yes?"

"Hello, sir," I say, introducing myself. "Did you get my fax?"

"Yes." His yes is followed by an awkward silence.

"Well?" I ask, "What do you think?"

"You certainly know where our sympathies lie," he says. My heart soars and beats so loudly in my ears that it takes a minute to calm down and hear the rest. ". . . nonpolitical, must respect the rights of the host country. We knew about the forced labor on the border before we came. We talked about it. We agreed we would not involve ourselves."

"Will you give the fax to others?" I ask. Kind Mr. Potter. Mr. Miller of the bright eyes and baby-clear skin. "I spoke to a few at church and some seemed interested. I can set up something here at our house. Those interested can come and find out what's happening. I can even offer that the whole thing be videotaped. Then, those who feel so moved can call attention to the problem when they get back to their homes."

"How can I even give your message to the others?" he asks. "I can't exactly put something like this on the bulletin board, can I?"

"You could pass it around. Quietly. You could announce it the next time you have a moment together just with your group."

"I suppose I could do that," he says, sounding as though he supposes no such thing.

"Will you?" I ask. "You could see if anyone is interested, and I could take it from there. All I ask is that you let each person make up his own mind. Please, sir. The refugees are in so much trouble. They need you so much." I'm on the verge of crying now. My voice is climbing, sounding high and shrill even to myself. I notice that in my fervent appeal to these men to speak publicly about the current threat, to be brave, to be bold, to speak the truth, I sound a lot like Matthew.

"I'm sorry," he says. But I do not think he is sorry. I think this is what you say when you want to get off the phone as quickly as possible. "We come here every year now for vacation, you know. After we visit Kanchanaburi, we go down to the island of Phuket. We must think of the future." He says this like a final statement. It is a final statement. It is also, perhaps, a plea for understanding. "You know where our sympathies lie," he says again. "We can imagine it. We can see just what it's like."

Yes, I think, as he hangs up. I know exactly where your sympathies are. Vacation in Phuket.

As I hang up the phone, I remember my recent quarrels with Matthew. I see the anger in his face when he read my statement, devoid of letterhead or identification. To a certain extent I am no better than these men who refused to listen and speak even though they had a natural audience and clear credibility. What is needed in my work is the courage to take risks. The risk of being thrown out of the country. The risk of looking like a fool. No one wants to risk these things. But to refuse, to stay safe and silent in the face of injustice, is to forfeit all we stand for. I think of Matthew's vehemence and anger and passion, and I admit to myself that I was wrong.

Simple as that. I was wrong.

* * *

I make up my mind to do what Mary asked and talk to the police directly about the rumor—to reveal that much, risk that much, at least, and if that decision yields nothing, I will think about where to go next with our story. The only question now is how to make it through the next week in one piece while I wait for the meeting with the Police High Command.

That night in my room, I stand against the window in the dark, looking out onto the distant lights of Bangkok. From one corner of the room, I can see the twinkling from a string of little lamps stretched along the length of a distant bridge. The city is peaceful and full of light. I press my cheek against the cool glass and cry. How can it be, I wonder, that the same animals who build bridges and mimic the stars also put children into dark, cramped prisons, build land mines with a careful eye and unwavering hand, or work an old man to death on a road in the jungle? And when the time comes to turn that pain into something useful, something holy, how can it be that those who have suffered most turn away and will not listen?

So much for thinking the Spirit arranges the daily events of our lives to help us participate in building the reign of God. Or maybe that is exactly what happens. Maybe every day is an opportunity to love one another more truly, more deeply, more tenderly. But if so, there is nothing to keep us from turning our backs, escaping from our own terrors, yet leaving our brothers in prison, or in the jungle, carrying the hard steel for a railroad on their backs.

Safe

At last the day comes for the meeting with the Police High Command. My heart is pounding so hard I am afraid I'll collapse. It turns out Theresa is gone that day, so I approach Gary, her assistant, and ask him to bring up the rumor we have heard that refugees will be handed over to the SLORC at Three Pagoda Pass. I tell him everything I know, including the conversation between me and Mary from the Australian embassy. In Asia, official authority counts for something, and I figure Gary's role as the vice president of this group makes him the logical candidate for bringing up unpleasant business. In a way, I'm glad, too, that Theresa is away, as it may be an advantage to have a man do the talking. Here, and maybe everywhere, men speak to men in a different way than women do. As much as I'd like things to be otherwise, this is especially true when dealing with an all-male, rigidly ordered, hierarchically minded group, like the Thai police.

As the meeting begins in the police office at the back of the detention center, I sit on the back bench, as far from the center of the action as I can. I drink the bottle of orange soda they offer me, and watch the proceedings.

Gary valiantly brings up the report of the threat of repatriation, complete with the veiled threat that the embassies have asked us to look into this matter. He barely has his first sentence out of his mouth before the police spokesman becomes irate. "Send them to the SLORC? If we did that they would be killed. We know that. Everyone knows that. Don't you know our policy? Our policy is to let them go at the border. There has been no change in that procedure. Don't the embassies know our policy? Who has made this accusation?"

Gary quails and turns to look at me. The entire room turns around to join him. I have the pop bottle in my mouth and dribble over myself in my haste to get it out.

"Which embassy has voiced these concerns?" The police superintendent looks at me steadily, perhaps trying to assess whether I am as insignificant as I look or whether this greasy-faced, somewhat unkempt, and obviously nervous person with an orange soda stain on her bosom might really have contacts he should worry about.

"Many embassies are concerned," I squeak. The words Mary has given me over the phone come back to me. "But in particular I have spoken with the Australian embassy. They have heard the reports from the detention center, as have I. They seek assurances that the detainees from Burma will not in any way be handed over to the SLORC. Can you give such an assurance?"

He glowers at me, but as I chew my lip nervously, his energy seems to dissipate. "I give them my assurance," he says. "I have not received any order to change the usual procedure. Detainees from Burma will be returned to the border as usual. Thailand has a humanitarian approach to these refugees. You should know that. You should know better. I have not heard any rumor that the refugees were to be given over to the Burmese military at Three Pagoda Pass. I can assure you of their safety."

His eyes slide away a little as he says he has not heard this rumor. But the rest of the statement rings true. It leaves me in some doubt as to whether there is still a plan afoot to eventually hand prisoners over, but if there is, it seems unlikely that the order has been given yet or that it will be realized in the next few weeks, and so these particular prisoners are not in imminent danger.

After the meeting I run up the stairs. A boy with a box of donated bakery cakes climbs the stairs ahead of me. I hop up and down impatiently, then nearly knock him down when he moves to one side to let me pass. I fly up to the first cell.

"Is Nai Tangay there?" I whisper through the bars.

Nai Jalai, a tall, handsome refugee with long hair swooping out like wings on either side of his face nods once, says nothing, hurries to the back of the cell. "Nai Tangay," I hear him call softly. "Nai Tangay."

There is urgency in his voice. Nai Tangay comes out quickly, his face a study in expectancy. He looks as if he cannot imagine I bring good news.

"We have spoken with the Police High Command. They say they will not hand you over to the SLORC. They have given assurances. I will be reporting to Mary. Perhaps the policeman who told you that you would be handed over had no real authority. The official word is that there will be no change in the policy for Burmese refugees. You will be released at the border as usual."

Nai Tangay's face is like wax melting. Lines I didn't notice were there are disappearing. He looks suddenly younger, though still very pale.

"Thank you," he says simply.

"You are safe," I say. "All of you. For now. Tell the others. It is difficult to know what the immigration policy will be in the long run. But you are safe for now."

He leans down to whisper to the others. A buzz begins among the refugees beside him and spreads to each huddled group of men throughout the room. It sounds like a hive of bees. They are speaking a language I do not know, but I can hear the meaning in the way the message is said, the cadence of relief.

I hurry away again, down the stairs, out to seek fresh air. I am tired and want to get away from the tension and the reek of two hundred sixty sweaty bodies enclosed in a small space. As I go through the door I can still hear them whispering behind me. "Safe. Buzz, buzz. All of us. For now. Safe."

After telling the refugees, I call Mary from the nearest pay phone. "I don't know if that really means they are safe for good," I say.

"I know," she says, thoughtful. "But we can only do what we can do."

I think about this statement, not sure whether to be comforted or disappointed. Then I shrug and sing my way toward the wat, on foot. I walk across the overpass on Satthorn Street and enjoy a moment of calm above the roar of cars and the smoke of exhaust and the stinging fumes. When I'm content, the city looks achingly beautiful to me. Glass skyscrapers glitter among the distant spires of temples and mosques. I gaze appreciatively over the sprawling mass of humanity and then head onward, following the small, orange, sinking sun toward the river and home.

The Sound of the Prison Gate

Although I have been successful at intervening for the student leaders, my attempts to help the prisoners who are kept beyond their sentences have been thoroughly useless. For someone deeply attached to the idea of being useful, I am getting awfully familiar with failure. Given the confusion about what really happens at the northern border, sometimes I think it does not matter one way or another whether they get there. They may never reach safety, no matter what we or they do. But then again, it is not my decision. We are not here to make decisions for the refugees. We should neither coax nor dissuade them. If we have information that may be of use to them, we should give it freely. And if we truly mean to be their equals, their brothers and sisters, we must help them find their own way through the maze of dangers, invite them to think through the risks they are willing to take, and then support, with all that is in us, the decisions they make for themselves.

My fear of being ineffectual is compounded by an argument I had with Theresa. I dropped off a few more lists of prisoners who have been kept beyond the terms of their sentence. My arms are full of ragged sheets of paper, rumpled from my bag, with notes taped to them. Theresa sighs and says they're incomprehensible. I suppose they are.

"I have gone to the cells with the lists you gave me," she says, looking at the papers on her desk as if she wished they would spontaneously combust. "I can't always find the people in the rooms where they are listed as being. They've been moved."

"Why were you trying to find them?" I ask, muddling through this new information. "Do you need me to double-check where they are?"

"How can I tell the police where they are," she asks, "if I'm not sure myself?"

I feel exasperated. "Each list has names, the room number, and the person's ID number. Why can't you just give the list to the police and ask them to find them?"

"The police have no idea from their records where anyone is."

I look at her aghast. She realizes she's made a tactical error with that last admission. "Let me get this straight. Hundreds of people are imprisoned, and the records are such a mess no one knows who is who, or where, or when they should be released? Worse, the police demand thirty-five hundred baht from those who need to get to the northern border? That's $140 U.S. How can they get away with asking for so much?"

"You know, you can't measure everything by *your* standards," she says. "Your standards of time and money are different from those of the police."

I'm not sure what this means. "No matter whose standards you use, it doesn't cost thirty-five hundred baht to get to Mae Sae."

She scowls. "They can't be frugal. They're police, not normal people."

"Let's see how much they're getting, total." I add it up. "Thirty-five hundred times fourteen people to a van. That's forty-nine thousand baht. That's almost two thousand dollars. Wouldn't you say that's excessive?"

She looks at me impatiently. "I have to tell you, it scares me when you talk like this. I am *not* going to the police with that kind of a question. And I don't want you to either."

I'm sure my face shows my surprise. "Of course I'm not going to go to the police myself, and of course you have to find a diplomatic way to broach the topic. I thought you understood that."

This seems better to her. She nods.

"However," I add, "I will keep asking you these questions. Because there are people who have been here six months, nine months, eleven months, a year. They don't see a reason to stay here. I don't see a reason for them to be here, either."

"O.K.," she says, "But about the money, you're forgetting the price of the van."

"So if we can get a cheaper van, the police are open to it? They'll charge the refugees less?"

"Yes," she says, "They're open. There's been a big change in personnel here among the police recently. Some of them are better now. Really. These new ones are trying. They know what everyone thinks of them. One of the big social service agencies used to donate the vans, but they don't anymore, so there really is a money problem."

I think for a moment, my mind scanning people I know who might loan us a van.

Theresa guesses what I'm calculating. "So now you're going to take on the transportation of the Burmese to Mae Sae?" she asks, incredulous.

"If need be. I'm trying to be helpful, Theresa. If we need a van, I'll work on it. I thought these lists would be useful. If they aren't, I'll do something else. Just tell me what you need, and I'll do it." I am all puffed up now with self-importance and a sense of my own heroic energy.

"Money," she says, laughing and looking at me the way those who have been in service a long time look at newcomers who have great enthusiasm but little staying power. It's an indulgent look, backed with a good dose of skepticism. "What we really need is money."

"Money." I repeat the word, defeated. "That's it?" She smiles kindly at my dismayed face. We're both aware we don't know anyone who has that kind of money. At least no one who would use it for a problem like this. Who wants to give money to people they have never heard of, people they can't form a relationship with, for a problem that is likely to go on and on? Every few weeks there's a new group of refugees from the north, and when their sentences are up they will need money to get home.

She laughs again. "Here we are arguing," she says, shaking her head, implying that it's not our fight, which is true.

I find myself hating the police. And I'm disappointed. I have worked and worked and am no closer to resolving anything.

"Don't burn out all at once, O.K.?" she says, as I turn to leave.

Fine speech, I think to myself on the way out. I sound like the intrepid warrior. I will keep questioning and pushing until the prisoners are free, but in reality my heart is edging out the door. Without the detention center work, my life just might be manageable. I cannot keep going the way I have been, working and working and yet seeing no progress. I am ashamed of the thought, but there it is.

The original crisis that gave us a few weeks to help the refugees threatened by repatriation is over. It has turned into four months of work on those kept beyond the term of their sentence. Every week I check on the ones whose names are on the lists. They are still there. They are still waiting for someone to help them. Some miracle.

I mention Theresa to Matthew. "Theresa is a saint," he says. "Did you know she prays three hours a day? And there she is working away in IDC year after year."

Every time anyone says her name these days, someone tells me she is a saint. It is an automatic response, like saying "Bless you" after someone sneezes. This would be grating under any circumstances, but it is especially so if the saint is perennially annoyed with you. Hmmph, I think. She's pretty cranky for a saint.

One day after four months of fighting and despairing and periodically giving up, Theresa calls me and is suspiciously sweet. She tells me there is a meeting of volunteers tomorrow. I have been out of town for two days, and returned just before her call.

"When did you get back?"

"Twenty minutes ago."

"Get some rest, don't work too hard."

After I hang up, I run into Matthew. "I just talked to Theresa," I say.

"Theresa is a saint," he says automatically.

"Sometimes," I say. "Sometimes she's just a pain in the butt."

Matthew shrugs. "Most saints are."

This leaves me momentarily wondering if, considering my reputation for being a pain in the butt, I might also be a saint. But I suppose the syllogism doesn't work that way. All saints may be pains, but not all pains are saintly.

The next day I discover the volunteers' meeting is being held in an apartment complex resembling a modern-day palace, complete with a medieval-looking tower, a pool, a fountain, wide halls, and marble floors. The windows are taupe-colored glass. Every inch of the upstairs hall is carpeted in plush, soft beige. One of the volunteers lives here; it dawns on me that someone among our mutual acquaintances is very, very well off.

We meet upstairs in a small conference room. It is Theresa's birthday, and we have a cake, the candles of which she blows out with one breath, delighted.

During a break, I wander down to the fountain out front. As I reenter the marble entranceway, I meet up with Theresa, who announces that she has at last given my lists of prisoners from the north to the police.

I try not to look as surprised as I feel. "You did?"

"I did."

"And?"

"They agree with you. They will release seventeen of those prisoners on Saturday."

I try to stand still while the building turns upside down, but then think better of it and do a little jig right there in the hallway of the posh apartment building, with the doormen looking on.

When the meeting resumes, the committee discusses how to apportion the funds it has raised so far for refugees in IDC, as well as how to acquire further donations. Theresa is about to ask the committee for money for the people from the northern border, when a volunteer leans over and says, "Don't bother asking. I'll pay for the whole thing."

The following day, Theresa calls again. It is not seventeen prisoners. It's twenty-seven. The new police staff have reviewed the records, and they agree that twenty-seven prisoners have been held beyond the terms of their sentences. Twenty-seven prisoners will return to their families at the northern border.

"However," says Theresa, her voice breaking in on my joy, "there is one small problem. You remember the woman who offered to pay for all of this?"

"Yes."

"When I told her it was twenty-seven prisoners, not seventeen, she said she couldn't pay that much. Then she realized they were Burmese, not Laotian, and she said she wouldn't pay for any of them. It seems she's partial to Laotians, and when I said the northern border, that's what she thought I meant."

This is an enormous blow. It is followed by another. "So can you pay?" asks Theresa. It is half-appeal, half-challenge.

"How much?"

"Twenty-eight thousand baht." This amount sinks into my consciousness like a stone in a well. That's a little more than a thousand dollars. On the one hand, it means that the police are being honorable. It is a reasonable amount, approximately a thousand baht per person, which is more than it would cost for me to get to Mae Sae but is probably legitimate considering guards, administrative expenses, and the bureaucratic inefficiency that plagues every country in the world. It is a tremendous show of goodwill and good faith on the part of the police.

On the other hand, I simply don't have that much in the account I have for such emergencies. "When do you need the money?" I ask, thinking if I have time, I could almost certainly raise money for such a worthy cause.

"How about by noon today?"

"I have some money," I say dimly. "But I don't have the whole amount." I mentally calculate the dollar amount, and try to figure out how much I have in the general account. Most of the donations we have are specifically for the medical work. Funds for discretionary emergencies like this one are hard to come by.

"Meet me here by noon," Theresa says. "Bring what you can."

I race upstairs, pull my account books out of the drawer with such force the drawer falls out of the desk. I leave it on the floor and run off to the bank. Then I board a bus and ride in a daze to IDC, with my hair uncombed and toothpaste on my cheeks, to hand over a thick roll of five hundred baht bills to Theresa. "I couldn't get it all," I say, breathing hard. "But here's ten thousand baht." I half expect her to be angry, but she has been working on getting funds from other sources all morning, phone call after phone call, asking each person to give what they can.

It's like the final scene of *It's a Wonderful Life*. We have each brought our pocketful of change, knowing if Theresa has asked it of us, then it is really needed.

There are some advantages to being a saint.

Together we have raised enough to allow us to squeak through. She smiles and uncharacteristically hugs me. Twice.

Outside again in the bright light, prisoners' faces drift through my mind. The anxious eyes, the fingers just touching through the bars. Free, free, all free.

That night I allow myself the luxury of being philosophical. Sometimes, on the edge of sleep, I hear a great shattering in my dreams, and the beating of wings. The image comes from an old Celtic story I learned in my student days that I can't get out of my head: two lovers turn into birds and fly out through the window to escape an evil king. I have internalized this image; it has become my private symbol for the dangerous eruption into freedom.

I hear it the night the twenty-seven are freed.

All the next day I hear in my heart the clanging of gates echoing in empty rooms where prisoners have been released.

This is how you have to measure the world—in prisoners gone home. Do not count the ones that come to take their places, the looks of animal despair when they see the cages in which they will be kept. In reality, there are no echoes in empty cells. The cells will never be empty. They are not empty now. A line of ragged detainees, with only the clothes they were arrested in, shuffles out to squat on the concrete and be counted before filing in to hunker down on the stinking floor of the cell to which they have been assigned.

I understand that conditions are not much better in other parts of the world, including in the United States, which surely has more wealth to share with the world than Thailand does. Even in my own country, asylum seekers are detained in overcrowded conditions, families are separated, and relatively little regard is given for the reasons that compel people to leave their homelands.

But I will not think of all that today. My life is only one. So I rejoice in my successes. Today is enough for me. Today I will not think of those refugees snared by the police and waiting for their sentences. I will not think about the fact that I don't know the end of the story for those refugees who were released. I won't dwell on Maria—I don't even know for sure whether she was whisked to the border by "our friend" or whether she left with the refugees set free at the northern border and tried to make her way home from there. And if the latter is true, I don't know whether we sent her to freedom or to death.

As Mary said, we can only do what we can do. And even that we don't do alone. We play a small part in any endeavor, and for what happens we cannot entirely claim either the credit or the blame. So tonight I will not think of my possible failures, of all that I do not know, or of how little difference my successes make in the grand scheme of things.

I will think instead of the long line of detainees handing in their yellow prison cards and boarding a dusty bus for the border.

A True Friend

They shall beat their swords into plowshares,
and their spears into pruning hooks;
One nation shall not raise the sword
against another, nor shall they train for war again.

MICAH 4:3

Better than a thousand hollow words
Is one word that brings peace.

Better than a thousand hollow verses
Is one verse that brings peace.

Better than a hundred hollow lines
Is one line of the law, bringing peace.

FROM THE DHAMMAPADA,
TRANSLATED BY THOMAS BYROM

The Stories We Tell

Given the constant tensions of refugee work, I am delighted when, shortly after the prisoners are set free, I am offered a much-needed respite. I am invited to go to the United States for a week, during which time I will take some resettled Mon refugees to Washington, D.C., to talk to the State Department about the situation in Thailand. This is an opportunity to interrupt my daily cycle of anxiety, though before the trip is over, I will have a more complex understanding of what is at stake for the Mon.

Before I go, the monks bid me farewell while we're at the hospital waiting for a patient. Phra Dhamma and Phra Dala Non sit with me in the waiting room, talking passionately in turns about life in America, our plans here, a patient's health. They ask repeatedly if I'm leaving for good, if I'm sure I'll be back. I assure them I'll return, but we still stand too long under a full moon, lingering in the parking lot, unable to say good-night.

In the world of the refugee, every parting may be forever, and I have caught their fever of reluctance to say good-bye. I finally peel away from them and climb into a bus, pressed against a hundred other people, rocking and roaring through the traffic. At home, I pack for my trip, somewhat dispirited, as if despite all the assurances I have made, I may never see them again.

My mood improves when I reach American soil. I am excited about the impending trip to Washington; accompanying refugees to the State Department is exciting, nerve-racking, energizing, and above all, undeniably *useful.*

Nai Kyaw Min, the first refugee to introduce himself and the evident leader of the group, is enamored of American idioms, a tendency I have noticed in many Asians. Their own languages are full of colorful expressions, and people who have not mastered such idioms identify themselves as outsiders. Thus, many Asians imagine that once they have memorized American expressions, proverbs, and jargon, they will have cracked open our culture like a nut.

"O.K., gentlemen, O.K., people," Nai Kyaw Min says, "I don't want to jump the gun, but time's a wastin', so let's get a move on."

"You guys want some breakfast?" I ask.

"No, we'll stop at McDonald's," says Nai Kyaw Min.

This begins a chorus of approval from the other refugees. "Mmm-mmm, McDonald's! Micky Dee's, my favorite!"

It is Nai Kyaw Min's car, and he drives—or, what passes for driving in New Jersey: fast and wild. I think we break the sound barrier a couple of times. The Mon are much better educated than I am, and they ask questions that threaten to reveal my ignorance, such as, "Oh look, it's the Monroe building, just like in the Monroe documents. What were they about again?"

"Nai Anukula," I say, addressing one of the men and changing the subject, "why don't you tell me a story to pass the time, a story of the Mon people."

"You would like to learn a little Mon history?"

"That sounds excellent."

"Very well," he says. "Mon history. It begins like this. One day the Lord Buddha was flying through the air with twenty of his monk-disciples flying behind him—"

"Excuse me," I say. "Flying through the air? I've never really understood that part. What do you mean he was flying through the air?"

New Jersey is whizzing past us at terrible speeds. Skyscrapers soar backward, and I cannot quite get my mind around the flying Buddha.

"Ah! He had reached enlightenment."

"I see."

"I shall continue?"

"Please."

"One day the Lord Buddha was flying through the air when he saw two golden bob, male and female—"

"Excuse me."

"What is it now?"

"What's a bob?"

"The golden bob. You know, sheldrake, like ducks. It's the Mon bird, the Mon symbol, which you walk under every day to enter the wat in Bangkok. Now one day the Lord Buddha saw two golden bob, male and female, on a land that was just coming out of the sea, and he knew this was a good land and would become a great kingdom. Do you know where this land was?"

"Where?"

"It was Monland. If you read more of Mon history, you will find many connections to Lord Buddha. We are very proud of these connections. For example, one day two Mon traders met the Lord Buddha in Nepal. I think Nepal is a long way to walk from Monland, don't you?"

"Certainly."

"Now have you heard of our most famous kingdom? The kingdom of Hongsawatoi? Hongsawatoi was made by a heavenly body. He created everything in the kingdom all at once. Buildings. Palaces. Houses."

I look out the window, feeling dizzy, partly because we are going so fast and partly because it is incongruous to be zipping along on the New Jersey turnpike, on our way to appointments with the State Department, and to be discussing flying Buddhas and heavenly bodies along the way. Nai Kyaw Min pulls off, and we stop under a sign that says Turnpike Hero and Quality Val, which further adds to my disorientation.

Still, I'm glad to be hearing these stories again. The Mon have not yet forgotten what all peoples know early on and later come to doubt: that our beginnings are miraculous and magical, that whatever spirits dwell in the heavens and the earth have had a hand in our making. Also, I know for the refugees there is continuity between the threat to individuals and the threat to the culture. They do not, as I do, consider the current political crisis to belong to modernity, and put the flying Buddha in some other category belonging to the past and myth. Their people are at risk, but so are their history and their culture. They grieve for both.

"Wasn't there a dragon princess at the beginning of that period? Tell me about the dragons," I beg, warming up to the storytelling.

"Oh, yes. That is an important part of our history. During the dragon generation, many dragons came in the shape of human beings. Then they married humans and had children. For some reason most of the dragons who do this are women."

"You're kidding."

"I'm not."

"Why is that? Why are most dragons in human form women?"

"I think it is because women get to know people better than men do. They are friendlier; men get to know them and marry them. There is a problem, though. The problem is that they do not born babies. They, how do you say, hatch them. Now, when the husband sees that his baby is an egg, he finds out his wife is a dragon. This is very embarrassing for the dragon. She is ashamed. So she goes back down to the dragon kingdom and disappears from his life forever.

"Now, the story of the dragon princess is this story. The mother was a dragon, and when her husband saw that his baby was to hatch instead of being born, the mother was ashamed and disappeared forever, down to the dragon kingdom. The child was sent into a forest, where she was raised by a hermit. She grew up, married, and had two sons of her own, who became the princes of the Mon kingdom. You like Mon history?" he asks.

"Sure."

He looks at me suspiciously for a minute. "I am telling you true stories, you know."

Our first night in Washington we visit the Lincoln and Jefferson monuments, and I tell the refugees some of our American stories. I read them the Declaration of Independence. "These are some of our most important words," I say.

At the State Department I talk too much and make myself and the refugees nervous. Despite this, the refugees are brilliant. They explain patiently about the situation in Burma and declare that the United States is missing the ethnic dimension of the problem, which means we are pretty much missing the whole point.

"You simply don't understand," says Nai Kyaw Min. "It is true there is no democracy. It is true there is a dictatorship. It is true the economic situation is terrible. But under all that is the real story: the ethnic problem. This is a very old problem. It is older than 8/8/88, when the demonstrators were massacred. Much older than 1948 when the British left and the beginnings of civil war crept across the country. Even older than 1757, the time we call the Mon holocaust, when Monland was invaded by the Burmese and more than three thousand monks were killed. You understand? This is *old*, and no one forgets. The fact is there are many peoples living in Burma, and they each have long memories. The Burmese and the Mon have hated each other for a long, long time. But you look at Burma as a modern nation state and worry about its political structure. You think of words like democracy. You have the Declaration of Independence on your mind. That's all well and good, but unless you understand how old and how deep the hatred is, Burma could be the next Rwanda."

The refugees also complain about the American interviewers for resettlement. Some are good, they tell us. Some understand the ethnic issues. "Others . . . ," they wave dismissively as if the others don't merit finishing the sentence.

"For example," says Nai Kyaw Min, "for a while you had two Americans doing the interviews in Bangkok. One was a white man. He knew nothing. Absolutely nothing, I'm telling you."

Nai Kyaw Min's idioms increase with the intensity of his feelings, and he's starting to get riled up. "This man seemed like he had never heard of the Mon— he wouldn't know an ethnic issue if it bit him in the nose. It's all over his head, I mean, he's out to lunch, man, I mean the guy hasn't got a clue. Then there's this other American, a black woman, and she has the whole ethnic deal down pat. I mean she's got it in the bag. I mean she *gets* it, you hear what I'm telling you? So here are these two interviewers, but they're like night and day, they're like oil and water, and the black woman gets it and the white man doesn't, and for the life of me I can't think why. I mean, are they both Americans or what?"

Weeks later I reminisce with Matthew about the stories Nai Anukula told me on the New Jersey turnpike. Matthew knows them all already, of course, knows them by heart. He tells me about a day in his English class when he was introducing the monks to words like myth and legend and faith. They were discussing the stories we tell as peoples, the stories that define us. They talked about the stories we live by, whether they are true or not, and the stories we recognize ourselves by—the ones we think of as "ours" as a people or a family or a religion.

He told them several stories from Jewish and Christian tradition, all the really good bits, about parting the Red Sea, and walking on water, people rising from the dead, and the pregnancy of a virgin. The monks listened appreciatively, smiled, applauded. "Good stories," they said.

"Now, do you have stories like that?" Matthew asked. "Stories about miraculous events that are special to your people?"

"No," they said. "Can't think of any. Not a single one."

"Hold on a minute," Matthew said. "What about the Lord Buddha flying through the air? What about the dragon princess? What about heavenly bodies creating kingdoms?"

"Not the same," said the monks. "No connection whatsoever."

"How do you figure that?" asked Matthew.

"Very simple," said a monk. "You see, our stories are true."

Before I leave the United States, I visit a prominent university to talk to various departments about the Mon. I wonder, aside from the few classic texts I'm acquainted with, what has been written about them. I am surprised to find the otherwise well-stocked university library lacking even those books with which I am familiar. My interviews with professors from relevant departments are even less fruitful. Everyone is friendly and tries very hard to be helpful, but their initial responses do not inspire me with confidence that the Mon are well understood in the United States. Here is a list of my favorite responses when I announce I am working with the Mon:

Professor of history: "The who?"

Professor of Southeast Asian Studies: "Ah, the Hmong from Laos, I know them well." (Sorry, that's the Mon from Burma. Wrong people, wrong country.)

Professor of anthropology: "Are they hunter-gatherers?"

While my attempts at increasing my practical knowledge of Mon texts are unsuccessful during my American trip, I do make some private discoveries. I find myself thinking about the monks a lot, especially Phra Dhamma.

One day I show my pictures of Thailand to a friend in the United States and surprise myself by my own announcement: "This is a water buffalo. This is a malnourished child. This is one of my best friends."

"Let me see the one of your friend again," my companion asks.

Yeah, I think, let me see that, too. It is a picture of three monks on a blue couch. Three bald heads. The picture is dark, and Phra Dhamma, the one identified as friend, has a feral red glow in his eyes.

I have said it without thinking and now discover that it's true. Phra Dhamma and I are not just coworkers or colleagues. We are close friends. What do we have in common that could make us close? I am Catholic, he is Buddhist. He is a monk; I am a layperson. I am an urban American; he comes from a village in

Mon State. I weigh as much as a small water buffalo, and he probably weighs about a hundred pounds and comes up to my shoulder. Still, we have found each other in the way of lost children—finding kinship in unexpected places.

In the last few months we have been spending more and more time together. It is funny how affection sneaks up on you. Mostly we are quiet together, standing at the foot of some hospital bed, where we have come to visit a patient. Or we are at work, helping each other enter mutually foreign worlds, creating between us a path for some refugee to be understood by those who can heal him. We spend a great deal of time simply staring out of taxi windows as we plod through Bangkok's congestion on some errand of mercy. We are two foreigners together, arriving at the same place through very different circumstances but with the camaraderie of explorers for whom everything is a discovery.

Now that I am away from him I realize how much his quiet presence means to me. It's as if I don't know what I'm seeing when there is no one standing by my side sharing my perceptions. Perhaps there is also a special connection, a special interdependence between a foreigner like myself and an interpreter. Phra Dhamma interprets his world for me, as all translators do, and I connect that world to a larger universe of international aid. It is only through him that I understand the deeper meanings of things, and now, without him, as I see my own culture and country anew, with the eyes of someone long-absent and easily surprised by once-familiar habits, I feel the lack of him keenly. As if some part of myself is missing. As if I should be able to turn at any moment and with the lifting of an eyebrow say, "Isn't the world strange? And isn't it good we have each other?"

When I return to Bangkok, I'm glad to be back, but I have a real sense of homecoming only when I reach the wat. When I arrive, there is Phra Dhamma, and seeing him I think, *It's true. This is my true friend.*

But there is no time to say anything; the wat is in chaos as usual. For several months Matthew and I have been working at enabling the orphans to attend a Thai wat for school. It is the only way we can think of for them to have some hope of growing up to be more than beggars if they stay in this country. We have raised money for their uniforms and books, and it turns out I have arrived just in time to hand out the new supplies to the children.

Phra Dhamma and I are unable to talk, because we must hurry up for the children's ceremony. John, one of our community members in Cambodia, has volunteered to help out today. We go up to the classroom, where the children are milling about in a state of excitement. Thirty-six barefoot, ragged urchins eye the mounds of merchandise. It's more than they have ever owned in their lives: a bright book bag, a pretty pencil box, a few schoolbooks with colorful pictures, a uniform, and best of all, a shoe box with a shiny new pair of shoes for each boy.

I think of Nai Oo scurrying across bubbling tar in his bare feet, and breathe deeply, relieved that this one small injustice has been eradicated at least for a while—at least until the children grow out of these shoes and we go on the search for money to buy more.

The monks stand in a line behind three tables, piling up the loot, and calling each child's name. The boys line up into three long lines, sitting on their heels, waiting to be called. When he hears his name, each one comes forward, wais, and holds out his arms.

The monks hand the boys' things to John first, because as a woman I can neither give nor receive directly from a monk's hand. When John has a grip on the pile, I put my hand on the gift to steady it. Or more accurately, ever conscious of my need to appear useful, I place my hand in the center of things, endeavoring to look as though I have some integral role in these proceedings. Together we place the gift into the child's arms. Matthew stands to one side shooting photos, mostly of our behinds and happy children's faces.

Some of the boys are so small and the gifts are so steep in their arms, that the child can't see over the top. He creeps back to his place, blind, feeling his way with his feet, his arms outstretched, like a sleepwalker.

After a while, Phra Dhamma gets weary of the whole business and hands me a set of school supplies directly. How like Phra Dhamma, I think, to be impatient with the ceremony, the religious restrictions that separate one human being from another. To go unthinkingly to the act of expedience, friendship, and equality. He chooses the human expression of companionship over the ritually correct behavior.

When the gift-giving is over, we hover and smile.

"How are you?" I ask.

"I'm in the pink," he says. "Fit as a fiddle."

"I'm so glad to see you," I say.

"I'm very glad, too," he says.

"I missed you."

"Me, too."

Together we go down to the sick room, joined by Matthew. The yard has flooded, and we wade through the waters toward the far room. The refugees have set up a plank between the stairs of one building and the dry walkway of the other. Gingerly I cross the wobbly plank.

In the refugee room, Nai Nya Naa is resting while his daughter, Kyang San, mills about Phra Dhamma; he puts his hand on her head and laughs. Heedless of tradition, he touches the female child with affection. She beams up at him and begins to dance. Not long, I think, will Phra Dhamma choose the celibate life, the life set apart. I can imagine him in some happy future, with a young wife, and his own dark-haired children looking up at him with the same trust that is in Kyang San's little, curious face.

Nai Nya Naa's infant son seems to have doubled in size since last week, rounding up like rising bread dough. He has also been improving his crawl. Or what I suppose must be called crawling, because it is on all fours. He is still too little to lift his belly off the floor. He drags it underneath him, like a man with a heavy sack. But his speed is incredible. It's a torpedo crawl. He makes a beeline for Phra Dhamma and me and his dancing sister, who laughs, delighted with Phra Dhamma's fingers stroking her silky black hair.

When the infant reaches my feet he lifts his huge head, heavy as a pail. I have him sit in the cradle of my hands then swing him up so high he's upside down. His mouth makes a happy "O" shape, and he giggles, his belly rolling.

So that Kyang San isn't jealous, I throw her at the ceiling a few times and catch her as she shrieks with pleasure on the way down. When I put her down, Kyang San runs to Matthew for the ritual gift of one baht, which he gives her with a flourish. She wais deeply, then gleefully dashes around with her treasure. She dances around the room, then dutifully deposits the small silver coin in her father's shirt pocket.

In the corner sits Nai Cham, a recent arrival, who is blind, mostly deaf, and missing one hand. He cups his remaining hand behind his better ear to try to figure out what is happening around him. "Miss Vicki has come," Matthew screams at him.

"Miss Wicki?" he hollers back.

"I am here."

"You have come back at last. I have been lonely for you. Has it really only been seven days? It feels like seven years."

"Yes," I say, "it has only been a week, but it felt very long to me, too."

"She has not been gone long," says Matthew. "She could not stay away. She has come back to get a Mon husband."

"That can be arranged," Nai Cham nods seriously. "And you too," he adds to Matthew. "We can find a wife for you."

"A wife for me?" Matthew asks, raising his eyebrows.

"Yes, but the Mon people have three kinds of wives, so you must decide what kind of wife you want. We have the wife who is a mother, the wife who is a slave, and the wife who is a sister. Which do you prefer? Mother, slave, or sister?"

Matthew laughs. "I'll have to think about it."

An old monk approaches from the shadows, holding prayer beads. "Hold out your hands," says Matthew, seeing my hesitation, my silent question about what is expected of me and what is permitted. "Hold your hands open. This he can give you. This you can receive." I stretch out my palms as if checking for rain. The old monk lifts the white beads high and slowly releases them, to curl down into my hands like a snake.

"Thank you," I say, moved.

"Put them over your head," says Matthew.

I obey, lifting them over my head, letting the halo of white rest on my shoulders, the small yellow tassel hanging down at my waist.

As I am ready to leave, one of the monks points out a refugee who is delirious with fever, and so my first day back at the wat turns into a hurried trip to the hospital with a flushed and miserable refugee. But the magic of return is still around me like an aura, and I finger my prayer beads all the way to the hospital.

Where the Poor Search for Justice

For several months the refugees in camps along the border have been afraid they will eventually be forced back into Burma by the Thai government. The leaders of the Mon meet with prominent people. They write letters to international human rights groups. They write to the UN General Assembly that the Mon are "in an impossible and desperate situation. We have no choice but to ask the world community to intervene on our behalf."

But the world community does not intervene, and no help comes.

Then all at once the reality is upon us. In January 1994, the Thai government orders that the refugees from Lohloe, the main Mon refugee camp at the border, be relocated to Burma against their will. The covenant between the world community and the refugees is broken. Refugees are forced back into the danger from which they fled.

A new refugee camp is constructed at Halockhani on the Burmese side of the border. Water is scarce. The SLORC is close by. At first we hear there is a Burmese military outpost half a day away, then we hear it is three hours away. Then it is an hour's walk. Finally, the refugees are practically living in the spill water of the Burmese military camp.

The NGOs and relief agencies keep mostly silent in public about the repatriation, but they soon begin to complain among themselves that there are signs of some change in Thai policy. I attend one of the monthly meetings of refugee workers. Each report from groups along the border is the same. Signs and checkpoints are appearing where a month ago there were none. New rules require people to sign as they cross the border in places where there had previously been free movement of people and supplies. In some places the way is barred entirely, and no one can pass.

Of course, the new stringency along the border does nothing to stem the tide of girls from Burma sold into prostitution across the border—they continue to flow in like blood from a sliced artery. But for refugees and relief groups, the border is seizing up like a fist.

In Bangkok the change is dramatic. The city is awash in police raids. The wat is raided daily, sometimes more than once. There are record arrests. The detention center is overflowing. Meanwhile, the UNHCR begins to cut allowances for refugees in Bangkok. The United States takes fewer and fewer refugees from Burma.

All of this is clear. What is not clear is the motivation. I always feel confusion about the roots of oppression. I believe in the evil I see before me, but the underlying reasons elude me. Why does the SLORC torment the Mon? Why does Thailand bother to round them up, imprison them, and force them to return to their enemy? Science-fiction novels have villains like these, characters or governments whose chief role is to create terror and inflict pain, who operate out of the shadows and commit atrocities because, simply, that is what they *do*. Real life, so I hear, should be more complicated.

Me, I have the brain of a mammal, not a politician. I understand the boy with the ruptured bladder, the man blinded by a mine. Their pain is real to me, urgent, an impetus for action. The rationale that could prompt such torture and harassment is beyond my comprehension. How can anyone benefit from the suffering of the poor?

To the two governments, Thai and Burmese, the Mon and other indigenous people must have some meaning beyond themselves. They are portents. They augur a future that causes the military leaders to sweat in their cots at night and cry out in their sleep. But portents of what? What kind of future? Trying to figure it out makes my head ache.

I am with Matthew when he figures it out. Or perhaps he figured it out long ago and tells the story again just to help himself believe it.

"Why?" he asks. "Why?" He prompts me as though I am a slow student, daring me to figure it out. I shake my head. I don't know why.

"Don't you understand? Thailand's government and business community must be expecting some mutually beneficial arrangement with Burma. The refugees are being systematically rounded up and isolated from the Thai population. That will put enormous pressure on them to sign a cease-fire with the

Burmese military. The more cease-fires there are, the more Thailand can put pressure on the refugees and migrants to go back to Burma, and the more the refugees are on the Burmese side of the border or at least isolated from foreign workers and reporters, the more the news to the West can be controlled. Back in Burma the refugees at best face 1984, and at worst 1944. Either way, businesses can exploit the resources in the ethnic homelands more or less unchecked."

Soon I begin seeing articles in the newspapers, implying the same thing. When the British left in 1948, Burma was one of the richest nations in Southeast Asia. The country is still rich in natural resources, though it has plummeted from a nation of plenty to a Least Developed Country. Logging, fishing, oil, and yes, heroin—it is plentiful in all, and most of these resources are located in the indigenous lands.

American and international oil companies are building a natural gas pipeline across the heart of Mon territory. The Burmese want to sell this gas to companies in Thailand. The Thai businesses want to use the gas, and they want a friendly relationship with Burma.

Cut off from international aid in 1988 after it massacred peaceful demonstrators, the SLORC is desperate for funds, especially international exchange. How else will it pay its debts? How else will it buy the weapons and pay the army with which it enslaves the peoples of Burma? It is a tight circle. The indigenous must be quelled in order for the government to get the riches from indigenous lands, and the riches must be got in order to pay for the war that controls the indigenous. Thus the Burmese government sells off the teak forests. It sells fishing interests to Thailand and other Asian nations, oil to companies from many nations, including the United States. Seventy percent of the heroin sold in the United States passes through Bangkok, but much of it originates in Burma. In general, the players in the global marketplace gather round to do to the indigenous lands what the men of many nations are doing to the young daughters of indigenous families.

The rest follows from these economic interests. Arrests, harassment of refugees, the forcing of the Mon across the border. Governments and multinational corporations look at Burma's countryside and see gems, lumber, opium, and natural gas. Thailand sees a seemingly unlimited supply of natural resources to be refined in Thai factories and then sold to an international market. The Burmese government sees the possibility of hard currency needed to support its military. Everybody looks at the land and sees the Mon and other indigenous standing in the way of their dreams.

And what do the Mon see when they look at the lush forests across the border? They simply see home.

Of course, in a way, even this is too simple. It explains the big picture. It does not explain what happens when one man stands in front of another and kicks him until blood comes from his mouth. It does not explain why one person plunges a cigarette into the flesh of a prisoner. Nor does it explain the underlying current of racism, the ethnic tensions, some of which are the fruit of battles fought centuries ago. The descendants of warriors long dead rehearse ancient transgressions at their evening storytelling, keeping old wounds fresh in their collective memories, until they look at one another and say, "This is my enemy."

Perhaps some of what enables human beings to cause the suffering of others is always a mystery. There is some capacity for seeing someone different than ourselves as entirely other and therefore unworthy. This tendency to dehumanize and demonize squeezes our cerebral cortexes like a vice. From that fundamental capacity, we proceed to invent war and burn villages and craft weapons with a careful eye and depth of concern we rarely apply to human beings. In short, we create every terror we have ever imagined on a dark night. I know this capacity myself. I recognize it when I catch myself hating those who hate the Mon. None of us is perfect. None of us is completely clean. Most of us just muddle along, doing the best we can.

Meanwhile, the implications of the increasing pressure on the refugees are stunning and close to home. Phra Dhamma and Phra Dala Non, too, are in danger. These brave monks, these men I work with each day and stand beside in the service of others, these men I admire. Their monks' robes will protect them for a little while, but we all know what is coming; we can smell it the way you can smell the coming of the monsoons the day before they begin. How long do they have? No one knows. But it is clear we must get them out, soon, to safety and a new life in a new country.

Phra Dhamma tries every avenue toward resettlement. He and many of the other monks who were prominent among their own people in Burma have been recognized as official political refugees by the UNHCR, the first step in the process of resettlement.

At the wat, we have people in all stages of application. Of the people I know, Nai Nya Naa and Phra Dhamma are the furthest along in the process, for they already have UNHCR status as "persons of concern" and have begun applying to various countries for resettlement. UNHCR refugee status does not mean they have full protection in Thailand. They are still illegal in Bangkok and subject to arrest. Nor does refugee status guarantee a person resettlement in a third country. After receiving a determination of refugee status by the UNHCR, every refugee must submit a separate application to each country in which he or she is interested. Given quotas and requirements for each country, it is perfectly possible that he or she will be rejected by all of them.

On the other hand, having been approved by the UNHCR is a start. Some refugees who have arrived more recently, like Phra Dala Non, have not even achieved that assurance yet. Phra Dala Non has applied to the UNHCR and has waited nearly six months without hearing one way or another. Still others are just at the beginning of the application process.

Another refugee in the process of obtaining refugee status is Nai Cham, who lost one arm, his sight, and most of his hearing in an explosion in Burma. I arrive at the wat one morning to find him sitting in the half-light by the wall. The sun streams in the open door, making his corner seem dimmer and cooler. His right sleeve hangs empty where his arm was severed. Little Kyang San, Nai Nya Naa's daughter, tugs at the sleeve playfully, twists it into a long coil, then lets go to watch it unwind. Nai Cham endures this in amiable silence. As I approach, Nai Cham cups his remaining hand around his better ear and leans toward me. His face emerges in the light, with its torn eyes, deep gouges in them, the blind whites staring out moist and unblinking, like the face of some underwater creature.

I sit down beside him on the floor in a patch of light. His wife, Palei, swipes at the dirty linoleum with a rag. I nod my thanks. I wait while they finish getting ready, then we head for the ear doctor who today will test whether a hearing aid would be helpful. Meanwhile, Nai Cham tells their story, which gives me a glimpse not only of his life but also of the situation in his village in Burma.

Nai Cham's first language is Mon, but as he was born when the British were present in Burma, his second language is English. "Only my third language is Burmese," he explains. "But it has been thirty years since I spoke so much English, and now it is all broken. I hope you can understand me a little."

He fingers his empty sleeve and looks toward his arm with the habit of one who once had sight and still dreams of a world with shape and color, a world of substance.

"This is the case of the Burmese soldiers nowadays," he says. "Whatever they ask, no one can say no to them. Whatever they request we must give. They come at night, and they drink, and they shoot. If they see a girl, even eleven or twelve years old, they take her and do to her as a wife, and then they leave."

Once when Nai Cham's daughter was in high school, a group of soldiers loitering in the village grabbed her. Palei ran out to help her daughter. A soldier seized Palei, boxed her head and kicked her, while the daughter ran away. The soldier was angry and shot in the air over Palei's head. After that, whenever the daughter saw a soldier she ran and hid. A year later she left the village and did not come back.

Nai Cham sent his oldest son to study in Rangoon, where the boy took part in the demonstrations that ended in the massacre in 1988. When he returned to his home village, he took part in the general strike, with Nai Cham and Palei supplying drinks, food, and advice for the demonstrators. Eventually the soldiers came for the young man, and he fled.

"When my son ran away, the soldiers came after me and captured me," says Nai Cham. "They asked me, 'Where is your son? Your son is a rebel, a revolutionary man. You must know where he is.' They struck me and kept me for half a day. But I did not know where my son was, then, and I do not know now.

"My second son was fifteen at that time. Soon after our oldest son escaped, he also disappeared. We believe he went to join his brother.

"Two miles from our village is another poor village. The soldiers destroyed that village like this. They asked for money, they asked for pigs, they asked for bullocks. If not given, the soldiers put the men in a wooden hole. They killed three men from that village. They killed one woman. They did to her as a wife, then they killed her with a gun. That was about a year ago. Now all the people have run away from that village. Two villagers were also killed in our village. The soldiers put them into a wooden hole and asked for money. The man's wife gave money but only about half of what they asked. So they took the man out from the hole, caught him in a rope, and shot him."

Nai Cham's family had both a house in the village and a farm about six miles outside of the village.

"One day the soldiers came and destroyed everything at the farm. They destroyed windows, doors, properties, pigs, hens, bullocks, ducks, crops, and cows. Everything. They stayed in the village about two weeks and at night they shot their guns.

"That year they seized my third son and hit him on the side of the head with a gun. Then they put him in a wooden hole. At night they hit him with their guns and kicked him with their boots. It was the end of four days when they released him, and he could not walk. When he coughed, blood came out of his mouth. We took him to a hospital, where he stayed for fifteen days. But when he left the hospital, the soldiers saw him back in the village, and they struck him. So he also fled, and we don't know where he is.

"Now I have lost all my children. My daughter is a teacher in Mon State. She does not know where we are, because we had no time to tell her before we left. I do not know where any of my sons are."

Nai Cham believes the real problem, even deeper than the ethnic struggle, may have been his relative wealth. He had a small mill that processed rice from the paddies. "The soldiers destroyed all the machines in 1993 and 1994, and now everyone must use only the machines owned by the government."

The antagonism continued between the family and the soldiers until one day when the military planted land mines all around the family's house and on the road. "That night they surrounded our house and they shot from every side. They shot from the north and from the south. They shot from the east and from the west. They were all around our house, crying into the loudspeaker that if we came out they would shoot us, and if we are dead, they don't care. They shot the house and broke the windows. Bullets came inside the house.

"Now how did we live through that night? I will tell you. Our lavatory is made with concrete and that is where we hid."

Near morning, the shooting stopped. But the soldiers were still in the village, nearby. For three days Nai Cham and Palei stayed inside the house, hiding, starving. "We thought we were going to die. We were afraid that if we came out of the house, they would shoot us. Or we would step on the mines and be killed. The soldiers destroyed many other houses, too, firing guns and smashing things. Many people fled.

"Finally, we escaped. We decided we couldn't stay there, because if we do, someday we will die. Maybe not today. Maybe not tomorrow. But sooner or later they will catch us and we will be killed. We went slowly, from village to village, staying one or two days in each place until at last we reached the border.

"Now we are searching for our first son, but we have not found him. We think he is in Thailand, but we hear no word from him. We have come to this wat, because if our son is in Thailand, someone here will have heard about him. We would go home if we could, but it is too difficult to live with all the fighting. We are getting old now, my wife and I. Even if we are too old to fight ourselves, when the Burmese soldiers come to find the forest men, we will be hurt. We are like grass, and the soldiers are like water buffalo. There is an expression: when two water buffalo fight, it is bad for the grass."

Meanwhile Nai Cham and Palei have applied for refugee status from the UNHCR. They hope to be approved as refugees and to apply for resettlement somewhere. "We wait and wait, but we hear nothing. So I ask you, can you call the UNHCR for us?" he asks. "Can you call and ask if we are refugees?"

I do not want to say yes, I do not intend to say yes. But I do. I imagine the UNHCR will not be particularly pleased to have a call. They are always over-worked, always behind. But I know Matthew calls for refugees often. He will know whom to ask. I suspect that while Nai Cham asks me to call only for in-formation, he really thinks the sound of my foreign voice expressing concern for his family will turn the UN decision in his favor. I have no such illusions, but I will do what I can.

After being misdirected then put on hold three times, I am put through to a woman who manages to sound pleasant and wary at once. It is a useful skill. I wish I could cultivate it. It does not quite put people off, yet does not inspire an excess of confidence either.

I give the woman Nai Cham's NI number, the number each applicant is given to identify them through the process of screening for refugee status. As perhaps Nai Cham expected, once in contact with someone who I think may have the power to make this family safe, I feel compelled to tell her their story, to plead for them. The UNHCR representative suffers this politely. "I'm very sorry, madam," she says. "I am not familiar with the case. It is not one I am working on."

"Yes, but do you think they have a chance? Do you think it is a strong case?"

She sighs. She must take twenty such calls a day. "I really couldn't say. They must go through the proper application procedures. There are so many factors that determine whether a refugee fits the profile."

"But I thought the definition of a refugee was a 'well-founded fear of perse-cution.'"

"You must understand that is the very beginning of a long description of what we must look for to determine status. I'm sorry. Really. It is never as simple as it looks. And I should not comment on a case I have not been personally involved in."

"Yes, of course," I admit, deflated.

"Let me just take a look at their file," she says, putting me on hold for the fourth time.

After several minutes, she returns. There is a new note in her voice, worry or urgency. "Mr. and Mrs. Cham should have received a letter from us. Are you sure they have not?"

"Not unless they received it just this morning. I know they have been anxious to receive news."

"Can you tell them to come to our office, please?"

Now I am annoyed. "No, I can't. Nai Cham is blind, partly deaf, and missing one arm. Neither he nor his wife speaks Thai. They do not exactly blend in with the crowd. I do not think I have to remind you that you require people to come to Bangkok to apply for refugee status from your office, but they are illegal and can be arrested at any time. They have been waiting for word and have asked me to call for it. Please do not ask them to come out of the relative safety of the temple to come to you. I think you can at least offer them the protection of an answer in some way that does not put them directly in the eye of the police."

"But surely they can come in a taxi? You could give them money for a taxi. Or you could come with them."

"No. I can't. I won't. I will not risk their safety, and I cannot take the time to come with them. And our funds are mostly for medical purposes. I have several medical cases waiting for my attention. Please give me the message or send it directly to the wat."

"I cannot give you the message. It is against the rules. If they are at the temple, I will send a letter. I'm sorry."

With this conversation in mind I go through that day's work and the next, wondering what will happen to Nai Cham and Palei and afraid to face them. On the third day I stop by to see if they have received the UNHCR letter yet. I find them sitting solemnly in the dark.

"How are you?" I ask. "Any news?"

Nai Cham signals to Palei, who takes a piece of paper out of her small plastic bag of worldly possessions. Wordlessly she unfolds it and hands it to me.

I read it slowly. It is brief and carries no explanation. Nai Cham and Palei have been determined not to be true refugees. They have no claim on international protection. They have been rejected. I stand there shocked but not surprised. Their rejection is a wound—for them a sentence to a life where they will never be safe, for me an unpleasant reminder that the world is neither just nor gentle, and neither my wishing, nor my love, nor the work of my hands can make it so.

"Can you help us, Miss Wicki?" Nai Cham asks. "You are our hope."

His wife looks at me from her beautiful face. She has been following this brief conversation with alert, trusting eyes.

"You must not hope too much," I say, unable to bear that look. "I think there is no chance for you. Once the UNHCR has decided, they will not change their minds. I am free, and I have the power of freedom. But I have no other power." In my heart I say, don't hope so much. Don't watch me like that. Don't need so much. I can't bear it.

"But will you write a letter? Will you write a letter for us to the UNHCR? Will you tell our story?"

"Yes, I will write a letter," I say. And I do, following it up with phone calls to the person working on their case. Despite the letter and the calls, I do not believe the UNHCR will change its determination. The appeal process, built in as a safeguard, rarely reverses an initial decision not to grant refugee status. The UNHCR publishes the discouraging statistics as proof of the accuracy of its initial assessment. Some skeptics suggest the opposite is true—that to defend its initial assessments, it keeps the successful appeals low. I do not know what to believe, except that the ways of bureaucracies are equally inscrutable to refugees like Nai Cham and to religious volunteers like me.

Many weeks pass. In the end, when the final letter comes, it is the same as the first. In the eyes of the UNHCR this family has no claim on the protection, little as it is, granted refugees.

These people tell a story of fifteen years of general and specific persecution. True, it is not the worst story I have heard. They were clearly well off by Mon standards. They had a farm. They had equipment. Their crime in Burma was that they had a little money and they had the misfortune to raise brave sons. And they were Mon.

For these crimes they were deprived of their property, their safety, and nearly their lives. There are more brutal stories. Stories of torture, of rape, of murder. But if the world measures a refugee according to the worst story, we will always excuse human suffering, saying it is not yet as bad as someone else's. There is only one true measure, and that is to hold a person's life against our deepest ideals of human dignity and freedom from persecution.

Nai Cham and his family were persecuted. Both as members of the Mon, who are generally at risk in Burma, and as individuals suspected of cheating the army of wealth from the mills. If the UNHCR says this is not a "well-founded fear of persecution" no matter how many pages of qualifiers it puts after that initial phrase, it makes those words meaningless. And if we make these words meaningless, where can the poor and oppressed turn for justice?

Now that we are certain of Nai Cham's status, our attention turns to Phra Dala Non. Before coming to Thailand, he was active in the resistance inside Burma, where he supplied the Mon people with "The Buddhist Way to Democracy" and other writings which call the indigenous to peaceful but firm resistance. He also got news of events inside Burma out to friends in Thailand, who, in turn, got it out to the world.

In 1992 he was discovered by Burmese authorities. He was away from his monastery when the military raided, finding within his small bundle of belongings some items of literary contraband that labeled him a subversive. His abbot sent hurried word not to return. And so a visit to a village turned into an exodus, the frightening journey away from homeland and family, across the border, into an unknown life.

Phra Dala Non has been waiting for months to hear whether he has been accepted as a legitimate political refugee. Meanwhile he, Phra Dhamma, and some of the other monks do a brave and astonishing thing. They take to the streets, holding signs and placards, calling for freedom and justice for the Mon. They demonstrate outside the UN building, hoping to attract the attention of the media. They risk everything—anonymity, safety—to speak their truth to the world.

Later, Phra Dala Non shows me pictures of the demonstrations, which do get some news coverage. "We were, how do you say it, quite a sight!" he says. "It is good to demonstrate. The Burmese army want to hide the many terrible things they do so the world won't know. And the Thai authorities want to hide that they do not really help us sometimes when we most need help. But what is being done to the Mon people is so bad it cannot be covered up. The Mon have a saying: You cannot hide a dead elephant under a handkerchief."

During the demonstrations, the UNHCR office invites the refugees to send someone inside the UN building to have a dialogue with officials and to explain the Mon position. Phra Dala Non's English is good, so he goes in to speak with them. They listen. In the end the talk becomes friendly. On Phra Dala Non's way out they ask whether there is anything else they can do for him.

"Yes," he says. "You can explain to me why I've waited six months and still don't know whether I have refugee status."

A few days later he gets the notification that he is officially a refugee. He can be resettled. This is wonderful news. It somewhat mitigates the ache I have over Nai Cham. At least some of the refugees will have a small portion of protection.

Soon after Phra Dala Non obtains refugee status, I am on my way to the hospital in a taxi with Phra Dhamma when he leans forward and asks, "Ah, Wicki, how many children do you have?"

I turn around in surprise, looking over the seat of the taxi. "Why, none!"

"You do not have two children?"

I shake my head, baffled. Where would he have gotten such an idea? Where does he think I've been hiding them?

"And your husband, is he very important?" he continues.

"Husband? What husband? I don't have a husband."

He looks thoughtful. "When you go back to America, will you live with your mother and father?"

"No, Phra Dhamma. I will live with my community, as I do now."

He slaps his head and mutters in Mon.

"What is it?" I ask.

"Phra Dala Non," he mutters. "He told me you have two children, and your husband is very important in the United States government, but that when you go back to America, you will live with your mother and father."

I snort. "Well, I happen to know, he told you he got refugee status because a woman in the UN was in love with him."

"You mean that's not true either?" he sputters, turning red.

"No." I laugh. "He got status because he's a true refugee, just like you."

We both shake our heads and laugh. Phra Dala Non!

The next day I am with Phra Dala Non. "I hear you told Phra Dhamma I have two children," I say.

He blushes, looking sheepish. "You should have seen Phra Dhamma's face," he says. "He was like this." He drops his jaw in astonishment and opens his eyes wide.

"And did you also tell him I have an important husband and will live with my mother and father when I go home?"

He laughs and nods.

"To get you back, I told Phra Dhamma you made up the story about the woman from the UN being in love with you."

For a second he looks as if he will be angry, but curiosity wins out. "You told him? What did he say?"

"He shook his head like this and said, 'Phra Dala Non!' " I do a fair imitation.

"You should have seen him," Phra Dala Non snorts. "He scolded me for leaving him waiting in the hall at the UN for a long time and said, 'How could you leave me here waiting, while you're inside talking to your lover?' "

A little later, he makes another confession. "I did make those things up, but it is also true that I had heard they were true. That you had children, that you had a husband."

I search through my memory, until I find a probable cause of the rumors. "I think some of the monks were with me one day when I was in a taxi, and I knew the monks were going to get out and leave me alone with the taxi driver. Taxi drivers always ask me if I am married, if I have children, if I have a Thai boyfriend, what I think of Thai men."

"They do?" Now it is Phra Dala Non's turn to be astonished.

"Yes, especially if I'm alone. So I always lie. Always. I say I am married. I always say my husband is *very* tall and very powerful. I usually say that I'm going to meet him right now. And then I say I have some children. Usually at least two. If I'm especially nervous, I say I have six."

"You do?" Now he is more perplexed than ever.

"Yep. In my culture it is a little bit rude to ask a woman personal questions, especially if you don't know her and she is alone. I know it is not rude here, but still, if I am alone, I feel a little afraid. I figure they will not bother to kidnap me if they think there is someone who knows where I am and who is waiting for me right now. And they will not rob me if they think my husband is big and will come after them with a gun. And maybe they won't rape or kill me if I'm a mother, because they'll feel sorry for my children."

"That's smart," he says with admiration.

Just then another monk, Phra Nantathara, passes by and waves. "How are your two children?" he asks.

The next night Phra Dhamma calls. "Phra Dala Non told me about you and taxi drivers," he says. "You tell them you are married because you are a woman and you are afraid."

"Yes," I say. "It's true."

"I think about this all night," says Phra Dhamma. "I feel very sad. I think about how the Mon people have, how do you call it, many injustices. But this also is injustice, that women are afraid."

"Yes, I suppose that's true, too."

"Some day," says Phra Dhamma wistfully. "Some day it will be all right for everyone. For Mon people. For women. We must all work together. We must look at all the injustices, one at a time, and make them end."

Phra Dhamma is in the midst of the anxious and arduous endeavor to be accepted for resettlement, and we, his friends, watch with a growing feeling of hopelessness while he applies to the United States and is rejected outright, and then turns to Canada for help. He is among the first to apply to Canada, and things look promising, but as time goes on and we hear nothing, he decides to check back with the embassy. We discover to our horror that the officials have lost his application. He has to start all over. He applies again, with a growing sense of unease.

More and more refugees apply for resettlement, but the number each country accepts does not increase to meet the increasing need. The odds turn against any individual, no matter how worthy his history or how desperate his fear. We are all tense and wish there were something we could do. But there is nothing we can do. The refugees' attitude is contagious, and we begin to look at the world out of their eyes. A sense of dread infects our daily activities, and we alternate between despondency and frantic hope.

One night the phone rings. On the other end are street sounds, the fuzzy connection of a pay phone, and the swish that comes from our own bad wireless. The traffic goes by like the sound of rain. An indeterminate sound, muffled, hesitant, comes out of the speaker's mouth.

This long pause, the motorcycle engines, the voice that says something like "Yezza," instead of "Hello." These are signs the call is for me.

"Phra Dhamma?" I ask.

"Yezza. Is me. There is a question I want to ask you. Do you know anyone in Australia?"

Australia. Big country. Do I know anyone? While I'm thinking, he continues. "You know Mary from the Australian embassy? Today she came to the wat. She explained to me. Now Australia is accepting refugees. All I need is a sponsor. But I don't know how to find a sponsor. Do you know someone who could sponsor me?"

I know it is important for him to apply to more than one country, even though he has a strong application. The United States has already rejected him, and Canada is an uncertainty, so seeking a possibility in Australia makes sense. I search my memory for any friends in Australia. Then the light goes on in my brain, and I think of Friends with a capital "F." I have a long-standing connection with Quakers in the region, and it happens that Asia and Australia are closely connected in the Quaker world. It's such a small world that I do, in fact, know Friends in Australia. Surely if they understand how desperate the situation is here, one of the Quaker Meetings can help.

"No problem," I say. "I think I can handle this."

His voice goes light with relief. "Uh, Wicki?"

"Yeah?"

"I think you really love me, is that right?"

This is sort of a shocking question, coming out of the blue. The answer is so emphatic, it makes my chest hurt. "Yes. I do."

He is silent for a moment. I hear sounds of traffic, constant as the ocean. "Very much?" he asks, with a kind of sympathy, as if he has had experience with the helplessness true friendship imposes on a human heart.

"Very much."

"And I think you love my people, the Mon people. Is it true?"

"True, Phra Dhamma."

Phra Dhamma thinks over my answer for a moment. "I thought so," he says. And then my favorite part of the conversation, the return to the ordinary rhythms of relationship after the grand confessions: "O.K., then. I see you tomorrow."

"See you tomorrow." I hang up, smiling. I go to my room and pull my address book off the shelf. I write a letter to everyone I know in Oz, asking for their help, explaining the situation here, telling of Phra Dhamma's heroism and his sweetness and his need. I write late into the night, and when I am done I have a small pile of letters. I say a little prayer over each one, then bundle them together for the post office, where I will go tomorrow, dropping my hopes and my desperation into the mysterious arms of the postal service, which will carry my plea for a miracle off to the land down under.

A few weeks later I receive word from one of my friends in Australia. She has contacted the Quaker Meeting she belongs to. They will sponsor Phra Dhamma. It will be a long process—my friend's letter warns me it will most likely take six months, and there are no guarantees. The Meeting will offer to sponsor him, and then he can officially apply for resettlement. After their papers and his are submitted, Australia will review his file and make a final decision whether to accept him.

I walk back to the wat to bring the news to Phra Dhamma. On the way I smell the characteristic scents of Thailand: exhaust and coconuts. I watch a man on the corner frying dough in a large vat of oil right on the street. The dough drops in solid blobs. Then it puffs up with the heat, and becomes hollow, crispy, and delicious, filling the air with the smell of fresh bread. I watch the world around me, whole families on the back of motorcycles, pretty girls riding sidesaddle behind the drivers. They ride without helmets, heedless of danger, their hair flying, their bare legs crossed prettily in an exceptional display of balance, their toes pointed toward heaven, while their flip-flops tremble and flap in the wind.

At the wat I look for Phra Dhamma but unearth Phra Dala Non instead. "Where's Phra Dhamma?" I ask Phra Dala Non. We poke around a bit, and Phra Dala Non announces he suspects we will find Phra Dhamma hiding on the uppermost staircase. "He's probably smoking," confides Phra Dala Non.

"Phra Dhamma smokes?" I ask, incredulous. This information conflicts with my image of monks.

"Like a chimney," says Phra Dala Non, who takes endless pleasure in English idioms. We peer up the stairs, and there he is, engulfed in a cloud of smoke. He looks as though he's been encased in dry ice, swirls of white billowing off his orange robe.

"You shouldn't smoke," says Phra Dala Non. "It's unhealthy."

Phra Dhamma smiles, looks embarrassed, then punches Phra Dala Non in the ribs.

I look at these two young men laughing with each other, and I think about this world of danger and beauty, and about all we attempt to accomplish in it. We come to a country like this wanting to bring structural change, wanting to walk beside the servants of justice, hoping to preserve a culture, wanting to save the world. But our expectations get smaller as time goes on. Our hearts settle on one goal: to save one man, one friend. Even then the odds seem against us. In the end, we go forward with our small pursuits, our only act of courage the fact that in a confusing world, we still dare to hope.

Snowy River

It is Songkhran, the New Year and the celebration of water. Riding buses is hazardous and very damp. People stand by the side of the road and throw bucketfuls of water through the open windows, sometimes followed by flour. Passengers disembark dripping and looking like the Pillsbury doughboy with white drizzle oozing down their backs. The point of this silliness is to give the sky the right idea—that's one of the main objectives of Songkhran. The people get tired of the dusty, dry weather, and they demonstrate to the sky what they expect of it.

They are successful this week. They claim they always are, every year. By the final night of the holiday there are flashes of electricity in the sky, and the first showers begin. Everyone goes home looking self-satisfied, as if to say, "You see, sometimes you call for rain, and the rain obeys."

I am planning a trip to Isaan, the northeastern part of Thailand, where our community has several projects. The night before I go, Phra Dhamma calls. "You must be careful when you go to the north," he says.

"I will. I'm always careful," I assure him.

"You're going alone?"

"I'm going alone, but when I get there, I'll be with community members."

He is in a philosophical and somewhat motherly mood. "There are a lot of bad guys out there, you know. Think about those taxi drivers who make you afraid."

Bad guys? Where has he picked up that expression? "I know. I'll be careful."

"It is dangerous to be alone so much. And you are often alone. I see you walking to the wat by yourself. Young and very fat and beautiful and wearing those black glasses."

I smile and for a moment I see myself as they must. A heavy white woman in baggy clothes, usually with some stain, eyes shrouded by dark glasses. Always mysteriously solitary. It is amazing to me that given the kind of danger the monks have faced and continue to face, that my safety would even occur to them as something to be concerned about, but I am touched nonetheless.

"I'll be careful," I promise again.

I spend a pleasant few days in the northeast visiting other members of the community and enjoying the Songkhran holiday. Many activities are afoot in the community. There will be an assembly in the summer for discussing our organization, our statutes, and our financial prospects. In the meantime we are engaged in local discussions about our dreams, our work, and our individual and collective futures.

I return to Bangkok on the train, no doubt smelling of garlic and cucumbers, which I have eaten for three days in a guesthouse by the river—dipping hunks of French bread dipped into garlic-suffused yogurt.

I ride the air-conditioned part of the overnight train, but the door opens onto a true tropical night, wet and hot. The evening monsoon creates a womb-like feeling—I am enclosed in the arms of a warm rain, its song all around me. All night the automatic door slides open and closed. Shuck, shuck. Thailand intrudes on my second-class, air-conditioned bed: rain, bugs, momentary glimpses of the night sky in an electric storm. Lightning erases every darkness across the horizon and then itself disappears. The night smells of wet clothes, overused train toilets, garlic, fish sauce, sweaty skin.

The train from Nongkhai pulls into Bangkok at a crisp 6:15 A.M., and I haul myself, sleepless, out of my upper bunk. I go home and read my mail. The first letter is from my Quaker friends in Australia. I rip open the thick package and read the cover letter. Then I fall on the bed, put my face in my pillow and begin to cry.

If this is how I react to good news, what is to become of me?

For it is good news. The sponsorship papers are almost completed. If one more signed document goes through, the Quakers will be accepted as sponsors. Once Phra Dhamma has a sponsor, he can officially apply for resettlement. If he's accepted, he could be in Sydney in a few months. I can't stand to think of how much I will miss him, of what it will be like to work here without his help and his companionship.

At the wat I run into Phra Dhamma right off. I have washed my face, but I look dreadful. I find him, seated, part of a quintessential Asian urban scene. There's something about how the tropical light reflects off the bleak architecture, how the dirty, convoluted constructions of brick and concrete, tower in cramped, angular shapes so unlike the small, vulnerable bodies of human beings.

Here in the city, the light is trapped, gauzy, and full of shadows. It hides rather than illuminates. It creeps like smoke, as if even in the dark halls of city streets, some ancient, malevolent spirit, unaware of human existence, lurks, waiting. History, the gods, even the walls built by our own hands, ultimately dwarf us, and turn their stone backs. We live in their shadows, animals without claws or shells.

In this case the smoky light, the palpable air, is not illusory or metaphorical. Phra Dhamma is sitting on the curb, smoking. I come up to him smiling. We are two soft-bellied creatures, meeting under the shadows of steel and concrete.

"Morning."

"Good morning."

"Caught you smoking," I laugh. He laughs, too, and puts out his cigarette.

Ashes or petals have fallen on him. His face and his nearly-bald head are covered with white buds. He looks like a baby chick. He looks sleepy. The sight of him fills me with tenderness.

We exchange pleasantries. He has been away, too. He has a letter I left for him before I went north, still in his pocket. It is damp and wrinkled as old parchment.

Silence falls around us through the smoke. "Can I talk to you?" I ask seriously. "Someplace quiet."

He leads me around the corner to the computer room and unlocks the door. Inside the room, I am momentarily blinded by the darkness. Slowly shapes reemerge. The computer, four or five chairs, the solid shape of Phra Dhamma.

"Please sit," he says, waving to a chair.

In the corner a monk lies curled up on the floor, asleep on his side. He turns his back to us and continues dreaming. I present Phra Dhamma with a wad of official papers from my bag. "This is about you," I say. "From Australia. It says we need one more form and then you can apply for resettlement. There is no guarantee your application will be accepted, but I think you have a chance. There's a lot of work to do between now and then, so you'll have to decide if you even want to try. What do you want to do? Have you heard from Canada?"

He shakes his head. "Not yet."

"You're lucky. You can probably go to either country. So, Canada, Australia. What do you think?"

He looks suitably serious. "What do *you* think?" he asks.

For once all my worldly wisdom fails me. For all my travels, these countries are mythical to me. I take them on faith. They are reported to exist. I have met people who say they have been there, lived there, been born there. But I do not know how to begin to imagine them. I try to assemble my mental pictures of Canada and find I have none. Maybe once I saw pictures of Niagara Falls from the Canadian side. And I've seen *Anne of Green Gables*, as it happens, on cable TV in a guesthouse in Penang, Malaysia. This is the entire stock of my knowledge.

About Oz I have little more. Isn't Sydney where the famous opera house is, the one that looks like a clam? In the picture in my memory it stands in strong sunlight. Isn't there water nearby? What will Phra Dhamma think of opera? Will this picture have anything to do with him?

I know there is information I should get, questions I should ask. What is the job situation? Will it ever be possible to be more than a janitor? A dishwasher? Will he ever be able to go to college? I try to picture daily life there. Do they have 7–11 stores and Magnum ice cream bars and Thai food? It is surprising what you wonder, what emerges as significant.

"If you go to Canada, after a while, maybe you could visit the United States. Maybe I could come to visit you."

"But we hear it is difficult to get a job there."

I nod. This may be true. "It is cold in Canada. It snows." I shrink from the thought of all that snow. He thinks about this in silence.

We sit and sweat; drops roll down my neck, keeping time. I have grown used to it that way. Phra Dhamma wears a vest over one shoulder and under one arm, one shoulder and one breast bare, like a cave man or an Amazon. He doesn't belong in a world where he could be surrounded by ice. This seems a convincing argument to him, too.

"Maybe you will not have to stay anywhere very long," I offer. "Maybe the war will end, and you can come back home, back to Monland."

For the first time he smiles and looks happy. "Oh, yes," he says, "someday I will come back. Someday I will return."

That's how it is. Those refugees who face repatriation dream of the West. And the lucky ones with the possibility of a plane ticket long for the homes of their childhood.

"So what do you think?" I ask again. "If you are accepted to both, will you go to Canada or Australia?"

He looks at the papers, frowns. "O.K., how about Australia?" There it is, settled. A future chosen, preferences expressed. Not based on hard facts, only fleeting impressions, and a moment's consideration of the weather.

I feel both pain and pride. Pride because, if this works, I will have been an instrument in this opportunity. It is my gift to him, my unique competence. It makes me magic. I write a letter to another country, and freedom comes back in the mail. The pain comes from the same source. He is going to a place neither of us can imagine. A place with an opera house and no other pictures. No reputation except distance. In my heart I am already trying to let him go. I am thinking I will never see him again.

Already more and more goes into the category of the lost. I am thirty-six, which is after all not so very old. But there is so much I expect not to accomplish, not to finish—things I have started that I will not see the end of. I contemplate a future without Phra Dhamma, and suddenly I miss him terribly, as if all the missing I will feel when he is gone is stretched out in a long line in front of us. Years and years of missing. Like the map of a journey I don't want to take.

Now that Phra Dhamma has chosen Australia as his first choice, we have to get him ready to make his final application, assuming signed papers come through. In the meantime, I try to think of something practical to offer. "I know," I say. "I saw a movie once: *Return to Snowy River*. They have it at the video rental place down the street. I think it is about Australia. You want to come over and watch it?"

"When?"

"It's up to you."

"No. Up to you, I think."

"O.K.," I say. "I'll get the video, and you can come over this weekend. You and Phra Dala Non and anyone else who's interested."

It occurs to me I am planning an entire orientation to a nation based on a children's movie about the Australian frontier. I suppose this is the equivalent to orienting someone to the United States with a John Wayne movie followed by a showing of *Bambi*. Not that that would be such a bad idea, come to think of it. Besides, showing this video is something practical to do, and it makes me feel better.

No sooner has Phra Dhamma made the choice in favor of Australia than the question becomes irrelevant. He calls to inform me that Canada has rejected his application for resettlement, which is shocking, given the strength of his leadership in Burma. We write letters of appeal, letters of disappointment, but to no avail. His only chance now is Australia. And now that I know it is possible to get as far as he did with Canada and finally be rejected, I realize that Australia is not a sure bet either, by any means. In fact, in the current political climate, there are no sure bets. It is possible in the end that all avenues of escape will fall through. And then what will we do?

I am determined to adopt a more Buddhist attitude about the risks, as I'm clear worrying won't help anything. But of course, any calm I project is a thin veneer over a deep well of panic. You can see that my tranquility is not even skin deep—for I immediately start biting my nails and soon have also bitten the sides of my fingers until they bleed.

Soon after being rejected by Canada, Phra Dhamma and I attend a refugee meeting at the community house. An International Human Rights group has sent Aung Thain, a resettled refugee, to interview the monks at the wat and students in Bangkok. Our community house seems like the safest place for the group to meet.

Two tuk tuks pull up in front of the house, and four or five monks pop out of each like pellets from a PEZ candy dispenser. I catch Phra Dhamma's eyes as he stands in the crowd. I smile at him and offer him a Coke.

Students crowd in at the door. I know most of them, but not all. I retreat to the kitchen to pour sodas for the thirsty travelers. This is my main role in a meeting at which I have no other purpose other than to play hostess. It's a role I enjoy. I take pleasure in a full house, a house in use. I love seeing both refugees and foreigners unload at the door, making me grateful there are so many of us in this common cause. It reminds me that though I may not always be aware of it, I am not alone.

When everyone has arrived, I ask whether we should stay downstairs or go upstairs to the sitting room. A tall student, one of the leaders, looks around him. The front of the house has many windows. "Upstairs," he says. "It is more secure."

So up we go. They conduct the meeting in Burmese. There is no Western sense of privacy or linearity. It is an entirely Asian affair, and to my Western eyes looks chaotic, everyone talking at once. Still, it is all theirs, and I feel content in my silence. The tall leader pulls up a chair for me so that I can sit nearby and feel part of the conversation.

Because I don't understand a word of Burmese and because everyone is speaking at the same time and this does not seem to be considered rude, I whisper to the other Westerners present, two young men, Sam and Ken, both of whom work with refugees here in Bangkok.

After a while the meeting begins to break up, and people start leaving slowly, drifting downstairs. Then one of the refugees rushes back upstairs. "Wicki," he says urgently. "Police. Two of them. Downstairs."

I am halfway down the stairs before I know it, calling to the remaining refugees over my shoulder, "Stay here. Close the door behind me."

Downstairs half the refugees are standing in the living room, looking perplexed. Just outside the door two policemen are eating their lunch at the noodle shop next door, unaware they are the objects of so much speculation and terror. I am about to step outside to see if there are more than two, but the refugees hold me back. "No. Don't go out," they plead.

I had never noticed that police eat at the shop next door. Though their presence is a real threat, I am relieved this is all we have to contend with at the moment. I had half-expected to find police with guns drawn, pounding on the front door.

We all sit and wait for the police to finish their lunch and leave. The monks decide it is not necessary for them to wait. They are safe for a little while still in Thailand. They adjust their robes tensely. They put on their sandals in silence, then edge out into the street single-file, looking straight ahead, not daring to speak, cutting a wide berth between themselves and the noodle shop. I wonder what the police and the restaurant people make of this. They must imagine they are eating beside an extremely devout Buddhist household, to have so many monks trail out at once.

By the time the police leave, everyone is hungry. The refugees decide to leave in two groups of four in order to be less conspicuous. They will meet half a block away at a cheap restaurant.

"No talking Mon," I admonish. They nod.

"Good Thai speakers in the first group," they say. The first group leaves. Fifteen minutes later one of them comes back, sticks his head in the door and smiles at the refugees who remain. "All clear. Follow me."

All this to go half a block for a bowl of noodles.

The tall leader lingers in the door and turns back to me. "You see how different your life is from ours," he says with bitterness. Then he turns and is gone, through the door, out to the dangerous streets.

By the end of the week I check in with Phra Dhamma at the wat. He asks to talk about the papers he has received from my friends in Australia. He has been slowly reading through them and has noticed that although the Friends will pay for him, the group who will officially receive him is a Burmese Community Center.

"Who is this man who signed the forms? Is he Burmese?"

"I think so, but in the West we also say 'Burmese' when we mean any of the ethnic groups. This Burmese Center may have within it many people from all the different ethnic groups."

Phra Dhamma unfolds a letter from a Mon friend who says there are almost no Mon in Australia. This is going to be a problem. He's going to have to think about this.

He stands by the wall wrapped in silence. We have finished the day's business, but there is something in the tightness of his shoulders contrasting with his downcast eyes. He has something to say, but he is afraid to speak.

"Anything else?" I ask.

It has begun to rain. Thunder rolls nearby, and though it's still early, the sky is growing dark. Occasionally the sky splits open, and light spills out of the crack.

"Will I be dependent on them?" he asks.

"Who?"

"The Burmese sponsors. Will I live with them?"

This had not occurred to me. "I don't think so. I think they will be there to help you find a place to live." I realize all he knows is the life of the temple, where many live together in absolute simplicity and complete community. He has no concept of separate apartments, of "simple" meaning still having what we consider basic: a refrigerator, a bed, some chairs, electricity, a phone. Even to go without a TV is deemed deprivation these days. Too many people sharing one bathroom practically makes the five o'clock news. The Burmese community is probably no more interested in living with Phra Dhamma than Phra Dhamma is in living with them.

"What will you do?" I ask. He looks at my shoes. I wait. "Shall I write and ask my Quaker friend about this? Shall I ask her where you'll live if you go to Australia and how dependent you'll be on the Burmese group?"

"O.K.," he says, but he is not enthusiastic. I cannot tell whether it is the yes that means yes, or the yes that really means thank you for asking, but no.

I chew on my tongue to keep from blurting out questions, suggestions. I know from experience that questions will not speed things up. It is likely my words will only interrupt the process of thought and courage-gathering that is happening deep within him, and then we will have to start at the beginning again. But after another moment of silence, despite my better judgment, I erupt into speech. "What about the friend who sent you this letter? Is there a possibility you can live with him? If my friend pays for the trip?"

He shakes off the question. "This Community Center, I think they are not Mon people. They are Burmese." He says it with distaste, with fear. "You understand? Burmese!"

We walk out from under the protection of the wall. If I'm going to go, I have to go now. The rain is coming down so hard it sounds like the roof is being pelted with grapefruit.

"O.K. I will write to my friend," I say. "I will explain. But you must tell me what you want. Do you want to be sponsored by your friend? Do you want to make sure you won't live with the Burmese community, if that is what they are planning?"

"Wicki," he says, turning to me with anguish, his face begging me to understand. "I want not to be dependent on Burmese. I cannot be dependent on Burmese. Cannot. Cannot. *Cannot!* You understand?"

I have never seen him adamant before, about anything. I nod. I understand. I steal away in the rain, astonished and guilty. Have I done the worst thing? Have I handed him over to his ancient enemy?

I walk home through the monsoon rain, soaked and shivering. My canvas bag, full of books and unprotected paper, is as absorbent as a sponge and growing heavier by the minute. Muttering to myself, I am aware I am wallowing in ego. Wounded and deflated ego, the worst kind. But the awareness does not lessen the onslaught. Self-blame turns to brooding. By the time I have reached the main street I feel thoroughly sorry for myself.

I am a failure, I tell myself. He is disappointed. I have let him down. Now I am also letting myself down by discovering that I seem to care less about his happiness than about my own importance. The more difficult Australia seems the more desperate I am to make it work. I want him happy and safe, which is noble. But I also want to be the one to have made him happy, which is not noble at all.

On Saturday morning, I am awakened by the sound of the phone. I am sorry to be awake but glad at the voice at the other end. "I called you yesterday," Phra Dhamma says, "but they say you are not in."

"What time did you call?"

"About four."

"I was in," I say sourly. I make a mental note to strangle my housemates. I am sleepy and still recovering from bad dreams.

"So what about the movie, *Snowy River*?" he asks.

"How about 2:30," I suggest, thinking that in addition to seeing the movie this will give us a chance to delve into the question of his sponsorship by the Burmese community. I am still sulky and bewildered after his outburst. I want to understand, to apologize, to get it right. I simultaneously look forward to and dread further conversation on the subject.

"O.K., 2:30." There is a long silence. "Are you O.K.?" he asks.

"Yes," I lie. The phone goes dead. I wait for it to ring again, but when it does, someone else answers. No one calls for me, so I decide it must be for someone else. I am tired of standing in the middle of the hall in my nightie with the moth holes chewed across the belly. I take a long shower, stumble into some clothes and go downstairs. After a while I call the wat to see if I can catch Phra Dhamma. They say he is gone.

I decide to go out for the morning and get some fresh air or at least a fresh perspective. On my way out the door, the phone rings again, and I grab it. "Is Brother Matthew there?"

"No. He's out of town."

"Then can I speak to Vicki?"

It's Ken from the Burma group meeting.

"Have you seen Aung Thain, the Burmese from the United States who has been interviewing refugees about the border situation?"

"No. Why?"

"He has disappeared. He reached the border and was staying in a guesthouse, but no one has seen him in days."

This is distressing news, and I have no information to make the picture brighter. I leave the house in a thoughtful mood.

I'm still out and beginning to worry about getting home on time when the rains begin. Every day now brings a storm of biblical proportions. During some part of it, I'm convinced I'm going to be struck by lightning or drown. Within an hour the whole city is submerged. Everyone has taken off their shoes and is wading through calf-deep muck, hoping their karma is such they won't step on anything with teeth that still work. All over the city, the sky darkens then splits open like a coconut to reveal its scar of white milk. The horizon is an empty room where the lights go on and off. Being caught outside, I decide to take a cab home. The water is halfway up the tires. The thunder is so near it could be coming from the car speakers.

"Are you afraid?" asks the driver.

"No," I say, biting my nails.

"Don't be afraid," he says nervously. "If you are a good person, lightning won't hit." At least this is what I think he says, with my indifferent Thai. It seems a comforting philosophy, if theologically weak. After a few more whips of lightning, each of which makes us flinch, the driver adds, "But it is pretty loud, isn't it?"

When it floods like this, you would think this must be something rare. You would think if it were like this all the time, something would be done. They would build wider and deeper gutters, unclog the drains. Something. But it is like this all during the monsoon season, and nothing is done. Streets everywhere turn into ponds. We pull up to our house through the beginning of a small lake.

Within two hours of the rain stopping, there won't be a trace left of the deluge. Well, maybe a trace. Maybe the streets will look as though it has drizzled lately. They glimmer darkly. But the sun is so hot, it dries everything out—bodies, the wet shirt I am wearing, even the flooded streets.

I make it back just before 2:30, but there's no Phra Dhamma. I step from the cab into the cold bath of street water and wade to the front door. Then I lie on the couch for two hours, fretting, conjecturing. Periodically I call the wat. They say something I don't understand and put me on hold. "Phra Dhamma, he not here, he go out," they say over and over in Thai and English with strained patience, with infinite pity for my slowness at comprehending, with amazement at Phra Dhamma's regard for his slightly retarded foreign friend.

So I sit by the window and watch for them while the waters subside by the minute. I blow on my damp shirt and hold myself close to a shaft of sunlight coming in slantways from the street. I don't know why other people's lateness makes me feel inadequate, but it does.

I'm disgusted with my own indecisiveness. Should I go upstairs? Read a book? Write them a note and leave? I am particularly grieved by lateness when I feel underneath that I may be at fault in some way, as now, when I'm afraid I have mangled Phra Dhamma's chance for a happy resettlement, and that perhaps he is reluctant to face me.

I put my feet up, write a letter, nap. At the other end of the room sits a French woman, bound for Cambodia, who is staying for a few days. She is snoozing, with her head flopped over her arm on the kitchen table, the newspaper sprawled around her. She also is waiting for someone who never comes. We make a pair, the two of us, with our air of disappointed expectation. The phone rings, and I am glad to see she opens her eyes. I was beginning to wonder if she had died in her sleep.

I leap up and grab the receiver. "Phra Dhamma?" But it is not Phra Dhamma.

"No. It's me, Sam, from the border group. Have you seen Aung Thain lately?"

"No," I say disconsolately. "This is the second time today someone has asked me that question."

Sam explains that Aung Thain was in Sangkhlaburi. He left the guesthouse one morning, but his things are still there. He hadn't paid his bill, he hadn't told them he was leaving. No one in Bangkok has seen him. Not his friends, not other refugee workers. He's been gone three days. "It's time to call the headquarters in New York," says Sam. "It's time to panic."

Most of the time I manage to put to the back of my mind how close by the conflict in Burma is. True, it is likely this man is safe. Perhaps he is just forgetful and peculiar. But when your heart lurches like this, for a moment you are forced to recognize that this is not an ordinary situation. People are taken. People are hurt. Someone missing for three days from that border is a serious matter. A Burmese refugee and activist missing from that border is catastrophe.

I hang up feeling unutterably sad. The missing man at the border has brought the Burmese ethnic conflict home, and Phra Dhamma's fear has brought it straight into my heart. Even though I mean well, it suddenly seems to me I am out of my depths. I am trying to arrange people's lives, but I am in the midst of a political situation that is bigger and more dangerous than I can comprehend.

It is not quite night yet, but the monsoon weather seems to be inside the room, with its cloak of wet air. I close and lock the front door, put our French guest to bed, go upstairs to watch a truly terrible video, an old Western with Kurt Russell and Susan Dey.

Halfway through the movie, the phone rings again. There, at last, is Phra Dhamma's voice. "Wicki, is it you?"

Relief floods through me, and tenderness. "Yes, Phra Dhamma, it is me, Vicki. How are you?"

"I'm fine. In the pink. And you?"

"Fine."

There is a pause. "Uh, Wicki?"

"Yes?"

"I am very sorry I did not come today. I miss the movie. It was my friend. He have the fever."

"Malaria?"

"Yezza. Malaria. I took him to the hospital. I did not get back until four o'clock. I called this morning to say I am going, but they tell me you are not home."

"Oh!" I begin to stamp my feet. "I hate that!" I bellow, laughing. "It happens all the time. They say I am not here, but I am. I am! I am right here."

Phra Dhamma laughs, too, at this outburst.

"But do you know," I continue, "that I called the wat many times today. At least once after four. They did the same thing. They told me you were gone."

He laughs, and I laugh. "It is the same. Your house. The wat."

"Yes, the same," I say. While we are laughing the phone cuts us off.

Thirty seconds later it rings again. "Uh, Wicki?"

"Phra Dhamma, hello again! I hate it when the phone does that." I begin to stomp my feet again. I am really enjoying my temper tantrum. "Hate it, hate it! This phone is no good!"

He laughs at me. "No. Phone works good. I must put one baht in. It only gives one minute."

"Oh," I say, understanding for the first time, thinking of him standing there by the street, cars zipping back and forth, while he patiently plugs one baht at a time into the machine.

"Wicki," he says. "I have one more question."

"Yes?"

"That letter. Did you write to Australia? Did you write to my sponsor?"

I had been up very late, typing and retyping it last night. After redoing it more than three times, I finally cut the last version with scissors, leaving the letter in two short pieces on my desk. I couldn't bring myself to try again. It is such a hard thing to explain politely that a refugee who we categorize as "Burmese" is afraid to be dependent on the Burmese Community Center. Now the two uneven scraps of paper give a brief list of questions. I hope my friend will think this is a new, exotic, and very short kind of stationary when she gets the two odd-length pieces of paper. I am planning to mail the letter on Monday.

"I wrote it," I say. "I finished it last night. But I did not send it yet."

"I'm glad you didn't send it," says Phra Dhamma. "I worry very much maybe you sent it already."

"No. Not yet." I am more confused than ever. "You don't want me to send it?"

"No. Please don't send it. I will explain all to you tomorrow."

We make a new time for seeing the video the next day. "I really worry I miss my appointment with you," he says.

"It is no problem," I say. "No problem at all."

"Goodnight."

"Goodnight."

Before I fall asleep the phone rings one more time. Aung Thain has been found. He's fine. The explanation for where he has been is so complicated I don't understand half of it. Never mind. The world is a dangerous place, and the people I love are at war, but at the moment, no one I care about is lost or captured or imprisoned. All is well, for tonight at least.

The next morning, Sunday, I am sitting in my seat by the window with a hot tea bag on my eyes (reported to be soothing) when the tuk tuk pulls up in front, full of monks. All four of them, including Phra Dhamma and Phra Dala Non, pop out of a space meant for two. They float in the door, right hand touching the left shoulder, like tin soldiers. I wipe the tea tears off my cheeks and fix them an assortment of drinks. Seven-Up. Orange Miranda. Even a Pepsi, which someone seems to have mistakenly bought instead of Coke.

We are boycotting Pepsi because of its bottling operation in Burma. (Pepsi has since withdrawn from Burma.) But the staff does not understand about boycotts. The truth is, I figure the monks won't know the difference, as long as I don't show them the bottle. "Mmm-mmm," says Phra Dhamma, appreciatively, emptying his Pepsi for me, like a small boy. "This is really good."

I lead them upstairs and settle them into chairs around the TV. Phra Dhamma is in the slouch chair, a lean-back affair meant for creatures made in the shape of lemon drops. If you sit back in the chair properly, the only thing you can look at without giving yourself whiplash is the ceiling.

Phra Dhamma curls up catlike and tucks his feet in, wrapping his robe neatly around his legs. Under the robe, a hands-breadth of bare calf is visible. It is quite a hairy calf.

For some reason I have been noticing his chunky legs lately. Maybe it is because he, like all the monks, has just gone through his monthly head shave. His scalp is as smooth as an egg. So his legs surprise me. They look innocent, somehow, in their natural state. They remind me of a story my mother used to tell about a priest who taught her in high school. The priest sat down and hitched up his priestly robes. There under the awesome exterior of the holy man, she spied golfing socks and shoes. It was in that exact moment that she ceased to be afraid of priests.

Phra Dhamma's hairy legs strike me similarly. They lack the conscious symbolism of his shaved head, as if the Sangha, or monastic community, demand priesthood and mystery only from the knee up. The poor bare calves, ankles, and toes are those of an ordinary boy.

Phra Dhamma is pleasantly chunky, like a child. I am struck by his fullness, the roundness of his arms, legs, face. The monks must have a metabolism of zero. They eat two spare meals a day, both before noon. They sleep in the afternoon heat. They survive on chanting and tropical sunshine and grow round on a daily bowl of water-rice.

We watch *Return to Snowy River*. I try to be sociable and cheerful to cover up my underlying anxiety. I provide unnecessary and probably irritating narration to accompany the movie. "Did you understand that bit? Those are poor people, see. They live on the mountain. Then there are the rich people. They live in the lowland. That's what we call a valley. The poor boy loves the rich girl. Get it?" They nod sagely and whisper to each other in Mon.

Our video, probably intended to be shown in bars, thoughtfully provides captions, including descriptions of sound effects. "Shhhh, shhhh, shhhh," goes the steam train; "Crackling of rifle in distance." The monks read these aloud. "Crack of thunder. BOOM."

I help out by adding my own sound effects, which I consider very good. I'm especially talented at the sharp gun sounds. I let go with my best loud cluck when the guns go off. The monks are duly impressed. They try to duplicate my performance. The room is thick with clucking.

At the end of the movie I ask, "What did you think?"

"Good movie!" says Phra Dala Non.

"So, Phra Dhamma," I ask. "What did you think of the pictures of Australia? Did you like it?"

"It's good," he says. "Please tell my sponsor I would like to live in those mountains."

"Fine. I'll have them buy you a horse." Everyone laughs.

We sit quietly for a minute while the tape rewinds. Then Phra Dhamma asks, "What about my sponsor?"

"Yes, what *about* your sponsor?"

Phra Dhamma turns to Phra Dala Non, who of the two of them has the better English. He is suddenly earnest. He talks in Mon for a long time. He seems to be pleading. I try not to be too obvious that I am curious, but I can't help looking intently at them. Is he saying something he wants and fears to say to me?

I raise my eyebrows at Phra Dala Non. He smiles apologetically and continues the conversation in Mon.

Will he translate for me later, I wonder? I want to ask many questions but don't know if Phra Dhamma wants to speak of such things in front of his friends. I look away, pretend to be busy with rewinding. I don't want them to see my eagerness, my emotional over-involvement, but probably they do see.

Phra Dala Non turns to me. "Are you O.K.?" he asks.

I nod, but the question makes me feel like crying.

Phra Dhamma breaks into another long speech, facing Phra Dala Non, his back to me. He speaks for a long time. Phra Dala Non laughs at him gently. "He is ashamed to talk to you in English," he says. I don't know whether he means he has something shameful to say, or whether he is ashamed of his English or both.

Phra Dhamma sits back in his chair at this point, and his face is a dangerous red. It can't be healthy to blush that color. He passes his hands over his face, hiding it, wipes at his eyes. I don't know whether this is serious, or just a boyish reaction to teasing. But it is unbearable for me. He is someone's lost child, trying to be brave.

"Well," says Phra Dala Non, standing up. "Are we ready to go?" He and the other monks troop downstairs, leaving without explaining the last ten minutes of Mon.

Phra Dhamma turns toward the wall and slowly readjusts his robe. I flick out the light and prepare to follow him down. Then Phra Dhamma turns back to me. Suddenly it is dusk and we are alone.

"I wanted Phra Dala Non to translate for you," he says.

"I see. Are you afraid your English is not good? I think it is very good, really. Do you believe me?" I smile at him. He is collecting himself for something difficult and cannot bother with these extraneous questions one way or the other. I try to center myself. I ask my next question into the growing darkness. "Phra Dhamma, why do you not want me to send the letter to your sponsor?"

"I think mistakenly about this before," he says. "Now I think I must thank you. I must thank your Australian friend and the Burmese Community Center." His face, over its shame, is calm again. His orange robe is tighter than I have ever seen it. It makes of him the perfect shape. A double arch. The arch of the head imposed on the small round shoulders. A perfectly tapered form, like a dipped candle, an Egyptian mummy. He is an orange cocoon. He is complete unto himself.

"I called my friends," he explains. "In Canada and Australia. They have explained to me. It is the same everywhere. The Mon refugee in Canada. The Mon refugee in Australia. The same. Both must sponsor by the Burmese groups. They must sponsor by the Burmese groups, and there are no Mon. No Mon groups anywhere. Not in Canada. Not in Australia. Only in New York."

"And the United States has rejected you, so you cannot go to New York," I say gently.

"No. I cannot go to New York. But it does not matter. These Burmese, they are good. My friends explained to me. If your friend and the Burmese Community Center will be so good, will sponsor me, I should say yes. I should say thank you. My friends have told me it will be all right. Everything all right now. I am sorry I think mistakenly about this before. Now I understand. Australia is O.K. Sponsor is O.K. Everything is O.K. I am not afraid anymore."

Welcome to the new world, I think. Welcome, little brother, to the best of what the West has to offer, and to the first crisis of your new life. On the other side of the globe you will be met by your oldest enemy. Your enemy will feed you and find a roof under which to shelter you. The people from whom you flee will be at the airport to welcome you with flowers. Their offering will be sincere. They will be your guides in the culture of malls and fast-food restaurants. You will all be foreigners together. In the West we are all equally brothers, or all equally enemies. Where you are going, the history of your people will mean no more to the ordinary person than yesterday's bread.

As we stand there in the dusk, his face begins to fade against the fading light. He is a child who has been chastised. He is mild, reformed, newly self-composed. He is sorry. He is relieved. He has re-found his peace. The one thing he could not bear to happen is going to happen, and this has changed him. He will be dependent on Burmese. He is resigned to his fate. This is the first of many heartbreaks.

Now he is O.K., but I am not. Before him I see loneliness stretching like a desert. He imagined danger. He imagined being handed over to his oppressors. This is worse. I am handing him over to a world where there are neither enemies nor brothers. I am handing him over to a world where there are no Mon. He will be more alone than he has thought possible. He will abandon himself, be unrecognizable to himself. The part of him that is uniquely Phra Dhamma will remain. But the part that is Mon will be transformed.

What have we done, I think. He will be lost, utterly lost. He will forget who he is. We will drive his identity out of him with every French fry he eats.

Oh my God, I think, great, terrible, and loving spirit of transformation. Watch over him. And you, Lord Buddha, if you are there, if you can hear me, I think you had better watch over him, too.

We join the others downstairs, but slowly. We stop at every one of the four flights to talk again. Of Australia. Of Canada. Of the Mon. When we reach the office floor, I look over the balcony. Three orange shapes sprawl across various chairs and the couch, reading newspapers. Their robes swirl around them. From above, they are round and bright as poppies.

Once downstairs, Phra Dala Non asks me when I will go to the United States. I had informed Phra Dhamma awhile back that I would be going home to our community headquarters at the end of the summer to attend a community assembly. And I have let them know that a year from now my term in Thailand will be up, and I will go home for good.

"I'll go to the United States this summer," I say.

"Really? But that is so soon! And you will never come back?"

"I will come back—at the end of September."

Phra Dhamma intervenes. "I think it is next June you will go away forever. Is that right?"

"That's right. I only told you early because I worry about our little orphan boys. Who will get them money for school? We need to think ahead."

The monks nod but do not take this seriously. It is very un-Buddhist, and perhaps un-Mon, to think so far into the future.

Phra Dala Non gives Phra Dhamma a teasing glance. "Phra Dhamma told me you will leave this summer. He told me in a very sad voice."

Everyone laughs, except Phra Dhamma and me. To lighten things up I say, "You'll be gone long before I will, resettled, all of you, you traitors." Now everyone laughs.

All four of them crowd into the little vestibule just outside our door, where the shoe racks are. Once they have put on their shoes, they go out into the evening light. "Thank you. Thank you for the good movie! Good-bye. Good-bye." They are wrapped snug as caramels. They lift their skirts, delicate as nuns, over the last slips from the afternoon rain, Phra Dhamma revealing his hairy calves. Out they drift, single file, into the noise of the hot city night.

Crossing Borders

Love your enemies, do good to those who hate you, bless those who curse you, and pray for those who mistreat you. To the person who strikes you on one cheek, offer the other one as well.

LUKE 6:27–29

In this world
Hate never yet dispelled hate.
Only love dispels hate.
This is the law,
Ancient and inexhaustible.

FROM THE DHAMMAPADA,
TRANSLATED BY THOMAS BYROM

Presidents and Kings

Matthew and I have been putting off a trip across the border to see the new refugee camp where the Mon were forced to relocate in January. It is now May. If we're ever going, we have to go now or we'll be cut off by the rains as the monsoon season progresses. We pack our bags and make arrangements to meet at the wat early in the morning.

Although it is a journey undertaken for sad reasons, it is an outing; it will take me into the countryside, into the sun, away from the dark cells of IDC or the cramped, fluorescent-lit halls of hospitals. It will prevent me from fretting about when the last form will come from Australia, allowing Phra Dhamma to apply officially for resettlement.

People like me who are dreadfully literal minded must always be doing something. It is hard for us to believe we are making progress, moving forward, unless our feet are moving. So climbing into a bus raises my spirits. I can't help it. We are going to visit thousands of refugees pushed back into the land from which they fled, but when I arrive at the wat, it feels like a holiday.

We begin our journey at 6 A.M. at the wat, me still in my glasses because I can't face contact lenses at that hour. Matthew greets me in admiration. "You pack light," he says approvingly.

It's true; I've brought one small backpack. I am just settling into feeling smug when Phra Dhamma and Phra Dala Non enter the courtyard, ready to accompany and guide us, looking disgustingly alert and cheerful for the hour. There they are, no extra robes, no extra shoes. No towels, novels, toothpaste, deodorant, shampoo, or bug spray. Each holds a small bag at his side. The bag is conspicuously flat, almost empty. Inside are bus money, toilet paper, and a watch. Good enough for a week's trip. Suddenly my bag seems ten pounds heavier.

Matthew stares at their bags, then shifts the weight of his clothes bag and his camera bag. He begins to quote: "Take nothing for the journey, neither walking staff nor traveling bag; no bread, no money. No one is to have two coats. . . ." He looks from them to our bags. "We have received the words of the Gospel. But look who's actually living it."

Little Nai Oo, still recovering from TB, stands on his spindly legs by the gate and waves us out. All the children stare, ragged and hungry-looking, waiting for the monks to return with begging bowls filled to the brim.

It is a long, drowsy bus ride to the border. The bus is crowded. I look over at the monks. Phra Dhamma and Phra Dala Non are asleep, their heads leaning together. They are apparently unperturbed by the blaring TV in the front of the bus, blasting Thai sitcoms at full volume. Matthew is in the seat ahead of me, and we occasionally shout friendly conversation to each other or sip flat soda served by the pretty bus attendant.

Five hours later we arrive in Sangkhlaburi, where we discover the usual dusty two-block Thai town. Row after row of two-story, white concrete shop-houses line the streets, with sliding tin doors that take up the whole front wall of each house. Every house is also a shop, stocked with endless supplies of plastic bins and laundry soap in colorful boxes. Ugly shirts hang from the rafters, covered with a fine layer of dust. The garish colors underneath are muted by dirt, blending everything into a uniform beige.

The two monks accompany Matthew and me through the town, pointing politely with their chins at scenes they don't want us to miss. By and large there's nothing out here. Even the lake looks shriveled somehow. There's a very nice bridge that the local people must think is their best claim to fame, because we have seen it everywhere we have stopped on postcards and calendars. A large, dreamy pagoda rises in the distance. That's it. That's Sangkhlaburi. It's nice, but you can see all the best bits, on foot, in half an hour.

Matthew says he can understand why people risk their lives to come to Bangkok from here, even if they are illegal and always on the run and have nothing to look forward to but backbreaking work for seventy baht a day. "If I were them, I'd come to Bangkok, too," he says. "Just to ride up and down the escalators in the Mah Boon Khrong mall or look at the TV sets in Central Department Store would be a real treat."

In the evening, we wander with the monks through the half-empty market, where I buy two skirts made of men's cloth. The women wear only flower patterns, whereas all the strong lines I prefer are on the men's wear. The only women's cloth I buy is the Mon national dress for women, a beautiful red fabric with small black checks and a white shawl that is meant to be worn over one shoulder. Phra Dhamma looks up from a pile of cloth he is inspecting while the proprietor nervously flutters and smoothes the edges of her merchandise, eager to make a good sale. At the sight of the Mon cloth, Phra Dhamma smiles. Phra Dala Non looks over his shoulder and nods approvingly. "You wear that, and you'll look just like a Mon woman," he says.

"Phra Dala Non, you charmer," I say. "Just how many green-eyed, freckled, two-hundred pound Mon women do you know?"

"Wicki," he says, "you'd be surprised."

I laugh. "You nut," I say, affectionately.

"No, really," he insists. "We have Mon women with red hair and green eyes, just like you."

For a moment I am inclined to disbelieve him, but then I remember Burma's long history with Britain. Of course. British men, some of them of Irish ancestry like my family, would have stopped to marry—or otherwise—mingling the blood of my people with that of the beautiful Mon women they saw wrapping their colorful sarongs around their slim hips. In such a world, how can you know for sure who is a stranger and who is just a long lost relative speaking a different language?

In the morning, Marie, a slender, gray-eyed nurse from France, comes to pick Matthew and me up. She's wearing a deep gray blouse from Chiang Mai that I covet. The monks have business at the Mon National Relief Committee headquarters, so they stay in town. Matthew and I climb into the back of Maria's truck and sit on the two narrow benches to either side.

Before long, the truck stops, and people start piling in. Two young refugee women hitch up their sarongs and step in, with infants slung over their arms like rice sacks. Three men follow them, and pretty soon we're snugly pressed together on the benches while the truck lurches over the broken ground. Matthew plays with one of the infants, and I offer my finger to the other, who promptly deposits it in his mouth with his fist wrapped around it like a hot dog bun. I stroke the baby's temple with another finger until he falls asleep, gradually letting go of my finger, which oozes out moist and wrinkled like a slug.

We stop at the Christian referral hospital, where refugees are sent if they have medical problems too complicated for the camps to handle. It is not a hospital of Bangkok's caliber. This is our first step out of the urban world and toward the jungle, but it is nonetheless a concrete structure and orderly, with people inside dressed in white coats, taking purposeful strides.

The nurse who shows us around explains they can't handle much more than minor surgery: emergency C-sections, an appendectomy here or there, and once a month when the eye team comes through, cataract surgery. They send anything more complicated on to Kanchanaburi, which can handle a few more procedures, but basically anything requiring more than a quick yank and a few stitches gets sent to Bangkok.

As the hospital staff explains to us, the problem is that the refugees sent to Bangkok are entitled to medical care only if it is a life-and-death emergency. This leaves hundreds of refugees with severe, debilitating ailments that limit their mobility and self-reliance, and can eventually kill them. If it won't kill them in a day or two, however, it's not considered an emergency, and it's difficult for them to get help in Thai hospitals.

A hemorrhaging limb is one thing, a missing limb another. The first will receive surgery, the second, nothing. That is where we and a few other NGOs come in, each of us specializing in aid to a particular group of refugees or in help for a particular type of problem, from prostheses to children's nutritional needs.

After a brief visit to this hospital we continue toward Halockhani, deeper toward the heart of the matter. The earth here is a deep russet, the color of my shirt. In dry spots it is the color of light bark. Elsewhere it is an unnatural and gorgeous red. The road is an hour-long gouge in the hills that rise around us in a tangle of torn branches and impassable, chaotic grasses.

I find myself depressed, thinking I wear the colors of the earth and espouse a return-to-nature ideology, but the thought of living in a place like this frightens me. Barefoot indigenous people bend up the trail with bulky bundles on their backs. Great trees lie smashed on the road or jut out of the hillside like huge splintered bones, the remains of something ancient and ominous. "Who cut these trees?" I ask, hoping that some industrious, though non-ecology-minded villagers have done this work.

"No one," says the driver. "It is the wind."

This is half what I expected to hear, half what I was afraid of. Nature wild and powerful tears down the ruined towers of trees. What must it feel like to live where you see daily the power of the elements? How small it must make a person feel. No wonder we build skyscrapers and machines that tower over us. No wonder we rip up the land and cut down the trees whenever we get the chance. We are trying to exorcize our primal terrors; we are trying to make something of ourselves. We thumb our noses at nature and say, "So there."

One waist-high tree blocks the road altogether. We bump to a stop, back up, the tires groaning through the mud. Then we turn off the road and bounce along a passage narrow as a footpath. It is overgrown and uneven and looks as if the forest has reached out to reclaim what humanity has sought to make its own.

We pass Karen villages and get stuck in the mud. Maria says that at the height of the rainy season the road will be completely impassable by truck.

"Then what?" I ask.

"Then we will stay," she says. "We will move in and not leave until the rains let up and the road opens. This is one of the last few weeks we can get through. You came just in time."

The truck passes through the border check, and there we are on the other side, in Burma at last, though it is a wandering, vague sort of border and like many things, contested. Maria says the authorities mark the border at a different tree each week.

The truck stops, and thinking we have arrived in some border village, I ask in surprise, "Where are we?"

"Halockhani, *thung leew*," says the driver. "Halockhani. We have arrived." I had assumed that what I saw before me was a long-standing settlement, a large one at that, not a makeshift camp erected in a hurry by people forced to move only a few months ago.

The truck parks, and I am sick with hunger and motion sickness and a strange sort of dread. Into this wilderness almost seven thousand people have been forced against their will along a road that will seal itself off in a few weeks.

Though dangerous, the camp is not without beauty. Obvious pride has been taken in the woven bamboo walls of the traditional Mon houses. On spacious porches babies bob up and down in nets of colorful string attached to the roof. A pig, two goats, a cow, and a pony wander down the muddy lanes of the valley.

Puppies tussle under the porches, and well-kept dogs, chickens, and a few chicks roll, peck, or squawk in the cool mud.

We walk to the end of the main part of the village, but there's another part hidden beyond the trees.

"The village gets bigger every time I walk through it," says Maria. "Now it takes an hour to walk the length of it. And every day more refugees come."

Children pass us carrying water buckets on their heads. Some stop to watch us watching them. Others shy away. Matthew, always great with a camera, gets stunning shots of small girls, resting in the shade a moment, with buckets half their size teetering on their heads.

Maria is eager to show us the hospital, a small thatched bamboo hut with maybe thirty people, mostly women and children, lying on a bare bamboo floor. One baby is dreadfully malnourished. Matthew explains that the swollen belly of this baby and some of the others is not just lack of food; it is a sign of chronic malaria.

A little boy lies in the corner, waiting for an injection. He screams and screams, while the cheerful and business-like medics get briskly to work.

It strikes me that something is not quite right, something is missing. "This is the hospital?"

"Yes, until we can build a bigger one on the cleared space next door."

I look around. It is not the size that bothers me. It's something else. I look up at the ceiling. I look at the bare walls. And it hits me. "You have no electricity."

"Of course not."

"There are no lights?"

"No."

"No generator?"

"Nope."

"So you have no x-ray machine."

"X-ray machine! Are you kidding?"

"Can you do any surgery here?"

She looks as though she might laugh. "Nuh-uh. No surgery."

"What do you treat here?"

"Come on, I'll show you the lab." She takes me three steps to the outside balcony and stops beside a small table with vitamins, a few basic medications, and syringes. I bump into her back, having expected a longer journey. "Well, here it is, everything we have," she says. "This is it," she says. "Voilà. Finis."

"What happens when people have malaria, particularly cerebral malaria?"

"A lot of them die. Especially during the rainy season."

"Have you had it?" I ask.

"Not yet." She smiles.

"If there is an emergency, if someone gets sick or seriously injured, what then?"

"There was a serious case just this week," she says. "It was at night. I had already left with the truck, so there was no vehicle. Two men put the injured refugee in a blanket that they tied to sticks, making a hammock. Then they walked over the mountain in the dark, through the mud, in their bare feet. It took them six hours, but they eventually got into Thailand and went to the Christian hospital where we were this morning."

Great, I think, and there, unless he needs a C-section or an appendectomy, he's pretty much out of luck.

Despite the hardships, the village is stunning in the tropical afternoon light. The sloping green hillsides are speckled with the bristly stumps of burned trees like a five o'clock shadow on the earth. Nestled in the cleft of the steep valley are hundreds of thatched-bamboo houses with the cross-woven walls particular to the Mon. Small stores have sprung up on peoples' porches with laundry soap, Coke, and dried squid.

While Maria chats with a refugee in Mon, a man walks by us with a video under his arm. Others fall in line behind him.

"Hey, I thought you said there's no electricity," I say.

"I said there's no regular electricity. Nothing for the hospital. But there's a small generator somewhere, and you can always find enough power for a video. Video is *very* important."

We sit and drink Cokes under an awning at a rattan table surrounded by stools. I have two and am still thirsty. I think I've never been this hot and thirsty in my life. Maria smokes.

Matthew tells us that it is the housewives of America who have the real power. "If we could just get them to boycott Thai goods, maybe we could pressure the Thais into turning this around."

Maria blows smoke out her mouth and waves dismissively. "That will never happen. People buy what's cheap."

Matthew falls silent after that, probably wondering if it's true, caught between faith in people's goodness and despair in their ignorance and worship of convenience. He is, after all, a man of faith. Like me, he is addicted to the belief that we can accomplish something, that we can take evil into our hearts and turn it into something good, that we can do something useful. There is something unsettling about Maria's casual dismissal of his analysis. He feels it. I feel it. We glance at each other and look away, slightly embarrassed.

Matthew and I have been in each other's company long enough that we make the same assumptions about the world. When we run into a perspective outside our circle of belief, when someone hears our dreams and our plans and raises an eyebrow that reveals more than they can say about how naive they feel we are, when they shrug and go on smoking, it is discouraging. It invites us to admit that underneath our own inflated rhetoric, we ourselves doubt whether anything can be done.

Doubt is not something we want to admit. So much of our identity and our faith are hinged on hope. If we allow ourselves to believe we have no power to change the world, it feels as if we are admitting we are impostors. It feels as if there is no God. So when Maria says change is not possible, we ignore her, not trusting ourselves even to argue with her, for fear our own doubts would be betrayed by the sounds of our voices. We take another swig of Coke. We look away. We change the subject.

While we sit, the earth transforms itself. The sun comes out, and the hillside gleams a golden green, like the underside of young leaves in a forest. Men are outside their huts, leveling small plots of earth on the nearly vertical hill, hollowing out tiny terrace gardens. Red-brown, bald patches of soil are scraped from the earth, ready to receive seed.

Maria follows my eye. "It is the only good thing about their being back in Burma. In Thailand they were forbidden to plant anything. Here, they can begin to grow their own food. That is, of course, as long as they aren't attacked. Every day the refugee camp gets bigger. As it spreads out, it gets closer to the Burmese military camp. So they plant, they pretend to hope, and no one says what we think, what we are afraid of. But in our hearts we know there is danger just around the next bend in the road."

* * *

We return to Bangkok, where every month reports come to border consortium, the gathering of NGOs who work with refugees. The recent reports are that the refugees at Halockhani are afraid. From the minute they were pushed across that border, the refugees have known that the peace would be temporary.

They repeatedly send word of their fears of attack to the NGOs. They beg the UNHCR to come see their situation. They write open letters to the international community. For months they have asked for help. But for months no help has come.

The inevitable finally happens on July 21, 1994. The Burmese 62nd Battalion overruns the refugee camp at Halockhani. They set fire to the huts, and one entire section of the camp burns to the ground. They kidnap sixteen refugees, some of whom later claim they were tortured.

The story makes Matthew so angry he can hardly speak. He is furious at the Thai and Burmese authorities, disgusted at the relief groups, and even irritated at the Mon themselves. "The Mon always want to do things quietly. But where does it get us? The Mon refugees, the monks, and all the NGOs have been very quiet during this whole process. The Mon are afraid if they make a fuss, they will be thrown out of Thailand or imprisoned. The NGOs are afraid that if they speak publicly, they will lose their visas. We have all sat by and tried to be polite. And while we were sitting by, the Thai soldiers relocated nearly seven thousand Mon across the border into Burma, against their will. While we sat by, more and more refugees were arrested. While we sat by, the temple was raided again and again by police. While we sat by, police robbed refugees of every baht, saying a bribe would keep them out of prison. Then they sent them to prison anyway, without even the money they need to get to the border at the end of their sentence. While we sat by, the UNHCR cut allowances to the Mon and other indigenous, making it impossible for them to survive while waiting for resettlement."

Matthew is close to shouting. There is a prophetic gleam in his eye, a note of absolute truth in his voice, the voice of someone willing to say the truth no one else will speak aloud. It is absolutely true that we all have been mostly silent, mostly acquiescent, and that the refugees have paid for our silence.

We NGOs always have an excuse; we have it ready at hand, in case anyone is interested. We claim we are looking at the bigger picture when we are really looking at our own self-interest. We ask, "If we are dismissed from Thailand, who will care for the refugees?" And we know if we make Thailand's inhumanity too public, we risk our visas. But what the refugees need most is not the sacks of rice the international agencies provide for them—which is so little that they still go hungry, so nutritionally incomplete, they get beriberi. What they need is justice. True justice is always the bigger picture, and while we were counting sacks of rice, I think perhaps we missed it.

The attack on Halockhani is brief—a warning, not a massacre. But the photos that reach us are dreadful. Mon woven houses smolder in the rain. Families with their one pot, their little bag of rice for the week, huddle under a blue tarp. Others try to dig their few belongings out of scarred patches of burned earth.

It may have been only a warning, but the Mon take it seriously. They do the only sensible thing. They pick up their children, their one change of clothes, their scraggly chickens, and they walk out of what is left of Halockhani, their huts still smoking behind them. They set out with everything they own on their backs, barefoot or in flip-flops, into the great lonely woodlands, over the hills, in the mud, toward the border, toward Sangkhlaburi, Thailand, and relative safety.

What happens next is unbelievable.

"Have you heard the news?" Phra Dala Non asks.

"What news?"

"The Thai authorities are blocking the roads at the border. They gave the Mon refugees until August 10 to return to Halockhani. The refugees refused. Now the refugees are trapped between Burmese soldiers on one side and Thai soldiers on the other. The Thai 9th Division is blocking all international relief supplies from getting to the refugees. The refugees are running out of food. They have no water, so are drinking whatever they find. Many are sick with diarrhea or malaria. Neither food nor medicine can reach them. One Mon man died from malaria because the soldiers would not let him go to the hospital on the Thai side of the border. The Thai and Burmese governments both want to force the Mon back to Burma. The Thai soldiers have told the refugees they will let the relief agencies get rice and medicine to them only if they will return to Halockhani."

"I don't believe it. They wouldn't. They couldn't. No human being would do that. Those Mon refugees are mostly children."

"Yes, they are mostly children. Now they are hungry children. They are down to one or two days of provisions, and even that is only rice soup with some roots."

"So what happens now?"

"Now they begin to starve."

Matthew decides our first and best recourse is to go public internationally. It's already public in Thailand, but maybe a little international pressure could be brought to bear. We contact the press in the United States. We are on the phone daily with the Mon National Relief Committee headquarters at the border. Monks from Bangkok shuttle between the border offices and Bangkok, bringing news in all directions, which we then send on to the States.

It is a futile effort, a complete failure. The American media aren't interested. I'm sorry, they say, but we already *have* our overseas story for the month—the American public isn't very interested in what happens in the rest of the world. Burma? they ask. The American public doesn't know much about Burma, unless it's about Aung San Suu Kyi. Now you get us a nice juicy story on her, and we'll print it. Who ever heard of the Mon? Too depressing, they say, but not exciting enough. How many refugees? Only seven thousand? That's not enough. Now if the children do actually starve to death, you call us back. That might be newsworthy.

"Now what?" I ask Matthew.

Matthew decides there's only one recourse left, only one person who might be called on to intervene: the president of the United States.

"You want us to write to the president?" I ask, alarmed.

Presidents are not my specialty. They're not in my line of vision. What would I say to a president? I get as far as "Dear Mr. President," then stare at the white paper. I think of writing HELP in big letters, but think it would be taken facetiously. I chew on my pen and go to answer the door. The Mon have begun to arrive to use the typewriter and computer for their own letters to various agencies and heads of state. They are writing to the Thai prime minister. They are writing to the king.

Soon the house is full of refugees. There are monks or students in every corner. Members of the Mon National Relief Committee are up at the border clicking away at their computers. Phones are ringing; faxes are humming in and out. The printer is chugging like a steam engine. Everywhere I step there is a refugee.

I go into the living room for a moment to rest and find Phra Dhamma curled up in a corner of the couch, sound asleep.

I return to my letter. It is still blank apart from the greeting. How silly I feel writing those three words, "Dear Mr. President." Will my little letter ever reach the president? He probably has more employees just opening letters than our community has members. And if it ever reaches him, what will he think of it? Yet I love the innocence of this—the belief our president might want to hear from us in this crisis, that he might do something to make things better. I'm unconvinced, but I don't have any better ideas.

In an hour, the Mon begin bringing drafts of their letters to Matthew to check over their English. Matthew reads, then shakes his head. He has been trying to get them to consider their audience, without much success. "No! No! No! No Golden Bob. No Burmese kings kidnapping Mon queens. No Lord Buddha flying through the air. No two hundred years of history! You tell me you have an emergency. So, O.K., what's your emergency? People in my country aren't very patient—they'll want to read your main point quickly. If you're upset about something, then tell us up front what it is, what is happening *now*! Today!"

Our enthusiasm for the present mostly baffles the Mon. "Um, Wicki," says Phra Dhamma, "where do I put the part about thirty years of cultural oppression?" He is writing a letter to the United States Congress.

"I've begun with a brief history of the Mon nation," says one of the students, showing me three pages of writing, every word of which is indecipherable, because it is in Mon. "This explains the significance of the Hongsawatoi period."

"You might want to begin with what is happening now," I suggest sweetly, thinking Matthew will have a nervous breakdown if he sees this. "This is an emergency, isn't it?"

"Ah," he says, surprised. "Start with today!"

It is not that the Mon don't care about the hungry children. They do. More than we and with more right. That is the concern that brought them to the house, which propelled them out of silence, and thus out of safety, and into speech. It is just that the fate of the children fits into a cultural landscape for them. Their hunger is a single point in a constellation of events that includes the slaughter of three thousand monks during what the Mon refer to as their "holocaust" more than two hundred years ago, forty years of civil war, the torture and imprisonment of Mon dissidents. It is not that they lack a sense of immediacy, it is just that nothing exists for them without its context.

Nor is it that we have a truer and deeper sense of the immediate. It is simply that we lack a sense of history and in its absence the present swells to fill the vacuum.

After a few days of chaotic letter writing, we settle down to wait. As Mary at the Australian embassy says, "We can only do what we can do." We have done everything we could think of and now have only a heaviness in the pit of our stomachs, as we wonder what will happen to the Mon who are caught between two nations. What will happen to the hungry children?

A week passes. Neither the UNHCR, nor our letters, nor anyone else has had any effect on the Thai government. It is an impasse.

I call the Mon National Relief Committee at the border. The Mon themselves have found a solution regarding the hunger of their children. They have begun moving back to Burma. We failed to rouse the world, and they accept our failure.

The refugees' fear of attack is something to worry about tomorrow. The hunger of their children is a constant, irreversible fact. It is now. They are too sensible and too practical to sacrifice their children today out of fear of what may happen tomorrow. So they carry their children away from starvation, even if it is to move back toward danger.

Phra Dala Non calls again. The news today is that although they have begun to move, the hungry refugees who have arrived at Halockhani have been told there will still be no food until everyone has returned. Diabolical, isn't it? Barbaric. And ingenious. Without burning one hut, without firing one weapon the Thai government has repatriated more than six thousand refugees against their will. If only those of us who claim to be servants of justice and peace could act with this level of creativity, this energy, this single-mindedness.

I think of writing to the president and begin to laugh. The naiveté of that gesture, the extravagance of it—whatever made us take ourselves so seriously? Neither the president nor anyone else intervened. They didn't even bother to answer, and now it is too late.

And yet, despite our failure, writing to presidents has a great appeal. There is a quirky kind of ambition in me, a kind of romance. The Mon seem to feel it, too. "I want a copy of the article from Sunday," says Phra Dhamma. "The one where the Mon appeal to the king. Be sure to save it for me."

I reread my own letter to Washington and feel delighted despite its absurdity. We're lost, I think. But we have written to presidents and kings.

When Monland Is Free

One day, after the crisis is over, Phra Dhamma looks up from a Coke he is nursing instead of eating lunch. "Wicki," he asks, "what do you think of the Mon going to live in other countries? Do you think we should go? Do you think I should really go if I am accepted?"

"What will happen if you don't?" I ask.

His face darkens. He says nothing.

"Will they arrest you if you go back to Burma?"

"Yes."

"Do you think you will be tortured? Killed?"

He doesn't answer.

I think back to my encounter with Phra Banyaa. I let him leave my life without listening to his stories. Determined not to make the same mistake with Phra Dhamma, I ask him what he is remembering.

He looks at me sadly. "I saw things. Terrible things."

"Tell me."

"I saw a man tortured in front of me. He was a Mon villager, and the Burmese military suspected him of helping the Mon army or being in the Mon army. So they stood around him with their guns. They took out a big knife. They asked him questions he wouldn't answer. He looked very scared, standing there with the soldiers around him. The soldiers said, 'What is the matter with you? What are you looking at with those big eyes of yours?' Then they cut his face, cut around his eyes. They said, 'Maybe you won't answer because you can't hear us. Maybe there is something wrong with your ears.' And they cut off his ear. Then they said, 'What? Still you cannot say anything? Then we know what is wrong with you.' And they cut his tongue. Then they said, 'Do you want to live? If you want to live, run. Run for your life.'"

"You saw all this? You saw it with your own eyes?"

"I was standing as close to him as I am to you now."

"So where is he now, this man they tortured? Did he live?"

Phra Dhamma looks surprised. He looks disappointed. I have not understood. "No. He is dead. They killed him."

"But you said . . . but they said . . . Were his injuries too great? Didn't he run? Couldn't he run?"

"He ran. He got up and ran, bleeding. He got about ten steps away. Then the soldiers picked up guns and shot him in the back."

I sit in silence for a while and think about what Phra Dhamma has told me. For every visible injury we treat, there are a thousand invisible ones that will never heal. Seeds of destruction take root in the human heart, and even among those who long for peace, they call to our darker instincts and urge us to violence. Perhaps Phra Dhamma is thinking something similar. He sits quietly, looking thoughtful. He has told me before of his struggles to remain true in his heart to Buddhist teaching, to be a man of peace in spirit as well as in word and deed. "Sometimes I just get so excited," he says, "I can't make myself calm down. My heart beats and beats its anger, and I cannot make the anger be quiet."

After a long silence I ask, "So what do you think you'll do? Will you go to Australia if they accept you?"

"Maybe," he says. "But what then? What if the Mon forget? What if they do nothing about Burma in these other countries? Then what good is it for them to go?"

"This is a difficult problem," I agree, "because they will forget. You will forget. You will go to Australia, and the first year you will think about the Mon. But then you will have to get a job, try to survive, fit in. For some years you will think only about coming back to Monland. But then you will meet someone and fall in love, get married. In the end you will think only about buying a television, a microwave, a car. You may not come back even if you can. You will try to tell your children about the Mon, about what it means to be Mon. But they will not want to be Mon. They will want to be Australian. They may even be ashamed if you speak Mon to them in front of their friends. I want you to go to Australia, if you want to go, if it will make you safe. But I worry about it, too. There is a lot about Western culture that will be hard for a Mon person to understand. You remember when you were afraid of being dependent on Burmese?"

He says simply, "I thought they would kill me."

I suppose I had understood this, but it is a surprise to hear it so starkly put.

"But this is the way the West is," I explain. "To people in the West, Mon and Burmese are the same thing. The things that matter to you are not important over there and can never be explained. I will be honest with you—it will be very lonely. You will be very far away from your people."

Phra Dhamma looks at his Coke can. "My people," he says sadly.

"If you all leave, the Mon leaders will be scattered," I go on. "This is something you must think about. You will be in many different nations. And who will be left to lead the Mon? These are the end times, Phra Dhamma. Not only for you, but for many peoples like you. All over the world. How long do the Mon have to remain what they are now? A generation? Less? Pretty soon there will be no people like the Mon—the whole world will forget who they once were."

He is silent in his thoughts. Then to my surprise he begins to speak of a free Mon State. "When Monland is free I will return," he promises.

Over the next few days I hear that phrase several times: "When Monland is free." The monks and students say this in the face of all evidence, in the face of their own lost hope. It is not so much a statement of human plans as an invocation of something mythic. An icon. An amulet. The sound of these words sends tingles up my spine.

I have heard these words before, I think. Not these words exactly, but something like them. These are the words of a people in exile.

This is a people who remember something good and holy but entirely human: a childhood in the village, the sound of their mothers' voices. Now cut off, alone, they invent a future in which this world is possible again. But in the wilderness of their exile the image acquires weight. It becomes more than a village, more than a mother's voice. It becomes redemptive, universal, perfect.

Yes, I have heard these words before, I think. I hear the cry of the Mon as it reverberates through my own culture, the history of my people. It is the call that grows luminous with time. It is the cry for the lost and future city. This is Camelot. This is the promise of the New Jerusalem. It is every story that comforts us, but that we do not believe.

As Phra Dhamma has revealed something of himself and his beliefs, perhaps he now wishes me to reveal something of mine. On the way home he asks, out of the blue, "Wicki, can you tell me the story of, how do you say it, Jesus Chreest?"

For a little while we chug down the road in silence while I think of how to begin. Then careening through the smoggy and congested streets of Bangkok, shuttling between the wat, where the wounded lie hidden, and the hospital, where pain and healing merge, I tell him the story of my ancestors, the people called the Jews, and of the Romans and the slaughter of the innocents, and of the life of Jesus. I tell him how in the end Jesus was murdered, executed as a criminal, betrayed by one of his friends. I tell him of the Christian beliefs in incarnation and resurrection.

I tell him what we believe Jesus left us, the teachings by which we who call ourselves his followers are trying to live, especially the one great commandment: to love our neighbors as ourselves.

Phra Dhamma listens to the story, but when I finish my exposition of Jesus' teaching, his eyes widen and he is speechless for a moment. "But," he exclaims at last, "don't you see? Don't you understand? It is the same for us. The teaching of the Buddha is this same teaching. All along we thought we were so different, but we have been walking the same path."

That night I turn out the lights and listen to music before bed. In the darkness you can see the city in its true shape. The abandoned warehouse behind our apartment, the empty parking lot, the man who goes out in his sarong to bathe in the gray concrete cistern in the corner, the buses whizzing by, and in the distance, lights, towers, the bridge. Clouds, stars. My heart searches for Phra Dhamma and finds him, as it always does, in some pocket of myself.

While I think of him, my imagination turns, as it does in moments of crisis or of revelation, to a hill in Aberystwyth, Wales, where I went to graduate school, and where I once had a vision. Wales is a pretty respectable place to have visions, with its wet, brooding weather, its mist-covered hills, and its respect for poets, romantics, and madmen.

One evening shortly after Christmas, I went up the hill in the darkness to nurse my loneliness and self-pity at being in a foreign country and without family during the holidays, even though I knew then as I know now that I choose such distant ports of call in part so I won't have to face the fact that I still feel lonely when I'm with my family.

It was very dark, and somewhere in the distance, very faintly, I could hear the Celtic Sea. As I listened, my breathing slowed, and I began to pray. Perhaps I fell asleep. All of a sudden I was overwhelmed with solitariness and terror and thought I was up in the deep emptiness of space, traveling between the cold and distant stars. Then I turned and looked beneath me, and there was our blue planet, spinning slowly in the darkness of space. Only, I did not see the earth flattened out, as in the pictures from the moon. I did not see it as one-dimensional or a globe cut up like the skin of an orange as in maps.

I saw it whole. I saw all sides of it at once. I saw, at the same time, the half turned toward darkness and the half turned toward the sun. I heard all the bustle of humanity, the prayers and the songs, the terror and the sleeping children, the fighting and the dancing, coming from millions of souls, all at once.

In that moment it seemed that the truest part of me spoke into my heart. And I knew that in my little life, I would travel far. I would see the other side of the globe. Sometimes when I lie down at night, particularly in moments of crisis or doubt, I see it still, the world complete, the world held whole, as in the eyes of God.

As I lie down tonight, I see it again, that earth spinning above me, seen from all sides at once. And I think I understand the image in a new way. I thought it meant I would travel. I thought it meant "Go and make yourself useful."

That's not what it means.

It means there is only one world. And it means the opposite. There are a million worlds within this world.

It is an image of the world we are sent not to build but to become together: a unified yet diverse human community. Unity is not assimilation. It is not same-ness. Nor does it flourish in situations of segregated equality. Unity is the companion of diversity, and it expresses itself through exchange and connectedness. Unity is a function not of identity but of relationship.

This is the dream of my generation, the dream of the unity of all life: to be content with our differences and not to be enemies; to find our essential unity without destroying our uniqueness.

The thought that I am part of a new kind of communal understanding comforts me but does not take away the pain of living. Perhaps it shouldn't. The human heart is made to understand departure, separation, death. And yet as I lie down to sleep, I feel a new kind of hope, a renewed commitment, a new clarity of vision. I don't know how far we will get, but I think our task is clear: to discover and celebrate the uniqueness of every person, every religion, every culture, and still to cross every boundary in love, until we find our true identity in being human together and our true family in one another.

One Step Forward

We have been waiting for what seems like forever for some news about Phra Dhamma's resettlement. We believe he needs only one more form from Australia and then we can go to the embassy to apply officially for his resettlement. That will not mean he is definitely going to be accepted, but it will be a step in that direction.

We wait and wait for the last form from Australia. Then one day the phone rings. "Uh, Wicki?" Phra Dhamma's voice briefly interrupts the noise of traffic.

"Hi, how are you, Phra Dhamma?"

"Fine." He says it distractedly, as if I have interrupted his train of thought. As if now he must start over, which probably he must, constructing sentences in his head, inventing, word by word, the syntax that will enlighten me.

"Today, Mary from the Australian embassy came to the wat. She looked at our papers. She says we have enough now. We can go to the embassy. Apply for resettlement. No need to wait for one more form."

"We can?" I burble. "When will we know for sure whether you can go to Australia? How long will it take to process the application? If they accept you, when would you leave?" I am like a child. Excitement and curiosity tumble out of my mouth. On the other end of the line, I can almost hear Phra Dhamma thinking. He draws in breath and tries to decide which of my questions to tackle first. As he tries to form an answer, I break the pool of his concentration with a new pebble, the question I want answered most urgently. "When can we go to the embassy to apply?"

We take turns suggesting different dates. Friday, Monday, sometime next week. He's O.K. with next week. I'm for yesterday. We settle on Friday. I do not say what I am afraid of: that soon I will return to the United States for a long assembly where the future of the community will be determined, and I desperately want to see Phra Dhamma's case secure before I go.

Early Friday morning I arrive at the wat with a ream of papers for him to fill out, cursing myself for not bringing them earlier. We compose ourselves on the floor. Not just Phra Dhamma and me, but also Phra Dala Non, who I hope will go through this soon enough himself and might as well learn the ropes.

Refugees and monks drift in and out to witness the flurry of activity. Another monk, Phra Tin Soe, is also applying for resettlement in Australia. He has already filled out his forms and written a neat essay on the back. Phra Dhamma's application is not nearly that far advanced. Spread around us are instructions in English, instructions in Burmese, and various documents, including Phra Dhamma's original autobiography, which is six pages long, and which he now needs to cram into the one page they give him on the back of an official form.

We take one question at a time. The first hurdle is the first line, which asks his "Given Name," "Family Name," and "Previous Name." Phra Dhamma pauses, his pen over the paper. Question number one, and we're already stumped. He looks at Phra Dala Non and me for help. I try to explain. "Family name. We also call it a 'last name.' Is any part of your name the same as the name of your father and mother? A name the whole family uses?"

He shakes his head. "No."

He can leave it blank, but it seems like a bad omen to apply to a Western country without a last name. On the other hand, there are no sensible categories on the form, such as "Monk's name" and "Layman's Name."

After conferring with Phra Dala Non, Phra Dhamma chooses to put the same thing in each of the three boxes: his monk's name and his layman's name all together.

We try to concentrate amid the clucks and coughs of curious onlookers leaning in at the door. The floor feels damp and cold under my thighs, and I shift my weight to get comfortable.

Things go better through the next several questions, until we hit the "character" part of the application. "Have you ever been declared mentally unsound?" Phra Dhamma reads us slowly from the form. He is scrunched down, his torso folded over his knees. Now he bobs up and puts his finger on the question. "What does this mean?"

"They're asking if anyone has ever told you you're crazy."

He gives me a look, bends back over, and checks the box "No."

He pops up again at "Do you have any hereditary disease?"

"It means do you have any disease that your mother, father, or grandparents also had?"

He shakes his head and bobs back down, ticking the "No" box. Another second, and he's up again. "Are you engaged in any activity, or do you plan to be engaged in any activity that would pose a threat to National Security?"

"They want to know if you are planning to overthrow the Australian government, do gun running, start a war, or anything like that."

He gives me an eloquent look, shakes his head, and begins to cluck and mutter. Down he goes again, and ticks "No."

The final time he comes up for air, it is for interpretation of a long passage that asks the applicant whether he has answered the questions truthfully and lists the unpleasant things they have in store for him if he has perjured himself.

"It means," I say, looking at his puzzled expression, "if you're telling the truth, sign here, and if you're lying about anything, you're in big trouble."

Phra Dhamma goes down again. Mutter, mutter. Cluck, cluck. He goes over the statement again, word by word, sounding it out.

"O.K.," he says, and confronts the signature box.

"Are you going to sign your monk's name or your lay name?" I ask, leaning over the form. He ignores me. He is concentrating. He is proud of his penmanship, which is usually extraordinary. He holds his pen above the paper with a painter's attention, pauses, then signs with a powerful artistic stroke. He looks up, pleased.

"Eh? What's that supposed to be?" I ask, alarmed. It is an exciting aesthetic experience but totally incomprehensible as a signature.

"It's my name!" Phra Dhamma says.

Phra Dala Non leans over to inspect. He nods. "Yes. That's his name. There's the D. There's the H. . . ."

"O.K., O.K.," I say. "Never mind." But I continue to glance surreptitiously over their shoulders, trying to make it out.

There is one more box before we get to the autobiography. It is for the person who assisted in filling out the form. "Now what?" asks Phra Dhamma.

"Did anyone help you with these forms?" I ask. He looks around him. The room is full of people who have each chipped in their two cents, and there are more at the windows. But there's room for only one name.

"How about you?" asks Phra Dhamma.

"How about Phra Dala Non?" I say, suspecting I have merely provided the entertainment. Any heavy-duty translating was done quietly by Phra Dala Non, without the drama and fuss I have brought to the proceedings. "It is Phra Dala Non who has translated into Mon."

Phra Dhamma prints Phra Dala Non's name in the box in neat letters and supplies the address. He leaves the "company" name blank. Beneath is another box to mark whether remuneration was required. They turn to me for clarification. "Does Phra Dhamma have to pay you for your assistance?" I ask.

They both look at me in amazement. Too bad, really, they think. So young to have lost her mind. "No?" I ask. "So O.K. So mark 'No.' "

Now it is Phra Dala Non's turn to sign that he has "translated these forms accurately into the language of the applicant." He takes the pen and pauses above the page. Then he flicks out his signature in a series of spins and flashes. He uses the pen aggressively like a weapon. I inspect the results as he hands the pen back to Phra Dhamma. It looks like a mangled spider web.

"What!? It looks like someone has had an accident here! It's totally unreadable! It's even worse than Phra Dhamma's!"

We collapse on the floor laughing. "I can read it," offers Phra Dhamma. "You see, D, A, L. . . ."

"Oh, brother," I say. "Never mind."

Now it is time for the autobiography. Phra Dhamma curls over himself, lying over his knee which is bent inward. He is very flexible. I have never seen anyone fold over himself so flatly and lie for so long. He's like a human paper clip, the bent angle of his leg lying beneath the arch of his shoulders. He reads each word softly while he writes it. The effect is a low buzzing sound, like a snore.

I think the Australian embassy will be glad to have this application over with. We have already called twice this morning, quick, nervous calls to ask what time they're open and whether we need an appointment. Phra Dala Non is afraid he hasn't understood, so he asks me to call again. I am afraid the embassy will be fed up with us before we even arrive. The voice on the other end of the phone tells me we must be there by 11:30. I look at the clock. It is close to eleven, and we're not nearly ready.

Finally, we squeeze into a cab and whiz up Satthorn Street. "What do we do if after all this they reject Phra Dhamma?" I ask.

"Tell them we'll demonstrate in front of the embassy," laughs Phra Dala Non.

We collect our tags at the gate and run up to the third floor, where it takes me ten minutes to figure out the system. I hear a woman behind the counter rudely telling someone else to take a number.

"Where is it?" he asks.

"By the wall."

"What wall?"

I am behind him in line to ask the same question, so I search the wall for the magic number, while the monks mill about in a clump. I take one number for all of us, and we edge into some seats, the monks sitting a row behind me.

"Look," says Phra Dhamma, leaning forward. "That man is Burmese."

It's true. The man next to me has the same forms Phra Dhamma and Phra Tin Soe have, only more of them. In fact, so many more it would take a briefcase to hold them all. His sponsor has written a letter for him. "Can I read it?" I ask, getting nosy. He hands it to me—it talks about a television show made about him and his wife and says there is no need to introduce him.

"There's a television show about you?" I ask jealously, thinking of the competition for resettlement. He smiles. I peruse the rest of his forms. "Phra Dhamma," I say, leaning over the back of the seat. "He has a birth certificate and certificates of education. Do you have any of these?"

"A what?"

"A birth certificate. You know, a paper saying you were born. Proof you were born."

He shakes his head impatiently. I don't know whether Mon people consider the fact that a person exists to be self-evident of birth, or whether when birth is in doubt, they lack confidence in the ability of a piece of paper to settle the matter. Or whether when the news comes that they are being hunted, the monks in hiding do not, in general, pause to stride out of their hiding place, approach the nearest soldier and say, "Excuse me, but before you torture and imprison me, I'd like a moment to go back for my birth certificate and perhaps some educational records in case they'll be wanting them in my application for asylum."

I hand the man's papers back to him and now he takes a look through ours. "Excuse me," he says, "but did you happen to read the instructions?"

"What instructions?"

"The very first line of the instructions says you must write in black ink and use only block letters."

I groan, looking at the pretty blue script of Phra Dhamma and Phra Tin Soe's applications. "Oh, well," says the man. "Do you have your pictures in order?"

Phra Tin Soe slaps his head and turns ash-colored. He has forgotten his pictures. "I brought," says Phra Dhamma, fishing in his pocket. He brings out two shots, one of him in a suit, one in a perfectly folded monk's robe, which cascades from his shoulder in equidistant pleats.

"Phra Dhamma!" I gasp. "When were these taken? They are supposed to be recent! You look like you're twelve years old in these!"

"Do not!" he says, insulted. "I did them only two months ago."

"Actually, he *is* twelve years old," supplies Phra Dala Non.

"What are your numbers?" asks the Burmese man.

"She has our number," says Phra Dhamma.

"One number?" The man shakes his head at us. "Each of you should have your own number."

Now Phra Dhamma and I slap our heads, and we all begin to giggle helplessly. According to the letter I originally received from the Quakers in Australia, we're still missing a form. We have no birth or educational records. One person has forgotten his pictures, we've written the applications in the wrong ink, and we can't figure out what to put in the name box. Now we've waited half an hour with the office about to close for lunch, and we have only one number between us.

I steal a look around the room. People are staring stolidly ahead in silence, like people in an elevator. Some have fallen asleep and are pitched at improbable angles, snoring slightly. Others are eyeing us back, no doubt trying to decide what to make of the three monks and the foreign woman giggling their heads off in the corner.

At last our number is called. Though the Burmese man has his own number, it comes after ours, and he suddenly jumps up and decides he will try his luck with us. Maybe he figures compared with us, he is a model of completeness. We go together and slide our applications under the counter window. The man's application goes through thickly, like a padded jacket. Phra Tin Soe's and Phra

Dhamma's slip through, looking meager. "Is it enough?" I ask the clerk, explaining the missing pictures and documents.

"It is enough," she says, smiling. "Go home now. We will let you know."

"Phew," I say on our way downstairs. "No need to demonstrate outside the embassy today."

When we get to the lobby we discover it has started to pour. The hard tropical rain drenches everything, flattening the grasses in the embassy gardens. We sit for a moment and contemplate our future.

"Hey," I say, suddenly getting an uncomfortable thought. "Phra Dhamma, did we write your NI number on the application?" That is the number that identifies him as a refugee.

He slaps his forehead again. "Ooo-eee! I forget," he says, disconsolate. "I'll go back." He goes to the door, but now it is lunch time, and the office will be closed for an hour. We wait another twenty minutes before it occurs to me that we were instructed to be here by 11:30. Maybe the office is not open on Friday afternoons. I ask the guard. Sure enough, immigration is closed for the day.

We go out into the rain slapping our foreheads.

The next morning Phra Dhamma stands by the computer looking at his bare feet and glancing at me shyly from the side.

"How are you?" I ask.

"Fit as a fiddle," he says, unconvincingly.

"Are you very worried about your application to Australia?" I ask with sympathy.

"Not that," he says, haltingly. "I think you are very angry with me yesterday when I forget my NI number. Is that right?"

I am shocked. "Angry? With you? No. Phra Dhamma, no! For something like that? Never, never. I promise."

"Oh," he says, not looking up. "I think you are angry." He is torn between relief and doubt. Tears come to my eyes. How will we ever understand each other? It could take years. And like a pressure behind my eyes is the thought that we don't have years. If this works, our time is almost up.

On Monday, I call the embassy to give them Phra Dhamma's NI number. "I see," says the pleasant voice on the other end. "What is your file number?"

"File number?" I ask stupidly.

"Yes, the number they gave you when you applied."

"But they didn't give us any number when we applied. Nothing at all."

"I see," she says again, this time more distantly. "Let me just check. What is his family name."

I groan. "That was a hard one," I say. "We couldn't quite figure out what to put in that box."

"You couldn't . . . !" she stops herself, battling between professional calm and astonishment. "What do you mean he doesn't know his family name?" she asks, still polite, but now resigned that this is not going to be an easy call.

"He's Mon. They don't have family names. Well, some do, but most don't. He doesn't. So we put all his names in the family box. His monk's name, his lay name, everything."

"I see," she says for the third time, but she sounds as though she's fading, as though she's growing transparent. "So, what are his names?"

I deliver them in the order we wrote them.

"We probably used the last one you listed as the family name," she says with renewed confidence. She checks the computer. "Hmmm. Nothing. Maybe we used the first one, then. What was that again?"

I supply it, and she clicks the computer keys. "Still nothing." She begins to type in other combinations. His names forward. His names backward. Nothing. His date of birth. His sponsor. His application date.

"It can't be," I wail. "Please. You can't lose this application. You can't!"

"Now, I'm sure that's a very rare thing," she says in a reassuring, motherly tone. "Imagine, an embassy losing an application!"

I happen to know that it's not rare at all. One refugee we know had his records lost three times by the UNHCR. And Phra Dhamma himself was one of the very first to apply to Canada, but they lost his application, and he had to start all over, not that it matters much, since they eventually rejected him anyway. Losses are made worse by the fact that many places, including the Australian embassy, warn you *not* to call and check up on an application, threatening that a call will slow things down. So people don't check for months. And only then do they realize the application is long gone.

I do not say all this to the woman on the phone—I just make a low moaning noise. "Don't worry," she says. "We'll find it. I promise. You send in the NI number. We'll do the rest."

I hang up and bite off what little is left of my nails, one after the other. Later, I report to Phra Dhamma, and we sigh together and shake our heads. Phra Dhamma slaps his forehead. "I meant to make a copy of my application, before we went. I wanted to make a copy to keep. But there was no time."

"Yes," I say, feeling guilty that I rushed us on Friday. "I meant to as well. And I was going to copy the blank forms in case we needed to redo them for any reason. But I forgot. So now we have no copy and no blank forms. All we can do is wait and hope."

I go home, and as I am unlocking the door the phone rings. It has stopped by the time the second bolt is undone, and I have missed it. As it is ringing I have the strongest sense it is Phra Dhamma. I rattle my way through the door into the kitchen, which is suddenly silent.

I go upstairs to the office and check my mail box. No letters from governments, TV shows, international organizations. No love letters. Nothing. I turn and find one of our community members pursuing me, cordless phone in hand. I have a sudden wave of exhaustion, a sense of my own inadequacy. "I didn't know where you were," she says, holding the phone out. I put the phone to my ear. It only emits a low, electric wail. I climb up two more flights of stairs to get nearer to the phone's source, but by now the caller is gone.

I sit glumly in my room and when the phone rings again, I run so hard I skid, afraid someone else will pick it up. It's Phra Dhamma. "How are you?" he asks.

"Fine, and you?"

"Fine. You tired?"

"Not really," I lie. "Are you?" We chitchat for a moment and then he says what is concerning him.

"Uh, Wicki, after you left I think I have forgotten something. I forgot to say thank you. Thank you so much."

I sit down in the hall and lean my back against the wall. "You don't have to thank me," I say. "I feel like I didn't do much."

"No," he says. "You try to help. I thank you all the way from the button to my heart."

"Well, you're welcome," I say, smiling. I am tempted to tell him the expression is "from the bottom of my heart," but then I realize he probably has it right. Certainly what I feel back for him has undone the buttons of my own heart.

Phra Dhamma has stood beside me in places where I have learned how deep human suffering can be, a companion on this journey of discovery and service. It is true we do not understand each other very well. Probably we never will. In its essence, every human relationship is a cultural journey, a leap into foreign territory. Who can say they understand each other? Most of us descend through layers of misunderstanding, until we arrive, if we are lucky, at the waters of intimacy. The willingness to take such a journey is important, maybe the most important thing, because for most of us, love does not come without conflict. Love does not seem to count for much, does not change much, does not save the world. But in the end it is all we have that really belongs to us.

Singing to the Dead

Things have been going well lately. Maybe too well. It makes me suspicious; things never go well for long.

Matthew is happier than I have seen him in a long time. He is spending more time with the children than usual and that always puts him in a good mood.

We have gotten the orphan boys into a Thai wat for school. They come home in the afternoon looking proud in their stiff uniforms. At school they are learning to be polite children, and someone must have taught them that politeness is expressed through waiing their parents and other adults when they arrive home. Lacking real parents, they have settled on Matthew and me.

One day Matthew and I are standing in the wat courtyard, our heads bent over receipts for the children when three of the boys come up beside us, wiggle themselves into the space between us, and give us both a wai. "*Sawatdii krup,*" each child murmurs over his folded hands. This is the essential Thai greeting for all occasions.

Matthew and I pause in our work and look suitably receptive, nodding at the three boys as each performs his gesture of respect. We smile indulgently at them, charmed, then go back to our fistfuls of papers, pointing to a questionable sum or routing through envelopes for elusive receipts. A few seconds later we hear a polite clearing of the throat and look down to find another child trying to step between us and catch our attention, his eyes tearing because he has been standing there with his hands folded in a wai and we have been ignoring him.

"Oh!" we say. "Sorry." We give him our most attentive, proud parental looks. He bows to us with a sigh of relief, and we begin to turn a third time toward our work. I happen to look behind us and realize the entire crop of orphan boys is standing there waiting to greet us in a line that stretches all the way across the courtyard.

Of course, the boys are not always quiet and orderly. Matthew sees to it that they are encouraged in creative play as well as in studious and demure behavior. Sometimes I think Matthew is the pied piper of Bangkok. After school hours his eye scans the compound and finds the wet boys spraying one another instead of washing, ten other boys playing with a jump rope, a small group lurking in the cool darkness at the back of the courtyard. "Time to study art," proclaims Matthew. "Follow me."

Boys come from everywhere, from nowhere. They steam about us, behind us, ahead of us, up the stairs, like foam on a wave. Up they go, taking the steep, narrow stairs two at a time in their tattered and ill-matching shorts and T-shirts. Up to the big cool room where we take off our shoes and sit on the slightly damp linoleum. The children line up in two or three rows. Most of them are between the ages of seven and ten.

"Today," says Matthew in Thai, "we will learn to draw a helicopter." They take the art pads he has bought them, large, rough pages for six baht a piece. They spread the paper and themselves over the floor. There are no chairs or desks in the room, only a big table up front. In the corner is a pile of blankets Matthew was able to get from a church down the street when the weather turned and the boys got cold. They live in this echoing, bare, cavelike room. They study here by day, and at night they roll themselves up in the wadded blankets and lie down on the damp floor in a row, curling together neatly like bowls in a dish rack.

Despite the emptiness, this is a pleasant room. The doors are big and wooden and swing out onto the small balcony and the stairs. Open, they let in a nice breeze. Diffuse light leaks through the windows, filling the room up softly. Maybe because it is so bare, the room has a sense of possibility in it. And because it is full of children, it is lively, like a word of joy on the verge of being shouted.

"This, children, is how to start." Matthew stands at a white board in front, his marker poised above the blank surface. The boys have sprawled over the floor now, cross-legged or on their bellies. One has fallen asleep in the corner, a bag on his rump like a turtle's shell. They are giggling and serious at once, their eyes on Matthew, their tongues between their teeth.

"First, draw a mango. You see, here it is. *Ma muang.*" Matthew draws a big mango on the board and the boys copy him. Lopsided mangos appear on all the white sheets. Mangos that look like moons, mangos that look like eggs. Mangos that look like mangos. "Now inside the mango you draw a banana. '*Kluay*.' See?"

Matthew has gotten this idea from a coloring book. There aren't enough to go around, so one has become his instructional art text. The children will draw the shapes themselves and then color them in. Voilà, instant coloring book. Matthew showed me the design earlier at the community house. The shape is remarkably simple and very effective. Just the sort of thing to attract a seven year old.

While he has plagiarized the shape, the pedagogical technique is uniquely his own: the order of the strokes, the mango and the banana: he has seen these possibilities in the forms on the page and called them out, named them, like Michelangelo calling shapes out of stone.

"Now add a Coke bottle top up here. Then a big circle even higher. Got it?"

All around me, helicopters are emerging on the sheets. Some look a little like space ships. Some look like fruit bowls. But most look very much like Matthew's. Matthew is now adding a little person inside the window of the helicopter. The person is waving.

Pleased with their success, the children are moving on to other things. They flip through their notebooks, where karate heroes throw kicks at strangely angled walls, or arthritic lions slouch through purple forests, and elephants bathe under the trumpeting fountains of their trunks. "Good," I say, nodding at the pictures they show me. "*Di di*." They do not seem to need this praise, but I feel useless otherwise and am not sure what other role I can play, and so settle for offering encouragement.

I roam the rows and come to a boy in back who has a reputation for being talented. He is bigger than the others and more passionate, laying large sweeps of color across the page. A group of admirers huddles around him, discussing his drawing. He has drawn his helicopter on a page with a blue ground and a green sky. "*Thammay na?* Why is the sky green?" I ask, hoping this literal-minded question will not interfere with his creativity.

He shakes his head, and the other children laugh. "*Thi ni, paa*," he explains. It is not sky but forest. The picture lurches for me into a new perspective. We are looking down on the helicopter, and beneath it are forest and sea. This is typical of my interactions with the Mon—they are always inviting me to see the world in a new way.

* * *

Matthew's concern for the Mon children goes beyond the temple boys. "A wo-man from the UNHCR called," he says one day, looking up from the typewriter, where he can usually be found for the hour between 10:30 and 11:30 A.M. on a work day. In between one class and the next, he pounds out letters to the editor, bulletins to Amnesty International, Human Rights Watch, or his congressman. Click, click on the keys. He rips the paper out as if he is snatching something away just in time. Then he rolls a new sheet in.

"Oh? What did she want?"

"She wants my help with a family," says Matthew. "The mother is dead. The father doesn't seem quite right. Maybe he's slightly retarded. Maybe he's just in shock, or malnourished. It's hard to tell. There are two children. A boy and a girl. Both very little. They've been living in the park. They have no money, no work, nowhere to go. I've got a room lined up for them, and I think I can find work for the father, but I'm worried."

"Why?"

"Because of the slowness of the father. How can a man like that look after two children? Especially while he's working. It's one thing to keep an eye on children in a village. But in the city, anything might happen. It's not as easy for a simple man here. Maybe I should have called a social service agency and had the children taken away, taken where they can be looked after properly, where they can be safe."

"You've decided not to?"

"The father may be simple, but he loves those children. They're all he has now. And they love him. They've already lost their mother. I couldn't bear to do it."

"Taking children away from a father is a serious decision. I'm sure you did the right thing. Perhaps you can keep an eye on the family. If the situation gets worse, you can reconsider."

The next time I hear about the family, they are doing well. Matthew has gotten them a room in a poor part of the city and found the man a job. "I think they'll be all right," he says. "With a room and some food in him, the father seemed to perk up."

A few weeks later I step into the office, wiping the salty sweat from my fore-head and asking cheerfully how everything is. Matthew wears his wild, sleepless look. He fiddles with his glasses while he tells me the story. I can tell from his face that I don't really want to hear his news. But when he finally ekes out the story, it is even worse than I expected. The little boy, left alone in the room while his father was at work, has electrocuted himself in the faulty wiring, and died.

Perhaps we take this family's story as an omen. It sours us. It seems to go against nature that children die. And when our efforts to keep them safe, to provide a future for them, result instead in death, we are disabused of any illusions that we have real power to make the world as we would wish it.

One might think we had had enough bad news for a while, but soon after the little boy's death, something happens that changes what I think is possible in the world.

One of the most chronic and frustrating problems of the refugees is cerebral malaria. Sometimes by the time the refugees realize it's not just the flu or regular malaria, it's too late to help them. They pick it up, unknowingly, as they cross the border, which seems to be one big cerebral malaria swamp.

Unfortunately, most refugees don't take their own pain seriously. They have so much of it. They have lived through regular, chronic malaria. They have lived through a war. They have seen their villages destroyed. They have lived through the arduous trip across the border. If they have the good fortune to make it all the way to Bangkok, at this point nothing worries them. Nothing hurries them. They are content.

So sometimes the fever surprises them. They tell themselves "Oh, it's nothing. It's the usual. It will pass." They take a little aspirin if they can get it. They lie down for a nap. And then as twenty-four hours go by and they realize they have never been this sick, that this is something untamed and unfamiliar, they find themselves slipping off into unconsciousness still in the middle of asking themselves what possibly could have gone wrong.

Matthew is stern with the monks at the wat. He tells them to call him right away if they notice someone has the fever. If they act in time, sometimes the refugee can be saved. And, to be honest, Matthew knows, it's so much cheaper if they get treatment early on. He's tired of the emergency calls that didn't need to be emergencies. The rush of adrenaline. The grief. The guilt.

One morning the monks greet him, then hang back at the classroom door. The older ones do not come in with the usual smiles and leisurely enthusiasm. The younger ones do not pull on each other's arms and tell jokes in Mon. They stand reluctantly at the door and politely ask him to come look at a sick man.

He is impatient to start teaching his English class. "O.K.," he says, "after class."

"You'd better come now," they say.

"Oh, God," Matthew says.

They never hurry him, they never insist. "Come now" means catastrophe, no matter how calmly they say it. Never mind the impassive faces, never mind the quiet hands, gently clasped in a posture of repose. He runs down the narrow stairs without stopping to put on his sandals.

In the refugee room a man is lying on the floor. He is barely breathing. Matthew carries him to a tuk tuk and attempts artificial respiration as they careen through the clogged and smoggy streets, the belching fumes. Matthew has no more money for the medical project, so signs the community's name to the hospital register as the responsible party.

The nurse figures out that this man is not Thai. He is a refugee. He is Burmese. He is illegal. She engages in a screaming match with Matthew. "What about the police?" she wails, wringing her hands.

"I'll take care of the police," growls Matthew. Then he adds, in a fury, "What's the matter with you? You should be an engineer, not a nurse."

The doctor is friendlier, efficient, and dressed in a crisp, white coat. He orders the dying man hooked up to what seems like every available machine. The man begins to breathe again and color comes back to his face.

Three days and several thousand dollars later, a full explanation comes from the doctor. The man has a mixture of ailments. He has TB. He has diabetes. He has cerebral malaria. All three are curable. The man is savable.

But it will cost.

"I have no more money," says Matthew. "No more." He is already nervous. The community is responsible for the bills so far, and the expense was unauthorized.

"It is regrettable," the doctor says. "If only we had seen him earlier." The doctor also has an organization to consider. The machines cost so much per hour, so much per day. He explains it all very carefully, adding it up for Matthew. To cure this man could take a month, two, three. "Who will pay?"

Matthew looks at the figure presented to him as if it is something distasteful. "I don't have that much," he says, "not nearly that much. Please. What can be done?"

"You must sign the release form," says the doctor. "He must be taken off these machines. He must leave the hospital. You must take him home."

"Leave the hospital? Home? This man is a refugee. He has no home. What will happen if he is taken off the machines?"

"He will die."

Matthew stares at the doctor, trying to think of something to say.

"You can see the problem, yes?" asks the doctor. "How can we treat this man? This man is not a citizen. He has no right to these services. Someone must pay for him. You say you cannot pay. How can we explain it if he dies here? Someone will ask questions. There is the law to think of. The police will ask why we took in this man who is not legal. He cannot die here. You should not have brought him here."

"I will not sign. I cannot. Have you no compassion? Are you not a Buddhist? This is not the way we do it in America," Matthew shouts, but he is not quite sure this is true.

Matthew begins to beg, and begging makes him angry. The doctor crosses his arms, and looks up at the clock behind Matthew's head. In his mind he has already left this scene, these unpleasant people with their loud voices and unreasonable demands.

"Someone must take responsibility," the doctor explains in his calmest voice. "It is your signature on the admittance form, no? You signed him in as the responsible party. Now you must sign to take him out."

"Give me time," says Matthew. "I will need some time."

"Time for what?"

"I need time to find a place for him to die."

The doctor nods. "I will give you an hour."

Matthew asks the monks if he can bring the man to the wat. They look at each other and at the floor. The Abbot is out of town. It is a big decision. An unexplainable body. It could bring trouble. "I will explain to the Abbot when he gets back," says Matthew. "I will take the responsibility." He is confident in the Abbot's answer.

Besides, it is one thing to ask; it is another thing just to come. A temple must take what is offered. The bowl of rice. The mangy dog. The broken bodies of the sick. They are all the same, they are all accepted. The monks can turn nothing away, neither gift nor burden.

When Matthew leaves the man to make arrangements at the wat, the man is lucid, though with the eyes of an animal that knows the smell of the butcher. When Matthew returns, the man is dazed. The doctor must have injected him with something powerful. Morphine maybe. Something to dull the edge of awareness. Matthew cannot decide whether this is some belated compassion or a last insult. He has no time to think about it.

The man is hooked up to some mobile machines to keep him alive on the journey back to the wat. The hospital is lending an ambulance. "There will be no charge for the ambulance," says the doctor, sheepish.

"Never mind that now," Matthew says angrily.

Everything is clear on the way out. The faces of the people in the waiting room, the two huge TVs on the wall. Matthew wants to smash one of them. Would the cost of them save this man's life? And if he destroyed them, would they spring up again, like magic, from some invisible and endless well of money that all nations in the world seem to have so long as it's not being spent on anything of worth?

Why is it, he wonders, that the debate is never about debatable things? No one questions the man-sized televisions. No one questions cars, or skyscrapers, or the amount spent on perfume or cosmetics or pet grooming or a thousand other silly enterprises. It is the things that seem obvious and irrefutable we end up arguing over. In this world, a man's life is debatable; television is not.

Matthew and the man and the monks and the ambulance driver move back through the dark streets in the ambulance, back the way they came, retracing the route from hope to silence. The screaming siren is annoying. It intrudes on their thoughts. One of the monks leans forward and taps the ambulance driver to turn the siren off. "We don't need that now," he says.

Matthew carries the man into the dark, empty room beneath the temple. He shoos out the curious and barks at adults to keep the children away. He lays the man on a rush mat on the cold, otherwise bare floor, and carefully unplugs all the machines as he has been taught to do. Then he sits down on the floor. Suddenly it is quiet. He is alone with the dying man.

He gathers the man up into his arms, holds him against his chest, rocks him for a little while. He talks to him quietly, "Don't be afraid." he whispers. "You are not alone."

And then Matthew begins to sing. He sings with the weight of the man leaning against him, the man's head slumped against his shoulder. He sings snatches of spirituals and songs from childhood half-remembered. He sings, though he knows the man does not understand English. And with whatever medication they have given him, perhaps he would not understand any language, not even his mother tongue. Perhaps some part of him is already gone, waiting somewhere else for the rest of him to catch up. Still, Matthew thinks, last moments may be important. Maybe as we leave the world, just as when we entered it, the small, lonely animal we are longs for some simple assurance beyond language. For a sense of companionship. A sense of ordinariness and humanity in the face of the immensity of the unknown, hovering just outside the perimeters of our lives.

So Matthew sings to him until he has no words left then trails off into wordless humming. He can feel the reverberations of his own deep voice in his chest, a comforting rumble, and he can hear his heart, also a kind of music, beating next to the man's ear.

After a while he notices the stillness in the room has deepened. He leans over and sees the rhythm of the man's breathing has stopped. It is shocking to have that rhythm stop. It seems unnatural. As if the oceans had stopped moving. As if he had just discovered this man was made out of wood. He feels like a solitary witness to something terrible. It is like being the only human being left on earth.

He lowers the man to the mat on the floor. Then he stands. He straightens his back, rubs his neck. He goes into the courtyard and calls the monks who enter the room behind him with a quiet bustle to make the funeral preparations.

He is both grateful for and resentful of this return of motion, of human noise, of purpose. He waits for a moment in silence, not doing anything, not going anywhere, just breathing in and out.

How long was he sitting in that room, he wonders, holding a dead man and singing to himself?

When Matthew tells me the story, I begin to despair. I am terrified by what Matthew has done. I am awed. This is what the world has reduced us to. This is what we are elevated to. To sing to the dying after we have exhausted all avenues, all possibilities, all our power. What sort of world is this, what sort of God is this, where those who work for good must relinquish the expectation that they can accomplish even simple things: to save one man dying of treatable diseases.

I suddenly feel the weight of all our failures. What have we really accomplished? I suppose when I set out to Asia, I expected to save the Mon, to save the world. But I have not saved it, whatever "saving" means. Sometimes it seems my goals have gotten smaller and smaller. I wanted to effect structural change, to ensure the future of a nation, a people. Perhaps Matthew started out the same way. We have learned to revise our expectations: mend one eye, get one man to freedom in a new country, save one family, one child, treat one man's treatable illness so that he may live to middle age.

To fail at the large, sweeping changes is one thing. Some steady self-knowledge may have held us back from taking ourselves quite that seriously. But to fail not only with the many but with the one—this is crushing. If we are this powerless, if we set our sights so small and still fall short, then what good is our work? And for those for whom work is our identity, it is hard to avoid asking what good are we ourselves? What do our lives mean?

Discouraged, I pour out my heart to two members of the community the next night. We are standing on the bus, squashed in with the multitudes, barreling down the garishly lit streets. The bus turns violently, wrenching our arms as we cling white-knuckled to the overhead bars. It is the least conducive place for a heart-to-heart, but once they ask me how I am, everything comes out in a torrent—all my disappointment and hopelessness and grief. "How can I continue to have hope in such a world?" I ask.

My friends listen to my long story in silence, their heads cocked with interest. "Do you know what Archbishop Romero said?" they ask.

"No."

"You must wean yourself from the need to have hope. Have faith instead."

I try on this concept. Faith, I think. Do I even know what that means anymore?

It is difficult not to feel orphaned, abandoned, and betrayed in moments of grief. We feel betrayed by religion as much as by circumstances. Buddhists believe in a reasonable and fair universe where what we give out ultimately returns to us. Jews and Christians believe in an all-powerful, good God who can rescue us, a God who can fix whatever is wrong like a parent soothing a fretful child.

But despite millennia of doctrine and philosophy, none of these traditions satisfactorily explains the chaos, brutality, and seeming randomness of life as we have come to know it. None of them gives enough reason, enough hope, enough of a promise of a bright future to heal the ache within us.

We get off the bus and enter the wat, where Matthew has joined the monks in evening prayer. We climb the stairs, and I see the familiar room, the many monks kowtowing to a statue of the Buddha. Incense curls up into the already spicy-smelling air. Many of the men have prayer beads wrapped around their wrists. They sit on their heels, their bare feet peeking out from beneath their orange robes, their soles dark with the dust from the floor. They bow to the Buddha not because the Buddha will come and save them but because he has shown them a way to cope with their pain.

Behind the monks sit the temple boys, sometimes praying, sometimes idly watching the ceiling or fidgeting.

And behind them all, alone, sits Matthew. He, too, sits on his heels, prayer beads wrapped in his hands. He doesn't know the chants, so he is simply silent. But he bows when the monks bow, setting his forehead against the floor in the oldest gesture of respect.

I look at Matthew praying not in the way of Catholics but not entirely in the way of Buddhist monks either, for we do not know the language, do not have the words. He prays this way not because he believes in the Buddha exactly, but because he wants to be one with this human community, who, like us, is engaged in the search for meaning and in the commitment to peace.

As I watch him it seems that we have gone beyond religion somehow, beyond the categories and laws and rituals that differentiate one tradition from another. We are in uncharted territory. If we have gone beyond where institutional religion can instruct us and comfort us, have we gone beyond faith as well, I wonder, or is faith something different? What was it Archbishop Romero was trying to say? Maybe this moment where we must choose between despair and ongoing courage is the threshold of a faith that cannot be destroyed by anything external.

The chanting of the monks rises around Matthew, enfolding him in the sound of prayer. I watch him and think that we have set down our idols, including our exaggerated attachment to the illusion of our own power. We have abandoned unrealistic expectations. We have set aside our overly simple childhood God who promised magic and a fair world. Without our illusions, our souls are bare. And maybe for the first time, whatever is true in the universe, whatever God really exists, will be able to break through and find us. Maybe for the first time we are ready to be found.

We are also ready to find and recognize one another, to commit to the difficult task of being community. Matthew closes his eyes and peace steals across his face. I breathe in the incense and the wet night air and think it is only our idols we have left behind, not one another, not love.

I think back to the day Phra Dhamma and I spoke of our religions. In the end, Phra Dhamma was right. We are on the same path. The wisest Christians and Buddhists teach the same lesson. We are not here for success. We are here to live the lives of human beings. The course of grace is more mysterious than a list of successes. The reign of God is not a checklist of tasks to be ticked off when completed. There is some goodness at work even in the growing room for compassion in a few hearts, in the loving encounter between people of very different cultures, in the reverent telling of the story.

Whatever salvation means, though in its final form it is a long way off for this world, whenever two strangers look at each other with understanding and love and commit themselves to a journey together, in some way maybe we are already saved.

The Face of God

For everyone who asks, receives; and the one who seeks,
finds; and to the one who knocks, the door will be opened.

MATTHEW 7:8

Who shall discover
The shining way of the law?

You shall, even as the man
Who seeks flowers
Finds the most beautiful,
The rarest.

FROM THE DHAMMAPADA,
TRANSLATED BY THOMAS BYROM

A Strange Reception

I expect to hear whether Phra Dhamma has been accepted for resettlement before I leave for the States to participate in a community assembly. But the bureaucratic process is sluggish, and we still have heard nothing one way or the other as I board the plane, so I leave in a state of unrelieved anxiety.

When I arrive in the States my life is rearranged for me. The assembly elects the leadership of the community. I am nominated, I am honored. But there are thirty-five other nominees, so I do not take it particularly seriously. I do not expect to be elected to the coordinating team. But I am.

I am thrilled. I am horrified. It is my dream job. It is about everything I believe in. The work will both use and expand my skills. But it is lousy timing. I accept the nomination with mixed feelings, and drink the celebratory champagne in tears.

The community gives me a month to wrap up my business in Thailand and return to headquarters in the United States to take up my new position.

I have been gone from Thailand less than two months, but by the time I get back to Bangkok, the city has rearranged itself. The gas station across from our house has been leveled. The Swenson's in Siam Center is gone, replaced by the more trendy Yogen Fruz, "The Taste of Tomorrow Today!" The sign on the plastic fruit display promises "*none fat.*"

Community members report that the traffic got so bad "even the Thais complained." The city tried rearranging the bus routes, but discovered that while this did nothing to improve the flow of traffic, it contributed significantly to the level of confusion. So they restored the original routes. The city changes so fast that I have been gone long enough for things to change and then revert. I find this depressing.

On my first day back in Bangkok, I stop by the river to feed the fish and think about how to break the news to Phra Dhamma and Phra Dala Non that I am leaving. A portion of the river is sectioned off by the nearby hotel to keep fish in an enclosure where they will be easily catchable at dinner time. Tourists stop to throw bread. As the bread falls into the water, the fish leap over one another in their hunger, writhing and wriggling, thrashing up into the dangerous air.

The fish with their flashing tails, their joy in the gift of bread, are unaware they are destined to be served up themselves for a tourist's dinner. Watching them, I think I understand why Buddhism, with its insistence on detachment, takes hold so deeply here. So many things, brief and glorious, present themselves in a flash, demanding to be loved. Our tendency is to hover somewhere between generosity and possession. To look with a kind of hunger at all we desire: the friend, the exotic culture, the child, the career, the illusion of self-importance. I think of all these and say, "*Mine. I want.*"

My own religion asks me to love without holding on too tight, and I suppose the Buddha knew everything would need our love, too, even though each bright thing would eventually leave us. Neither prophet meant for us to stop loving, I think, only to understand that what we love is not ours to keep.

The wat compound seems to have deteriorated since I was last here. Dirt, mud, ragged laundry, and trash are everywhere. Nai Nya Naa's daughter, Kyang San, is in the courtyard when I arrive. She looks at me sideways, as if she doesn't want to be caught staring. It is a look that says, "It can't be, can it?" She comes toward me, peering up intently, her smile growing. At last she puts up her arms to be lifted. I throw her up in the air, and then she recognizes me for sure. She begins to laugh.

She has borrowed some grown-up's flip-flops and they both fall off. They are three times bigger than her feet. My sunglasses fall off my head twice. I put her down and she picks them up for me, shaking her head at me. She takes my hand and tugs me toward the refugee room and her father. "Not yet," I say, though I know she doesn't understand. I tug in the other direction. Toward Phra Dhamma.

I find him in the computer room with Phra Dala Non. The monks have recently had their monthly head shaving and look lighter, newly shorn. The few hairs left on their bare scalps stick out at unlikely angles. There are old scars and small clear gouges where the hair will never grow again, whorls and swirls of hair follicles, individual as thumb prints. I look at them and feel so much for a minute I think of the metaphor in the movie *Little Buddha*, which I saw in the butchered airplane version on the way back to Thailand. "We are like tea. You can break the cup, but the tea is still tea." Here with these refugees I feel the integrity and fluidity of the human spirit. We seem to be all of one piece. Tea from a single pot, poured into separate cups.

Now comes the moment of truth. "Did anyone tell you about my new job?" I ask, half hoping someone will have filled them in, but knowing I'll be furious if they have.

They look at each other. "New job?"

"Phra Dhamma, you remember that dream you wrote me about when I was in the United States? The dream where you believe I will not come back to Thailand?"

"A lot of my dreams come true," he says.

"The dream about me was also true, in a way. There was an election in New York. A vote. You know 'vote'? I have been selected to be one of the leaders in our organization. I will be returning to New York to live. I have just come back to Thailand to say good-bye."

My voice breaks as I say this. Pain and pride mingle inside me. I look at them expectantly, waiting for the traditional Western response, the congratulations, the professions of undying friendship. There's only silence.

"How long will you be here?" Phra Dhamma asks at last.

"One month."

More silence.

"Why did you do it?" asks Phra Dhamma. "Why? You didn't have to take the job."

This is not the reception I was expecting, to say the least. "But I've been asked to be a leader," I say, noticing I sound more defensive than proud. "This is an important job. An opportunity. An honor."

Phra Dala Non is absolutely still. Phra Dhamma is unmoved. "You tell us this, and you aren't even crying? Teacher Jim cried when he left. He cried so hard his tears dripped off his chin. But you leave us, and you do not cry."

"Who is teacher Jim?" I ask helplessly. They point to a picture on the wall. A white American grins out among many monks' faces. In another picture he sits on the floor and wais a long line of monks. "What's he doing?"

"Presenting a monk's robe."

"When was he here?"

"He was here for six weeks. He went back to New York now. We wanted to see him off at the airport, but he said he'd cry so hard he'd never stop."

I look at the pictures and feel wildly jealous. I've been replaced and I haven't even left yet. I am afraid I will start crying, so I slip to the floor and try to change the subject. I ask for a piece of paper. "We need to plan for the meeting with the congressional delegation," I say, referring to one of our few recent triumphs. The United States Congress is sending a delegation to figure out what on earth is really happening on the Thai-Burma border.

The monks also scoot to the floor, but Phra Dhamma is not to be put off. "Is it because you're a lay person?" he asks. "You cannot stay and work with the priests because you are lay?"

"Not exactly," I say.

"Why then? Explain it to me. Try."

I sigh. "I know we Americans look very secure to you. Our organization looks stable and rich, but it's not. We have a lot of problems. I think I can help. I think I can make a difference."

"You knew about this before you left." It is an accusation. "You are fed up with us."

"Phra Dhamma," I say, incredulous, "are you mad at me?"

"Yes. Mad."

To myself, I acknowledge how completely unfair it is to leave them now. What made me think I could breeze in and out of their lives, fix a few things or imagine I had fixed a few things, and when it suited me, trot on home, pleased with myself. I struggle to be honest with him, to tell the most complicated version of the truth. "It is true it is sometimes hard to work here in Thailand. This is a hard job. I have been away from America for six years. That's a long time."

"I do understand you," he says more gently. "I understand it is good to take a job in your own country. I am happy for my friend who is a leader, who is elected. But I am sad because you are leaving. I feel I am losing one of my best friends."

"You're not losing me. I'm just going to be your friend from a little farther away."

"I'm already missing you," he says.

"No need to miss me yet. I'm still here."

The next day I am at the wat with Phra Dhamma and Phra Dala Non in the computer room. I chat with Phra Dala Non awhile. Phra Dhamma is silent. "What are you doing?" I ask.

"I am refusing to miss you," he says.

A Case of Stomachache

I am halfway packed and beginning to feel restless when Phra Dhamma calls. "Oh, hello, Phra Dhamma," I say, pleased with the distraction. "How are you?"

"Fit as a fiddle."

"I'm glad to hear it."

"Wicki," he asks, "are you very busy now?"

"Actually, I'm not. What's up?"

"Do you have time for one more sick refugee? We have one more patient."

"Sure," I say. "Who is it?"

"Is me."

"You! But you said you're fit as a fiddle!"

"Oh," says Phra Dhamma. "Was lying."

"What's the matter?"

"Stomachache," he says miserably.

For a moment I am alarmed. I think of all the things we've listed as stomachache. Surely Phra Dhamma has not been shot through the abdomen? His colon can't have fallen out, can it? "What is it really?" I ask anxiously.

"Is really stomachache," says Phra Dhamma. "I only lied about fit as a fiddle. About stomachache I am telling you true."

"Well, I'm sorry you're not feeling well. I'd be delighted to take you to the doctor. I'll meet you at the wat in an hour."

After his examination at the hospital, we mill about in the gleaming concrete lobby, which is big and empty and echoing and somehow reminds me of the hull of a ship in which we are human cargo. When the doctor comes out to find us and tell Phra Dhamma the result of his exam, he reports that Phra Dhamma, like many of the monks, has ulcers. "Eat regularly, three times a day," he instructs, handing him a prescription. "Take this medicine for two months and then you will be cured. Oh, and no hot food."

"No hot, no hot," Phra Dhamma moans as we wait at the pharmacy to fill his prescription. "I love, what do you call them, chilies." He makes the gesture all chili lovers make in this part of the world, pressing his thumbnail against his pinky, turning his finger tip into the shape of a chili.

"Shall we go eat breakfast?" I ask, while he pokes through his bag of medicine. We left the wat early, so both of us have missed the morning meal.

"I don't eat breakfast," he says in disgust.

"What! What did the doctor tell you, not two minutes ago?" I scold.

"O.K., O.K." he says, laughing. "We'll eat breakfast."

We proceed to the hospital cafeteria and while he finds us a table, I order *khao phat* (fried rice). The waitress points toward Phra Dhamma with her chin. "You are taking care of the monk?"

I nod.

She places a bowl of fruit salad on my tray for him. "For free," she says. It strikes me that generosity is the most contagious thing of all. And of all the gifts the monks give, maybe the most important is being humble enough to let others minister to them. That is, in fact, what they say their true vocation is—they do not beg in order to get what they need. They beg in order to give others the opportunity to be generous.

I carry the tray back to Phra Dhamma and set it in front of him. "Here we go. Breakfast. What will you do without me to boss you around?" I tease. It's a bad move.

"I'll be sad," he says.

I look at him, my appetite completely gone. "Me, too," I say.

The hardest blows come from the most unexpected places.

Today my father died.

Or rather, today I got a letter from my mother saying he died ten days ago. I don't know why no one called. Despite the fact my mother has been to Thailand, everyone is still convinced we live in huts without phones or electricity. My sister-in-law writes that she admires my fortitude. She's not sure how I make it in a place without McDonald's.

Of course nothing could be further from the truth. I eat Chicken McNuggets frequently—in between trips to A&W, Swenson's, and Pizza Hut. They are all right there in the mall she also does not believe in. Our house has not only electricity but a phone on every floor. It has air conditioning. It has a fax machine and a computer.

All this is irrelevant to my family. Even the evidence of their eyes cannot outweigh what "everyone knows," which is that religious workers ride mules to work, live in mud huts, and have their mail delivered by canoe.

Whatever the reason, they have written, not phoned. So for a week the world I have lived in was not the real world. In my world, nothing broke the surface of my consciousness but the lives of the refugees. In the real world I lost my father. He went through ten hours of brain surgery, died on the operating table, and his body was put to the fire. The two who knew him best, his sister and the lover he took after leaving my mother, collected his ashes and scattered them into the sea.

My father's death was unexpected. A tumor was discovered two weeks before the surgery, or at least this is when my aunt first heard of it. If my father knew of it earlier, he kept it secret, and his secrets have now gone with his ashes, into silence.

I was not close to my father. Stepfather, I should say, but since he was the one who raised me from the time I was six until I left home at seventeen, I suppose he at least deserves that from me, to be claimed as father.

We had not spoken in years. I cannot say he was a warm man or a kind man. I don't even know if I loved him. He was an alcoholic and the son of alcoholics. There were more terrible wounds, too, which he carried from childhood, wounds I think he tried to keep us from discovering, the way you protect a child from a sharp knife or a hot burner. Despite these attempts to shield us, his pain washed over into his relationship with us, kept him from us. His failures as a parent added to his shame, driving an even greater wedge between us.

In the end perhaps his most intimate relationship was with the demons of his own memories, and his energy went toward battling shadows into which he permitted no intrusion and invited no help. To us he seemed remote at best. At worst he was brooding, watchful, secretive, and capable of anything. His silences were not companionable; they were wells of quiet rage.

Given this strained relationship, I had often wondered what would happen when he died. Would I be called back for the funeral? Would I want to go? Would I grieve for him? Would I be asked to speak at the ceremony? Would I seem brave or aloof or lost?

It never occurred to me that he might die without warning, less than a month before I would return to the United States. It never occurred to me that there would be no time for reconciliation or good-byes. Most major changes in life require you to give prior notice. You don't leave a job or an apartment without notification. So how could I adjust to the death of a parent with no preparation whatsoever?

Then again, if anyone was likely to slip away without a word, it was my father. He was always disappearing. During my childhood, I would be speaking to him and would turn around to find him gone. I would discover him later, sitting alone in the dark, curtains drawn shut, unwilling to answer when we called his name.

In the end, his social life had deteriorated to the point that there was no funeral, no gathering of friends and clan to wish him a final farewell. No return is asked of me, no brave and poetic speech. None of his children came to see his ashes scattered, even those who live nearby.

And so, nothing is expected of me, and there is nothing left to do, except to sit in my room, thirteen thousand miles away, and answer my own question: yes, I would grieve for him.

After receiving my mother's letter, I sit on my bed for a long time and do not come down for dinner. I sit until the sun goes down, rocking myself by my window. For the next few days everything is out of focus. It is like living in that time between sleep and waking, when you can't remember where you are and parts of your dreams seem more real than your life.

At the end of the week, Phra Dhamma calls. I take the cordless phone and crawl back into my bed, fetal position. I curl up with the phone against my ear and close my eyes.

"You are so quiet," says Phra Dhamma. "Are you sad?"

"Yes." I begin to cry silently into the pillow.

"Please don't be sad," he says. "I don't want you to be."

That makes me cry harder. "How can I not be sad?" I ask. "My father died, and I am alone in a foreign country."

He thinks for a moment. "It is true you are in a foreign country. It is not true you are alone. I am here with you. And if you will let me, from now on I will be your brother."

I am crying hard now, and he continues. "I feel like your brother. I want to call you my sister, but I don't know if you would like it. You have been my family here in Thailand. So now I ask, can I call you my sister?"

"Yes," I cry into the phone, unable to say more.

He covers my awkwardness by beginning to talk about his day, about tomorrow, about plans we have for the coming week. The sound of his voice is soothing. My head begins to clear a little from its haze of pain.

"Good-night, then, my sister," he says at last, into my ear.

"Good-night." I hang up and flick out the lights. "Good night, brother," I say into the dark.

The Lion and the Dragon

Now that I know I'm leaving, everything moves in triple speed. I have packed my clothes and trinkets while making last-minute trips to the wat to bark final instructions to refugees about their appointments with various doctors. News has traveled fast that I will soon be gone, and the refugees also want last moments with me. Whatever truth has not yet been spoken, whatever secrets not revealed, must now be unveiled or they will remain in silence forever. And so there are refugees who I considered to be healed and well but out of some longing I have no name for, take me into the back room to lift up their shirts to show me their scars.

Two days before I am set to leave, I visit Phra Dhamma. "When you go back to America, where will you live?" he asks.

"New York."

"New York!" he gasps. "*The* New York? Oh, that is terrible. Very dangerous. You will be shot for sure."

"Don't worry," I say, smiling. "It's not nearly as bad as the newspapers make it seem."

"You must be careful, Wicki. Promise me."

"I promise."

He asks if I would like to hear some traditional Mon music. "I'd love to," I say. Then he fills my bags with gifts. He gives me six or seven music tapes, a T-shirt with the Golden Bob on it, a badge that says Mon students in front and has a map of Monland on the back. There is also a red sarong—the Mon national dress for women.

"I wanted to give you these tomorrow before you left," he says, "but I couldn't wait."

The next morning, Phra Dhamma sees me when I enter the compound, hands me a Coke, and invites me to sit with him for a moment in the computer room. "I have been thinking," he says. "If you are going to New York, I have something to protect you. There is a famous monk, Phra Utama. He can protect anyone who carries a picture of him. Many battalions go to war with this medal, and no one was wounded, not one man. It is very powerful."

He takes two amulets out of his bag. One is a copper likeness of Phra Utama. The other is a gold-speckled globe inside a clear plastic sphere. Phra Utama's face floats in the globe, turning to reveal its glimmer of gold, a glittering decapitation. I look at Phra Utama's kind, calm face. "Keep it with you at all times," he says. "It will also keep your plane from crashing."

I feel awed and guilty taking the gift. Is this Phra Dhamma's own safety in my pocket? And if so, who will look after him? That is when I get the idea of giving Phra Dhamma my own icon of the Mother of Perpetual Help.

I suppose most people would think I am too modern to have such an icon or to attach such importance to it. But the truth is I bought this little icon on Caldey Island, off Wales, nearly a decade ago. I had stayed the night in the town of Tenby, and in the morning the monks from the island had come for me in their small ferry, which waits for the tides, crossing only once each day between the mainland and the island. There I found the Mother of Perpetual Help, a Russian icon of a mother looking serenely over her child, and I bought her in a spirit of deep peace, near the end of my first great year of adventure and travel beyond the borders of my native land. I have never been parted from her since.

If you ask me what the perfect metaphor for the universe is, I would show you this picture. Many people think the universe is like a machine, and some think it is an empty room, and some a wilderness. But the image that appeals to me best is this: maybe the universe is like a family. Maybe it is like a mother absorbed in her child and the child looking back with love. And if it isn't true, if this is not what the universe is like, it's what it should be like. And if I act on this version of the world, if I live my life with the kind of tenderness such a vision calls for, I think my life and the lives of those I love will be the fuller for it.

I go home and take the icon down from its place above my bed where it has watched over me from many houses in four different nations. I carry it back to the wat and hand it to Phra Dhamma. He takes it respectfully. Later, I wonder if he can feel the tug from his medals as I feel the tug from the icon. It is not that

I think the icon or the medal are themselves magic, but they are reminders of a vision of compassion: the face of a mother, gazing with love at her child; the face of Phra Utama, the living saint, who comforts a beleaguered people. And most important is this simple exchange of gifts between two friends from different traditions. Of course there is magic here, if not in the objects, then in us.

On my last day at work, as I walk self-absorbed to the wat, not looking where I am going, I nearly tread on a small person. The little boy squawks a complaint, then recognizing me, tugs at my sleeve. It is one of our temple boys.

I look up to find the street full of Mon orphans walking purposefully, their hair washed, their smiles proclaiming pride in their Thai school uniforms, the crisp, white shirts with the name of the school embroidered on them.

We began with thirty-six barefoot orphan boys. Now nearly seventy orphans are on their way to school. They take up the whole street, as far as I can see, around the bend in the road. They have stopped traffic in both directions; tuk tuks, taxis, motorcycles, and pedestrians are pushed to the side of the road, staring, while the little boys carry on, unconcerned, uncontainable, as if to say, "So what if the bus didn't come for us? So what if we didn't get enough to eat? We are undeterred. We will walk if we have to, go hungry if we have to. The day is fine, and we're going to school, wearing our shining new shoes."

When they see me, being polite boys, they do the polite thing. They put down their books and their pencil cases. They wiggle out of their book bags and set down everything they are carrying, which in most cases is all they own in the world. They set it all down in the road and they lift their hands to greet me with a wai, all seventy of them, putting their palms together in front of their faces in a pose like the traditional posture of Christian prayer. It's a gesture of greeting, a salute to the fragments of God we each carry inside us.

As an adult no response is expected of me; nothing is required, except perhaps a nod. But how can I help it? I raise my own hands to wai them back.

They pick up their books and bags and resume their journey, and I resume mine, going in the opposite direction, against the flow of human traffic, wading through this flood of little boys, nodding and smiling a greeting at each one, as we pass. Perhaps after all, I think, we are building something for the future.

When I arrive at the wat, I find the refugees preparing for a festival. The courtyard is like a beehive. Monks chant incessantly over the loudspeaker. Every spare body is busy cooking, peeling small, succulent fruits, stirring vats of food. Women squat together, throwing naked onion bulbs into a basket, onion after onion. Bare-chested, a monk leans over a huge wok and stirs brown cakes that smell of sugar and chilies.

I have come to say good-bye. Phra Dhamma and Phra Dala Non and I walk to the refugee room, where we find Nai Nya Naa and his family tucked away in a corner, behind a screen. Kyang San asks to be held and held and held. Every time I put her down, she puts her arms up again, and I swing her up, telling myself, "One more time, just one more time."

I remind Nai Nya Naa that he has an appointment tomorrow. "How's his eye today?" I ask.

Phra Dhamma translates. "O.K., no pain, though he feels it. It's painful when he takes the bandage off, because of the light."

I begin to fuss and worry. "Tell his wife, she must keep track of his appointments and be sure to tell the monks when he is supposed to go to the doctor. The most important thing is he must keep clean. He must wash every day, and this floor needs to be mopped."

Phra Dhamma instructs them while I look around me in despair. The family, like most of the sick, has sought out a dark corner of the already dark room. Their living space is as dank as a petri dish. They sleep on the chilly floor, which at the moment is littered with scraps of food, reeking plastic bags, and the still-damp remains of something spilled during breakfast.

A lump is forming in my throat as I realize my time to take care of them is coming to an end. There is so much I wanted. I wanted to be here when Nai Nya Naa first looked out of his new eye and saw more than a painful blaze of light. This is one last lesson for me. Sometimes we fail in what we set out to do. Sometimes we simply don't know: the work begins without us, and ends without us, and we never know what contribution we made, what came of the seeds we planted.

"Tell them it was very good to meet them," I say. "Tell them I'll miss them."

Nai Nya Naa nods and smiles and speaks. "He asks when you are coming back," says Phra Dhamma, trying not to look at me accusingly.

"Tell him I am going far away. Very, very far. I don't think I am coming back."

I go from refugee to refugee, saying good-bye. All the while I squeeze Kyang San and put her down, only to have her dance around my legs, cling to my pants, and leap up again. Nai Nya Naa follows at a little distance, standing just to the side, with his head cocked, listening to the melee around him.

"Do you want to take this child?" the refugees tease me. "Kyang San, do you want to go to America with this woman?"

"Sure," she chatters, dancing, "if my father can come, too."

Everyone laughs.

"You see," I say, "this is what I have learned from this family. They love each other very much."

I wai Nai Soh. I wai Nai Han. "Thank you. Thank you. Good-bye. Good-bye."

An old monk brings out two perfect apples and puts them into my hands, eager to take care of me even to the final moment.

At last I release Kyang San and walk out to the edge of the walkway. One of the women throws her arms around me, pressing her beautiful, powdered face to my cheek. She holds my hand all the way out to the gate, where I wave a final farewell and turn to take one last look at the wat.

"Good-bye," I call, and to Phra Dhamma I say, "I will see you tomorrow with Phra Dala Non."

My heart is cracking like an egg. I look up at the wall, where Lord Buddha's image flies through the air with his disciples, discovering the land of the Golden Bob. For the last time, I pass under the twin golden birds perched on the gate and walk out into the last of the monsoon rains.

On the way home I take my last trip on a water taxi. I say good-bye to Wat Arun, the Temple of the Dawn, in the distance. I love this monument, not so much for its imposing silhouette, but for the story around its ornamentation. Following a tradition of the times during which it was built in the mid-nineteenth century, it is covered with fragments of colorful Chinese porcelain, arranged in a mosaic that represents the thirty-three heavens of Hindu mythology. Before the work was done, the builders ran out of porcelain and had to call for broken crockery from local people.

Somehow it seems fitting that the most sacred and most beautiful things we build are made of the most earthly and mundane items. We build our image of heaven out of ceramics, which is only clay, after all, only earth. Out of what is most broken and most ordinary, we build something that is holy. Out of what is scattered and fragmented, we create something with a pattern, a striking unity. Out of what we hold and use every day, we piece together glimpses of the eternal.

And out of what is most fragile, we build something that lasts, that towers, that shines.

Nothing is as black as a moonless tropical night. To take me to the airport, the monks have rented the biggest van I have ever seen , and it pulls up to the curb like a white ghost emerging out of the sticky darkness.

We ride in complete silence for an hour, then sit in the airport for another hour. Phra Dhamma looks off vaguely and whispers in a dignified way, "Can I cry here? I think I would like very much to cry."

"I know just how you feel," I say, my eyes beginning to sting.

"Don't start," says Phra Dala Non. "Don't."

The van driver lines us up in a long row and takes our picture. "I was sorry I did not bless you last night," says Phra Dhamma, referring to the good-bye prayer we had at the community house, where my friends and fellow community members said their good-byes. "They gave me the water and I wanted to bless you but I couldn't."

"Did you feel shy?"

"Yes. Very shy." He passes his hand, palm outward, fingers flexed like a Thai dancer, over his face.

"I have told your Mon fortune," he says. "I looked it up. You are like a ship setting out from a town by the sea. Your mind can never be still. You were born on a Friday. So you are a mouse."

"What are you?" I ask.

"I am a dragon."

"And Phra Dala Non?"

Phra Dhamma turns to him. "You were born on a Wednesday?"

"No. Tuesday."

"Oh," explains Phra Dhamma. "He has changed his name. You can always tell the day of birth by the name, but if you change your name, then no one knows any more what kind of animal you are. He was born on a Tuesday. That makes him a lion."

"Wait a minute," I say. "You're a dragon and Phra Dala Non is a lion, and I'm just a mouse?"

"Yes," nods Phra Dala Non. "A small, anxious creature. Busy and nervous all the time."

"Well!" I say, marveling.

"Did you listen to the tapes of traditional Mon music I gave you yet?" Phra Dhamma asks.

I had. The first song was "Tie a Yellow Ribbon 'Round the Old Oak Tree" sung in Mon, with a heavy rock backbeat. "Yes," I say, trying tactfully to explain that "Tie a Yellow Ribbon" doesn't sound like traditional Mon culture to me.

"Not that song," he laughs. "I mean the song 'Ramanya.' *Ramanya* is another name for the Mon people. There was a song written around eighty or ninety years ago, though some modern singers also have a version of it. The story goes something like this. 'We Hongsas [Mon sheldrakes] escaped and flew through the jungle from mountain to mountain, wet with dew. We were tired, weak, thirsty, hungry, sad, and lonely, and rested by a stream in the jungle, which had many ghosts. We arrived at Chiang Mai, but we were not happy. The place where we were happy was Pegu. Remember our language, literature, and religion, and then when our sons' feathers are grown full, we will fly back to Hongsawatoi.' "

"Wow. That's beautiful."

"When the Mon hear this song, they weep." He asks for my notebook, and I hand it to him so that he can write the name of the song in Mon. Below the name he writes, "I will be missing you, my sister."

It is time to go, late in fact. "Well," I say again. "Well." We stand in front of the passport control gate, which says "Passengers Only." Just inside the door, a woman is squatting, vomiting quietly into a bag. I know how she feels.

"I guess that's me," I say, pointing to the passenger sign. We have been standing in a line. Now I step out of the shape we make together and turn to face them. "Good luck with everything," I say, unable to put into words everything I feel, everything I wish for them.

"Bless you," says Phra Dhamma at last. "Buddha bless you and God bless you. Bless you with mercy and with compassion." I still stand there, unable to move. "Two monks and a woman. We cannot touch. We cannot even shake hands," he says.

Finally, I wave and turn into the passport control area, beginning to cry, disappearing into the beginning of the long journey home.

So I return to my homeland. Just as the work began before me, it continues without me. I thought singing to a man while he died of treatable illnesses might crush Matthew's spirit. That trauma, coming hard on the heels of the death of the little boy, after the attack at Halockhani, and the attempt to manipulate the Mon refugees by starving their children, means he had one blow after another. I thought such a succession of tragedies might rob Matthew of his fire and his passion.

I was wrong.

Matthew is a man of large visions, and global, universal dreams. But he has the wisdom and maturity to be content with the smallest act.

Police raids of the wat continue after I leave, and during one of them, the police arrest Naing Bai, a Mon woman with two children. The boy, a five year old, is with one of the monks when the police arrive. Helpless to assist in any other way, the monk steps in front of the child, sheltering him behind his robes while the police shout and hurry through the compound, rounding up the refugees.

The other child, We Lai, is an infant, only eight months old, sleeping in her mother's arms. When the police arrest Naing Bai, the baby, being too young to be separated from her mother, must share her mother's fate. Mother and child are carted away and locked up in the detention center.

Inside the hot cell, the baby begins to fuss and toss feverishly. She eats only fitfully. At last she sinks into a deep sleep. Naing Bai strokes the forehead of her dreaming infant, inspects the curled shell of her ear, absorbed in the child as if nothing else matters. As the baby's breathing turns shallow, Naing Bai begins to be afraid.

Something is wrong. Very wrong. The heat and the filth and the crowding and poor food don't help. She is not sure, she doesn't like to think about it, but she begins to suspect she has escaped Burma and come this long way into a foreign land only to watch her baby die in a Thai detention center before she herself is returned to the border.

Naing Bai thinks ahead, calculating the distance to Halockhani, weighing her baby's chances against the stories she has heard. She thinks of the long, hot trip, the thirst and hunger and dust, followed by another week's imprisonment in Kanchanaburi. She imagines the walk over the muddy mountain, wearing only flimsy plastic sandals, carrying We Lai strapped to her back. She thinks of arriving in Halockhani where there will be little medical care. She looks at We Lai, listless now, with her head cradled against her shoulder. And deep inside herself she acknowledges the child will never survive this trip.

Eventually the police announce that Naing Bai will be sent back to Burma the following day. Unable to get medical help for her child, the mother sends word to the wat that We Lai is dying, and her only chance for life is to get to a hospital in Thailand. She begs for the monks to send someone to come and take her child in the one moment of relative freedom she will have—as she is getting on the bus to the border.

On the day of deportation, the police bus waits outside the detention center while the refugees squat in the tropical sun, the mother rocking her dying baby. The wat sends a Thai-Mon woman, someone with legal residency in Thailand, to intercept Naing Bai before she is deported. The woman is delayed in traffic, and Naing Bai looks despairingly up and down the street while refugees begin boarding the police bus. She holds We Lai tight, believing one way or another these are their last moments together. Either someone will come, and she will hand the baby to her, or no one will come, and the baby will die in her arms on the road.

She cannot delay any longer. She stands on the bottom step of the bus, and turns to board. A hand on her elbow stops her. The woman from the wat has arrived, breathless, apologetic. Naing Bai leans to place her infant into the arms of the stranger. She does not know if she is saving her life or only condemning her to die alone, in a foreign country, surrounded by the sounds of a foreign language and people who do not really care.

Matthew makes sure the child gets to the hospital. There he hears that the doctors do not expect the baby to survive. The child has pneumonia, liver failure, cardiac distress, malnutrition. There are too many complications. She is too little to withstand so much.

On the night doctors expect her to die, We Lai wakes up and gives a reassuring howl. Despite everything, she's not ready to give up on the world. The doctors are surprised, Matthew is surprised, maybe We Lai herself is surprised, but here she is, separated from her mother by a national border, waking up under the fluorescent lights of a hospital in Thailand. She's going to live.

Now there is a new problem. Here is an eight-month-old Mon baby all alone in a Thai hospital, and a five year old in hiding—and the mother is somewhere on the road to Burma. And so Matthew is drawn further into the story, along with the monks. Unable to solve the bigger problems, they concentrate on the smaller ones. The most immediate is also the smallest—We Lai herself. Like all of us, the baby needs loving human contact. Matthew marshals help from other community members, and they make sure the baby is held every day. It's not much, but at least the child will have some sense she is not alone. The monks join in to make sure she has around her some familiar faces, and the sound of voices speaking Mon.

As he did with the dying man, Matthew, and others in the community, rock and sing to the sleeping child through the long days and nights. Despite modern technology and sophisticated theories of development, much of what one human being can offer another comes down to this: we hold each other in the dark.

Eventually word comes, through new refugees, that We Lai's mother has arrived in Burma, at Halockhani. So Matthew packs up the now-healthy baby and the little boy the monks have been sheltering, and together they begin the long journey to take the children back to their mother.

Sometimes when I close my eyes at night, I imagine We Lai's mother on the steps of the dusty bus, looking down at the face of her dying child, as she places the baby into a stranger's arms, not knowing if they will meet again. That image of courage, of hope in the midst of hopelessness, will stay with me for the rest of my life. Like so much of my experience with the Mon, this story brings me to the place of greatest mystery in human experience, the place where hope and despair weigh equally, where the cross and the manger meet.

My dreams are a jumble of images, signifying both heroism and brutality. I keep mental pictures tucked away in my subconscious as signs pointing to the deeper meaning of our lives. Images flash before me of police rushing across the courtyard of the wat. I see women and children huddled on the floor of Thai prisons. I see the Burmese military setting fire to the huts in Halockhani. I see the crushed limbs and the scars of refugees.

But I also see an old Mon monk, quietly placing a five-year-old boy behind him, shadowing him with his robes and adopting a tranquil pose as the police climb over the temple wall and run through the courtyard, rounding up frightened refugees. I see Matthew humming softly in the dim light of a Thai hospital room, rocking a sleeping infant. I see him later, undaunted by past pain or future uncertainty, doing what he can in the moment. After a long journey, with a baby in one arm and a five year old clinging to his hand, he enters the refugee camp in Burma to reunite a family.

And I ask you: Have I not seen the face of God?

And what of the other faces I have known? What happened to them? Where are they now?

The day Nai Nya Naa is arrested, I am thirteen thousand miles away in my office in New York. But when the fax comes, I see the events described to me in my mind's eye.

It is five o'clock when the police swarm the temple grounds, like bees on a honey comb. They move to the left, past the flooded dips in the courtyard, past the rotting board that bridges a puddle, past the cage where two monkeys scream monkey obscenities at anyone they think might pay attention, might slip them a bit of apple.

The police don't stop to feed the monkeys or appreciate the thoughtfulness of that board across the flood. They are up the steps in a minute, entering the bottom floor of the building, where they're blinded by the dark.

What do the police think when they uncover their human contraband, this ragged group of torture victims and wounded refugees? What do they think, bursting in on a room bare except for humanity, finding no chairs, no tables, no beds, only frightened asylum seekers—Nai Soh limping slightly with his healing broken back, Nai Lon massaging his crushed leg, others waving stumps for arms, looking out of bandages that hide their faces.

And the ones we had so carefully hidden for so long, what do they do? Does Nai Nya Naa's little son let go of his mother's breast and turn to stare at the silhouette of strangers coming in at the door? Do the refugees feel their spirits turning to stone as they think, "They are coming for me, for me. They have found me at last."

A monk hurries down the stairs toward the room where the refugees stare at the police, surprise still on their faces. He tries not to breathe too hard, tries not to betray that he is frightened, tries not to think that behind the temporary protection of his robes is the body of a refugee, no different from those who today will be taken to prison.

The monk translates for the police. They ask what the police always ask—they want money. Nai Nya Naa shakes his head. Nothing. "No?" ask the police. "Then you must come with us."

Matthew arrives at the wat too late to do anything but stare after the police cars as they carry away their human cargo. He follows, down the congested streets to the police station, where he pleads for mercy.

Mercy is denied, so he finds the holding cell where they have put Nai Nya Naa. The cagelike room is in the bowels of the building, and without a fan or a window, the temperature is over 105 degrees and climbing. Nai Nya Naa's children huddle on the floor with their mother. Kyang San, seeing a friendly and familiar face, jumps up to reach a hand through the bars, calling out to be held.

Of the many problems, Nai Nya Naa's is the most immediate. He is sentenced to incarceration along with the others. Never mind that he has UNHCR recognition as a refugee and in any other nation could not be arrested. Never mind his maimed face, the wad of gauze over his eye, his need for ongoing medical care. This simple man stands blindly with all his poverty, at the center of international political and business interests.

For Nai Nya Naa this means disaster. Without antirejection medicine, cleanliness, and frequent medical monitoring, he will lose his newly restored sight. Locked up in the Immigration Detention Center, separated from his wife, he will be helpless. With no arms and limited sight, he cannot feed or dress himself, or go to the bathroom. His wife improvises a sign language to talk with the other prisoners, who speak no Mon. She is trying to teach the men how to care for her husband, how to bathe him, how to know when he is hungry.

She isn't sure what happens next, but she knows it will not be long before she and the children are locked in the cheerless rooms upstairs with the other women, while Nai Nya Naa is led away by a guard, holding him above the elbow where his arm ends. He will disappear down the corridor where the musty smell of sweat announces the presence of many men, herded together like animals.

At last Matthew is able to arrange a concession for Nai Nya Naa, and he is kept in a special room with his family. But he is still at risk, given his medical needs, and Matthew tries to get him released as soon as possible. Matthew calls on everyone he knows in Thailand and throughout the world to help, including me, of course. It takes letters to everyone we can think of and newspaper articles and eventually an intervention from high up in the Thai government to set Nai Nya Naa free, and even then he isn't free. He is sent to the so-called student safe area, a prison-like refugee camp, which, if anything, reminds refugees how completely unsafe they are. It reminds them how Thailand promised refuge to some of the first students to come out of Burma after the 1988 massacre.

Thailand offered refuge, then rounded the students up and handed them over to the SLORC, sending some, according to later humans rights reports, to prison or to death.

By the end, the predictable happens. An infection creeps into Nai Nya Naa's eye, a fire that burns and burns and will not be quenched. As if all that Nai Nya Naa had lived, all that the Mon had lived, had taken physical form in a deep, inexhaustible pain.

Can Nai Nya Naa see? Of course he can see. But not, I think, with his eye.

No one discusses it with me, which generally means the worst. It means they are afraid I will think what they are already thinking: all that effort, the search for a cornea and a surgeon's care, the waiting, the wishing, and the pain—they were more or less a waste, more or less a failure.

So much for my attempts at making myself useful in this world. So much for making a difference. If there is meaning in my time with the refugees, it must be in something other than my accomplishments, or lack thereof, for it seems that our small acts of goodness are often swept away in a tide of injustice.

Eventually, Nai Nya Naa receives permission to resettle in the United States. I visit him soon after his arrival, feeling a mixture of anticipation and dread. He and his family arrive with the clothes on their backs, illiterate in any language, speaking only Mon. He confirms that he lives in darkness now. It is worse than when he first came to us for help, when a little light fluttered through the shutters of his blindness. Now the shutters are closed. He is locked in tight. He tells me this with no hint of bitterness. "What should we do now?" he asks cheerfully.

I want to tell him something, offer something, but no matter how long I think, I don't know what to answer.

As for the others, the last time the police come to the wat, they fulfill a threat made long ago. They had come for the refugees, they had come for the wounded, and now they come for the monks themselves. They clear the wat, taking the remaining refugees, the little orphan boys, one hundred twenty monks and novices, everyone.

A few avoid the police and remain, a few return, a few come to take the place of those who have left. They begin again.

When the police take the monks away, two are missing, already gone. Phra Dhamma receives his papers and boards a plane for Australia. He had so little, you cannot measure his absence at the wat by what he took with him. You must memorize the space under the window where he rolled up to sleep side by side with the other men. You must know which is the now-empty chair in the office where he liked to sit.

Phra Dala Non is also resettled in Australia, with the same Quaker sponsor. Now these two friends lay down their monks' robes to take up again the clothes of ordinary men. They lay down their monks' names to take up the names their mothers gave them. They disembark in a new life, bringing their culture and my culture one step closer, forming a bridge between worlds. I think of them often and with gratitude. Somewhere on the other side of the world are two people I love, people I feel related to.

As Phra Dhamma and Phra Dala Non enter the West, my world, they join me in telling the story of the Mon. They are the story. They enter my world as strangers, along with thousands of others, not only from Burma but from many nations. The cities of the West are full of refugees, migrants, foreigners. They have an important story to tell. Will we welcome them? Will we make them feel at home? Will we listen?

I had told Phra Dhamma I thought these were the end times. The end for the indigenous of our world, the last few generations for the Mon to remain Mon. The work of the end times is to preserve what we can, to tell the story. That is what I am here to do. I am like the boy who runs behind King Arthur on the last day, the survivor charged with the only power he has in him—to tell the story so that what has passed before us will never be entirely forgotten.

What lies ahead for the resettled men is the most difficult part. I know they will work hard to do what they can for those they left behind. But I also know it is possible to give all and to have the current go against you. Not all passionate and just causes prevail. Not all sacrifices result in the great good that was desired. Yet we are obligated to make the sacrifice, and to make it without knowing whether we will succeed.

The world does not stand still, not for the Mon, not for anyone. The things we sing in refrain rarely come to pass. We sing of being one people; we sing of justice, of peace. We proclaim our longings, not our beliefs. We do not speak of what we know but of what sustains us, despite what we know. In the end, what makes us human is the ability to set our hearts on an unlikely future, to commit ourselves to what is important, what deserves our love. To give ourselves over to the work given us to do, undistracted by fear or failure. To commit ourselves is to agree to hold hands with God in the dark.

As for me, my own health seems to have fallen apart in Asia. There are scientific explanations, diagnoses. I have pleurisy, an inflammation of the lining around the lungs. But if you ask me, it's something both more mysterious and inevitable, a natural consequence of my life in Asia, and the grief of separation. One lung partially collapses, and I end up in the hospital for eight days. Even after I'm released, I can feel the rub of inflammation like sandpaper. For more than a year, every breath hurts.

When I lie down at night it is especially bad, as if there is a string attached under my ribs to people on the other side of the world and whenever they move, if they so much as roll over in their sleep, I feel the painful tug.

Well, all right, then. All right. This is what I learned from the Mon: I learned that God is not a fairy godmother and that hope is not a belief in happy endings. It is the willingness to accept the human journey, complete with its dangers, its equal potential for happiness or disaster. And this is what I take with me: courage for the journey. A willingness to take the risks most likely to bring life, to walk the unknown and dangerous road in search of joy, even though we can see from where we stand that this is the road through fire. There is no other road, no such thing as safety. None. Certainly our hearts are not safe. Not as long as we love, not as long as we remain vulnerable to the painful possibility of hope. And the only consolation is, if we are not safe, we also are not alone. In the end, in a world as small as this one, we all carry one another's futures in our hands.